The Tattered Autumn Sky

The Tattered Autumn Sky

BIRD HUNTING IN THE HEARTLAND

Tom Davis

THE LYONS PRESS

Guilford, Connecticut
An imprint of The Globe Pequot Press

The Lyons Press is an imprint of The Globe Pequot Press

10 9 8 7 6 5 4 3 2 1

Printed in the United States of America

"Opening Day," "The Practice," "Heart of the Sandhills," and "Lost in the 20th Century" appeared in *Gray's Sporting Journal.*

"Upland Afternoons" appeared in *Wing & Shot.*

"Blood" appeared in *Gun Dog.*

"Closing Day," "This Peninsula," "Emmy's Pheasants," "In Peshtigo Country," "Woodcock Camp Revisited," "One Grouse," "A Pheasant for Al," and "Shooting Guests" appeared in *Shooting Sportsman.*

"Hypnotized," "The Promise," and "Back at Andy's Acres" appeared in *Sporting Classics.*

"How I Got My Nickname" appeared in *Ducks Unlimited.*

"Letting Go," "The Principality of Woodcock," "The Sportsman's Bird," "Something So Right," "A Boy and his Dog," "Guerilla Quail," and "Prairie Fires" appeared in *Pointing Dog Journal.*

ISBN 1-59228-379-9

Library of Congress Cataloging-in-Publication Data is available on file.

This book is dedicated to the memory of Robert F. Jones
1934–2002

ACKNOWLEDGMENTS

Were it not for the late Robert F. Jones—writer's writer and man's man; mentor, exemplar, and friend—this book would not exist. It was Bob who set it in motion, prodding me to send him my work, culling the pieces he deemed inferior, mustering the survivors into a rough collection, and mailing it off to The Lyons Press with an embarrassingly flattering cover letter. One of my great regrets is that Bob passed away before learning that his efforts had finally borne fruit—although as a friend and fellow writer of a somewhat metaphysical bent assures me, "Bob knows."

I like to think that's true.

And I'd like the members of Bob's family—his wife, Louise, daughter Leslie, and son Benno—to know how deeply and abidingly grateful I am for his labors on my behalf. Dedicating this book to Bob's memory doesn't begin to repay the debt I owe him. It only serves to acknowledge it.

I'm also indebted to Mike Gaddis—another writer's writer, and by a wide margin the most skilled outdoorsman I've ever met—for penning the Foreword, which is generous to a fault (and makes the prose that follows suffer grievously by comparison). Thanks, too, to Cole Johnson for providing the exquisite illustrations, to Lilly

Golden for her tough yet sympathetic editing, and, for their encouragement and support over these many years, to the editors of the magazines in which these pieces first appeared: Ed Gray and Steve Bodio at *Gray's Sporting Journal;* the late Dave Meisner, Steve Smith, Bob Butz, and Jason Smith at *Pointing Dog Journal* and *Retriever Journal;* David Wonderlich, Bill Buckley, and Ralph Stuart at *Shooting Sportsman;* Bob Wilbanks at *Gun Dog* and *Wing & Shot;* Chuck Wechsler at *Sporting Classics;* and Chuck Petrie at *Ducks Unlimited.*

I apologize if I've left anyone out, but you know what they say: The memory is the first thing to go.

Writing is often characterized as an essentially solitary occupation, but this is a bit misleading. While the *act* of writing is solitary, the language you have at your disposal, along with the knowledge and experiences that inform it and the attitudes and perceptions that give it shape, reflect the influence of countless individuals. For my part, the list of people who, in one way or another, helped make these stories possible is literally endless. Some gave me tools; some gave me opportunities; some shared their time, expertise, and/or resources; some simply provided grist for the mill. To all, my most profound and heartfelt thanks.

As for the dogs whose stories have come to mark the chapters of my personal history, I shudder to think where—or what—I'd be without them. I suppose I'd exhibit the usual clinical signs of life, but I wouldn't be very alive. And my soul would be as hollow as an empty shell.

CONTENTS

CONTENTS

FOREWORD

————————

On a brittle morning an October ago, two shooting men climbed a high Montana plain to settle the faith with a stand of pointing dogs. Crowning its crest were three blue-bred English pointers—two promised to scent, one posted to honor. Guns-at-port, they climbed evenly, gathering as they went the moments they lived for. As far as the eye could carry, forty miles across the billowing prairie to the snowcapped spires of the Crazy Woman, frost imprisoned the tall grass like powdered sugar, shimmering under the waking rays of the sun much as firelight in crystal.

So imperatively was the scene poised upon their senses, and so bold and grand was it set upon the country, that for the ephemeral moment it encapsulated the very epitome of the upland equation: the welding of birds, dogs, guns, men, and land into a singular religion of the soul, not unakin to a consecration.

I recall that without a word, both men paused once to marvel at the swell of it all. While ahead the dogs stood true, transfixed behind the gauzy glimmer of the cover—a chimera of moment and mystery—like a bride behind a veil.

Then the birds were up, a rusty clamor of Huns, shots were fired, birds retrieved, and the pieces of it all returned molecularly to the air, to wait there until some extraordinary time the dogs might again unravel its presence. All's left is the memory.

Remember I will. For I had the privilege of that morning and all it endowed, maybe foremostly, the company of Tom Davis, the man who shared it.

Over sixty years of dogs and birds, I've known a lot of people with bird dogs and a lot of people who hunted birds. I've known only a few who were dog men and bird hunters. They don't necessarily exist in the same package. Truthfully, they rarely do. There are many people who love to hunt birds. There are scores more who like to shoot birds. Many of them own dogs; the rest rely on the benevolence of others who own dogs; surprisingly few of either category really know either birds or dogs. Not like a man knows his soul.

In "The Rose," the romantic ballad brought to popularity in the seventies, there's a line that goes "Love, it is a hunger . . . an endless, aching need."

With a few dogs, and fewer men, it is like that.

Of the thousands of pointing dogs whelped in a given year, only a relative few will be so gifted that the desire for birds and the hunt burns within them like a white-hot ingot. So emphatically that it never cools, but consumes their psyche and their physiology, their every reason for being. It's not just passion, but uncompromising necessity. Likewise, of the bird hunters and dog men whelped in a century, I'm convinced a similarly small percentage will be so impassioned as the best of their dogs. So driven by the pageant of upland bird hunting that pursuing every whisker-and-feather of it will become essential to a lifelong well-being. So inspired by its beauty and intricacies that it will become compulsory for them to relish it, celebrate it, revere it, hunger to know it as intimately as a dearest lover . . . as much as they can even know themselves . . . for every day of their lives. All else—save dire-or-death—put aside.

Obsession? Perhaps. But out of it rises genius.

I'm convinced the obligatory nature of this phenomenon in a man . . . some might argue affliction . . . stems largely genetic—and that to flux, somewhere rather early into its journey, there must be the grafting of human and canine souls, i.e., the meeting of eyes between a boy and a dog . . . ideally a pointing or flushing dog.

I am fortunate to count a few such men, so bitten they want never to be cured, among my closest friends. Unequivocally, all have excelled in the world of dogs and birds, and in life at large. On any given day, sharing gunning company with any one of them is a spiritual experience, aside and apart from what other blessings the dogs, birds, or country might bestow. I can augment the profile, just in case you're uncertain you've ever met one. From September to February, depending on the part of the country, you'll find him under a curious felt hat in chaps and boots and hunting duds. He'll be traveling visibly in the company of at least one dog; the other ever-how-many are in the box or on the trailer. The glaze in his eyes is not insobriety, just wanderlust. He'll be drifting around noticeably lost as a part of the twentieth century, reluctant to cross into the uncertain waters of the twenty-first, and—if he could tell you the straight of the thing—wishing most days he could return to the nineteenth. Back at the house, he'll kennel at minimum three to four dogs more—if he's down a couple, check for puppies on order. More of his income than is disposed siphons into dog gear, horse tack, trip savings, shotgun shells, shooting paraphernalia, training books, and a recent shotgun receipt, and on the dash of his truck there'll be a brilliant likeness of his latest pup, though he has to fumble through his wallet a bit to find the yellowed simile of his son or daughter.

On his good days he can recite every National Field Trial Champion from Count Gladstone to present, tell you who judged each of the renewals, and how many birds got pointed. He's too antediluvian to own a GPS, but he's benchmarked every good grouse and woodcock cover in his head from Louisiana to Minnesota. He'll shoot a Parker and yearn for a Purdey. In his kitchen there's an anonymous, framed dime-store print of a basket of fruit on the wall; in the den over his dreaming chair, originals or limited editions of Osthaus, Goodwin, Foster, Abbett, and Hunt. If he's not on a shooting trip, he's planning a shooting trip, and if he's not planning one he's remembering one. He might forget Valentine's Day . . . even his own wedding anniversary, but be assured he'll remember opening day like the girl that got away.

All of which checkcords us back to Tom Davis.

You learn something every trip. I might have guessed, should have suspected, but in previewing the manuscript for this rendering, it also comes to light that Tom is a philosophy major. Certainly to the many of us familiar with his sporting ruminations from previous outings, this will come as little surprise. Though, having learned so, after equal enlightenment from the plain-time friendship and company of the man for a decade or more, I am sure whatever formal schooling was applied merely basted and steeped what was already in the oven.

No one scales the steep and misty cordilleras of the upland bird-hunting mindset—the exhilarating ether of wings and wonder—with greater aplomb, nor manages to more profoundly account for what he has found, than Tom Davis. In the doing, he enables those of us, who might never otherwise, to climb there as well. And to his enduring credit, he has the grace and good sense as he gleans, untangles, and embellishes the wispy emotions, the multicolored ascent of the senses, the sunlight and shadows of place, life and time, not to leave behind the things even one so gifted cannot unravel: the magic and the mystery.

So you'll not soon forget within these pages the haunting conclusion of "Opening Day," wonder at the souls of fallen heroes in "Blood," and marvel at the invisible weight of molecules in "Letting Go." There's real-time magic as well: the hammer-over-percussion cap drama of a trembling point, the leap and follow of a favorite gun, the simple, home-is-where-the-heart-is serenity of a woodcock camp. Crisp doubles right and left, the flaming feathers of a cock pheasant under the mellow blaze of the autumn sun, the lumpy-soft, small-of-the-back completion of birds in the bag. Little things, great and tall, that finish a shooting day.

Beneath all is the everpliant mood and majesty of the land, the "Heart of the Sandhills, Soul of the Prairie," the vicarious secrets of "The Principality of Woodcock," and all the quiet, happy places between that harbor a soul.

Behind the hunt, from the crossroads of the heartland, come the people too. People that share, enliven, and color the universe of the uplands. Mates and lovers, friends and others, daughters and mothers, fathers and brothers. Losers and winners, saints and sinners—above all, the good folks from Wisconsin to the Dakotas, on down through Kansas and Nebraska by way of Iowa and Illinois, on to south Georgia and up through Mississippi—and back again—

who shared homesake and holdings to make it all possible. Tom has remembered them well, in characterizations as clean and brilliant as a newly struck coin.

Most of all, richly to the core, there are dogs. For an upland bird hunt without a dog is an orchestra without a symphony.

I've often thought when I lay dying, lingering by the shadowy portals of eternity, I'll remember the best times of my life and their names will be Pat, and Jake, and Jodie, and Susie, and Katie, and Ben. . . . Here, while the memories still brightly live, are the joyful canine travels of Tom Davis's life, from a beginnings-and-beloved Irish setter bitch named Sheila, to Ernie, the most recent Hell-and-Hiawatha, see-you-a-week-from-Sunday firebrand of puppy-flesh. Hype and happy Gabe, teetering on the tightrope between break-and-brilliance; precocious but doomed little Maggie; Traveler—old Trav—loyal to his name; Hannah strung one star too tight; intrepid old Zack; *flawlessly-forever* EmmyLou. These, and others, each with a day and a destiny, all shared in resounding and reminiscent tones that will lead you happily down the path to your own best times.

I have anticipated this book. Unlike a host of other distinguished works, such as *Wild Harvest, To the Point,* and *The Art of Remington Arms,* collaborative outings in which Davis's gift with text embroidered the kindred talents of others, the stories here are as exclusive as his signature. Here is Tom Davis as Tom Davis—the way we would like him to be—off the cord and given the whistle.

—MIKE GADDIS
NOVEMBER KENNELS,
CREEDMOOR, NORTH CAROLINA

The Tattered Autumn Sky

1

Opening Day

W̶e counted our options around the supper table. "I damn near called to tell you not to bother comin' down," Merle volunteered, wincing behind his black-rimmed glasses, pointing with his pipe. His hands were ruined from decades of work with stock and farm machinery—"Aw, I ain't got no strength left in my hands," he'd admit—and the enlarged knuckles bulged out from his fingers like knots in a thick, hemp rope. When the old Garrison place he and Alvina rented went up in flames, burning in a hurry as if it were running late for an appointment, a few brittle photographs had been salvaged, and not much else; now they were kept in the roll-top desk, inside a small greeting card box. One showed Merle as a young man, curbing a brace of foxhounds with a leather strap gripped in his right hand, the tiny hand of his son, a child of four or five, enveloped in his left. The sleeves of a white cotton shirt were rolled above his elbows, baring a pair of awesome, incongruously large forearms; as if his jaw, which jutted out and at an angle so that the cleft in his chin lay to the right of the perpendicular described by the peak of his slicked hairline and the divide of his nose, and his smoldering eyes, which might have ignited dry tinder, weren't enough to cottonmouth anyone who thought to call him a liar or claim his hounds ran trash. Merle chuckles when he says "I was stout as a mule in them days."

He'd retired from farming four years back, and he and Alvina had moved into a comfortable pre-fab in town. He held on to a couple parcels of land, not the best in this part of Iowa, but not bad, and he could draw money from any bank within 50 miles simply on his word. Not that he was particularly cash-rich, but he'd lived and worked in this country over half a century, and people knew he said and did nothing without just cause, good reason, and the will to see it through. And although the skin covering his arms had slackened, and his stance was a little stooped, he still walked miles to the music of black-and-tans running coon, even when his knees hurt so badly he wanted to cry out, and once in a while he'd come bird hunting with us, mostly to check the creek bottoms for coon sign, watch our dogs make game, and just get out of the house.

This family I married into took their hunting seriously, and importance had accrued around opening day of the pheasant season like interest on principal, until only Thanksgiving and Christmas exerted similar gravity, and then mainly because they fell within the bird season as well. It was not something to miss, even if the prospects for good shooting were poor. There was always Alvina's cooking, the ham and baked beans and potato salad on Saturday, and the fried pheasant in mushroom gravy with bread dressing on Sunday, all followed by apple and pumpkin pies: these were meals that could reduce a proud man to beggary. And there were the night hunts with Merle, feeling through the woods by the glow of his wheat light, listening to Roxie's sweet bawl coat the darkness like honey on buckwheat cakes, oozing back and forth across the timbered bottoms of the smooth-flowing, chocolate-colored Skunk River.

It had been a queerly wet fall. Farmers in Keokuk and Jefferson Counties were sitting on their hands, waiting for the fields to dry, antsy to get their corn out. They were keeping time in the restaurants, worrying, dragging on cigarettes and letting black coffee go cold. If they thought of the pheasant season at all, it was in terms of minor nuisances: the polite or begrudging replies of "Sure, go on ahead" to the requests of some hunters, the firm "No" to others, the occasional need to put the fear of God into trespassers. A number working land still too muddy to harvest might uncase their shotguns for an hour or two on opening morning, dumping a ration of naïve young birds, and educating the survivors.

Our possibilities momentarily exhausted, the table fell silent. Merle tamped Velvet in the bowl of his pipe, while the rest of us nibbled molasses cookies and apple-raisin cake. Gene sat sideways to the table, left elbow resting near an ashtray, index finger curled around the stem of his briar. Merle's son, my father-in-law, he'd inherited more of his features from Alvina: nose tapering to a sharp point above thin lips, hawkish blue eyes, hair at once thinning and silvering. It was the kind of face that needed to be well and thoroughly provoked before breaking into a smile. Bruce, another of Gene's sons-in-law, tilted back a head of wavy brown hair to coolly expel a funnel of cigarette smoke, pretending not to hear the reedy calls of his wife, who was changing their baby son's diapers. Ken was my shooting guest, and he sat stiffly, shy around people he'd just met, his powerful bulk impressive beneath touseled red hair and small, laugh-lined eyes.

We'd assembled to find standing corn everywhere. As we drove in, I'd pointed out familiar draws and fields to Ken, punctuating each description of past triumphs with curses of "Damn!" and worse. The unbroken ranks of tall corn marched from roadside to the limits of vision, until the laws of perspective mustered them into single file. I greeted Gene with the bad news—"They haven't gotten any corn out"—when he stepped from his station wagon into the gray November twilight, and from his expression understood why the lives of innocent messengers have historically been at risk.

So here we were, four gunners hauling six bird dogs—Gene had his two German shorthairs, Ken had a setter, and I'd brought all three of my longhairs—and after ten months of feeding and training, practicing on clay pigeons, planning strategies, fretting and antici-pating and preparing, we didn't know where to hunt. We'd mulled it over through a jar of cookies and half a pan of cake before Gene knocked the ashes from his pipe, turned to me, as he does only when he feels all alternatives have been explored and found barren, and asked "Well, do *you* have any ideas?" The words sprang more out of courtesy than from any real hope.

I played a trump card. "Maybe Doran has his corn out," I mused. Doran's place was 25 miles southeast, and while his land held some nice cover, the best shooting was on his neighbor's, who didn't seem to mind if we forded the beaver-dammed creek separating their property to hunt the brushy ditches that drained the gently sloping hillside, the abandoned pastures reclaimed by Osage orange and blackberry, and the grassy waterways winding through corn stubble. It was via an intricate nexus of acquaintanceships, stemming from his wife having been a sorority sister of my spouse, that Doran allowed us to hunt. He did not extend this privilege to many, and threatened every season to take up the sport himself, denying any who would intrude upon his private preserve. We handled our relationship with Doran as if it were an antique, Damascus-barreled fowling piece, keeping it clean and oiled, daring once, or, at most, twice a year to lift it from above the mantel, to see if it would stand up to use, or blow up in our faces. We preferred to wait until December, when the generous Christmas spirit was at large, and there always remained, in this lightly-gunned cover, some careless cockbirds parading about like drunken Santas. My wife, who was not along, had been the mediator in all previous dealings with Doran, but if we were to shoot the way we wanted to, behind dogs, rather than ride around aimlessly like feckless road hunters, one of us had to approach him.

I dialed the phone. Doran was in an expansive mood ("Must be gettin' a good price for his hogs," Gene concluded later), offering that his corn and his neighbor's had been picked, that there were plenty of birds in the vicinity, and that it'd be nice to see us again. Eagerness crept back into our outlook, like watercolor spreading over laid paper.

We rose before dawn, gulping coffee, toast, and cereal, filling the space in our guts next to the butterflies of expectation that flutter from their cocoons on opening day. Gene and Bruce in the former's wagon, Ken and I in his pickup, we caravanned to our hunting groups, passing carloads of sportsmen motoring west, and, as daylight slowly clarified the shapes of the countryside, others already queuing up at cornfields, the dogless gunners who would post and drive the standing rows. A right at the Methodist Church and a left down a long lane took us to Doran's fastidiously groomed farmyard, dominated by a two-story house, black-shuttered, gleaming white. Doran greeted us, a suspicious Australian heeler at his side, and we clustered in the mud room, shaking hands, oohing and ahhing over the baby girl his wife cradled, making small talk, asking Doran about his crops and about the hog market, leaning into the doorway to exclaim about the furniture he creates in his workshop. We thanked them, and they wished us luck as we retreated up the lane, parking at the head of a deep ditch. Legal shooting time—eight A.M.—was "close enough;" we chambered shells and let out our complement of dogs: Gene's shorthairs, lean, white-and-liver Gretel and fat, shambling Heidi; Drummer, Ken's huge, handsome orange belton; and my Gabe, compact, muscular, high-strung. It was a promising day, clear, a whisper of breeze, light frost beginning to melt.

We split up, working both sides of the parenthesis-shaped ravine, the dogs embroidering their patterns through the fingers of brome reaching into the chiseled corn and the briars tangling the ditch proper. It was chilly in the long shadows of morning, and it took time to loosen up, for the blood to circulate freely through the toes and fingertips, the knees and hips and ankles to flex smoothly. The frail, tense wings of the butterflies still beat, but now other sensations crowded them: the sickly-sweet aroma of rotting cornstalks and mellow manure; the distant clank of hog feeder covers and the vague hum of grain dryers; dogs busting brush, looking to their masters for direction before plunging ahead; companions walking abreast in tattered shooting coats, the round, faded patches of bird dog clubs sewn on their shoulders. Iowa in November.

The cover thinned where a double fence—four strands of barbed wire on the outside, a single extrusion of live electric inside—divided the cornfield from a pasture, the grazed down ditch curving sinuously to its confluence with the creek. From the top of the pasture, the landscape unrolled like a Grant Wood canvas, floodlit by the sun arcing across an immaculate blue emptiness: to the south, white-faced Herefords ruminated dumbly in corn stubble flanking a shallow ravine picketed by spare, gray canes, beyond which, past a textured ribbon of gravel road, the navy enamel of silos bathed in a warm, orange glow; shards of light splintered from the surface of the creek to the east, where it emerged from a canopy of cottonwoods and silver maples to fan demurely between canary grass banks, the hillside above clad in a stippled yellow fur of cut cornstalks, striped by the dark banks of wild plum edging the gullys draining east-to-west; north, over the massed, leafless treetops gesturing weakly like old men and the dim squares of the brooding, abandoned pastures, past the whitewashed clapboards of the Methodist Church, the land swelled up from this comely valley and spread into a broad prairie, flat as a fleshed hide stretched tight to dry, flecked to the horizon by the bright dabs of farmhouses.

This painting, however, was not without flaws. A party of hunters swept the far hilltop, a brace of dogs scuttling in the vanguard, but, unless they chose to turn west toward the main creek, they were welcome to that territory. Of more concern were two gunners working their way up the creek from the road, on a course that would intersect ours. A dog accompanied them, and from that distance it appeared to be a springer, quartering methodically to the front.

Bruce grumbled "Those bastards," in his accentless, Midwestern version of a drawl, and Gene added "Horseshit." We hadn't expected company, but had no choice but to forge ahead. Ken and Bruce hunted down a fenceline woven with brome and foxtail, while Gene and I shooed the Herefords and made a quick pass along the cane-guarded ravine. Heidi pointed a cockbird at the base of a scoured indentation, but it flushed before Gene could position himself. We watched the cackling rooster soar downhill, brilliant in the sunshine, accelerating as it neared the pair of shooters working the creek, and saw them shudder from recoil before hearing the reports of their guns. The dog—I could tell now it was a setter—made no effort to pursue the unruffled bird as it merely altered its path, disappearing behind the cottonwoods.

Our parties converged. The two men were ordinary-looking, in their mid-twenties, hatless, carrying pump guns and wearing brown canvas coats that had seen little use. Only hair distinguished them at a glance: longish black locks shone from the head of one, the other, a wispy blond, wore his in a shorter cut.

It was their setter that riveted my attention. A tri-color female, she was short-coupled, nicely put together, looking to weigh about 40 pounds. Her black eye patches were trimmed in tan, her muzzle was full and square, and her silky ears were well-placed on a blocky head. Yet any judge of dogflesh would have noticed that all was not right: her tail, in most English setters a glorious plume rippling gaily with each stride, hung from her rump lifelessly like a length of frayed twine, and her gait, though mechanically sound, was sluggish. When the men paused near a pile of bulldozed slash, the dog lay down between them, calmly, head raised.

Gene launched into his pat routine, at the very least aiming to determine where they intended to hunt next, at best perhaps nudging them off course, securing better cover for ourselves. "Doin' any good?" he asked.

The dark-haired one replied "Nah. Only bird we seen was that one you kicked up, and it was really motatin'"—he stressed the *mo*—"by the time it got to us."

"You from around here?" Gene inquired. He felt proprietary about bird hunting in this section of Iowa, and hated to discover gunners from out of state.

"Over to Mount Pleasant," the same man spoke. Locals.

"Do a lot of huntin' on Doran?" Gene's line of reasoning was that if they hadn't actually received permission to hunt here, the mention of Doran's name might worry them enough to cause their abdication.

The dark-haired man shot Gene an accusing glance. "Ya know, this ain't Doran's land, not here past that last fence. Ain't all that much to hunt on Doran, anyway."

Of course, Gene knew the limits of Doran's property; his ruse had failed. Might as well get down to it. "So where you headin' now?" he asked.

The blond man fingered a pack of Marlboros and said "Guess we'll work up the creek aways, then back through the corn. Check out them ditches." He lit a cigarette and smiled. "Havin' a smoke first, though," he declared, tossing the smoking match inches from the dog's ear. She didn't blink.

This was precisely the area we hoped to hunt, but Gene nonchalanted it. "Our luck's always bad along the creek," he lied, "and did you see those guys up the hill? Looks like they're gonna hit those draws first."

The bait brought no reaction, so Gene threw in his hand. "I suppose we'll work that ditch north and west of Doran's, and that little woodlot. Then cut over and try those old pastures."

The black-haired man spoke again. "I wouldn't recommend that. The man who owns those pastures lives right over that rise"—he beckoned to the northeast—"and he's mean to post his land."

Gene had played this game too long to be bluffed. "I doubt he'll run *me* off," he snickered, and stepped back to form a knot with Ken and Bruce, lighting his pipe while Bruce sucked on a Camel and Ken chewed a blade of bluegrass. Our dogs padded around, except for plump Heidi, who rubbed against Gene's trousers like a cat until he complained "Heidi, you old fool," and knelt to scratch a leathery ear.

But I stood apart, nearer the young men, transfixed by their dog. No one else paid her any attention; the two men smoked and laughed over some whispered joke, while she lay quietly, seeming barely to breathe, motionless as a sphinx. Someone wrote that the eye of the English setter is the jewel of the animal kingdom, and I'd believed it, passionately, until I looked into hers as she rested in the fawn-colored brome, gazing off without emotion, aware, yet in a dimensionless plane beyond defeat or resignation. Her eyes were flat brown pools, fathomless, reflecting or betraying nothing, mere conduits to some dark, unmapped region of the soul, a place where a man could lose himself, wandering ceaselessly without landmark or lifeline, a breathless swimmer, hopeless of rescue. I thought of my own setters, the way their eyes blazed furiously when hunting birds, slashing recklessly through the cover. I thought of their affections, souls welling up in their gleaming eyes like hot springs, and the enormity of what it had taken to choke that pure upwelling, to extinguish that spark that once had surely fueled this dog's spirit, shook me.

"Like that dog's looks, do ya?" It was the blond man that spoke. I searched his face for a clue, a sign that he was capable of smothering a carefully preserved flame, but it was a face lacking malevolence. I saw him as a friendly clerk in a hardware store, pencil behind one ear, steel tape measure clipped to his belt, or as an assistant pharmacist, plastic nameplate pinned above the pocket of a light green shirt.

"I have to admit I was admiring her. I keep setters myself," I said, motioning to Gabe rooting for mice. A frantic, insane plan was forming, as stupid and shortsighted as it was irresistible. "What's her name?" My will was no longer my own.

He spat into the bulldozed slash and said "Cindy."

"Yep, I sure do like her looks." I was convincing the part of me still waging protest. God, this was idiotic: my consulting business had dried up, and my prospects for steady work were grim. We needed a new car. I had three setters already, two half-trained at best, another that, for all practical purposes, didn't know her name. I spoke quietly, not wanting Gene and Ken and Bruce to hear. "You know, I could use a pretty little bitch like that. Interested in selling?" I had eighty dollars cash in my wallet, and a blank check for emergencies. My fevered brain reasoned that this was the kind of man who would jump at the chance to unload a dog.

"Never really thought about it," he shrugged. "I've spent a lot of time with her, ya know, and she's just gettin' to where she's workin' nice for me."

I was thinking *If Cindy were mine, she'd be one of the family, like Gabe and Zack and Maggie, and she'd spend time in the house, curled on the sofa or the braided rug. I'd brush her, and scratch her belly, and feed her table scraps, and I'd take her out in the fields and woods and leave her alone. She could chase birds and rabbits, and I'd bring her along slow like a new pup. We'd go for long walks, and I'd bring my lunch and give her a piece of sandwich and part of a brownie, and one day I'd look her in the eye and she'd be back.*

"I'll give four hundred dollars for her," I said, as if it were no big deal.

"Hell, I paid a hundred and fifty for her at ten weeks, and now she's near four. I spent a wad of money just on feed and vet bills," he snorted. "And she's bred the best, too."

OK, I can play the game, I thought. "Five hundred bucks," I said. Jesus, we didn't have that much in the bank, but I could liquidate some stocks.

"I expect it'd take a thousand dollars to buy her, what with all the time I put in and everything."

The words "a thousand dollars" brought me to my senses like smelling salts reviving a dazed prizefighter. I whipped myself mentally, amazed I'd even considered it. Cindy had lain silent, without the slightest indication that we were speaking of her, and shunting my gaze from the dog I said "Christ. I don't need a dog that bad." I was in no mood to haggle; I wanted to walk away, to leave it behind. "Good luck," I said.

He made no attempt to retrieve me. "Sure, you too," he nodded. They turned and headed into the woods, Cindy casting automatically, almost somnolently, the heartless playing-out of a role. The entire conversation had lasted maybe a minute, but it occurred in a kind of expanded time, the way a hot hitter sees every stitch of the fast-ball's seams, and the pitch seems forever in crossing the plate. Bruce was drawing a last puff on his cigarette, and Gene still fondled fat, insistent Heidi.

I did my best to act casually. "Talking dogs," I said pleasantly, as we headed north along a fenceline. A wide belt of trees screened us from the creek for a quarter-mile, and the dogs dug into it before we swung west up a brushy draw that skirted the far side of Doran's hog lot. I began remembering that it was opening day, that we hadn't shot any birds yet. I started noticing our dogs: Drummer and Heidi combing the cover at close range; Gretel farther out, moving grace-fully, powerfully; Gabe running the widest, a miniature torch of nerve endings, teetering on the knife-edge between control and wildness. I refocused on bird hunting, on the reason I was there, and the already blurred episode of trying to buy the dog was discarded, like the digressions of a filmmaker coiled on the cutting room floor. "Should be birds in here, dammit," Gene muttered as we worked down the draw's other side, toward the creek.

Below us, Cindy and the two men hove into view, where the trees bounding the creek yielded to grasses for a space of 75 yards. They walked slowly, guns at port arms, through snapping goldenrod and the maroon splashes of big bluestem. Cindy had ranged out farther than before, and the blonde man was hollering "Bring it in! Bring it in, Cindy!"; I could see his mouth forming the words before their sound carried to us. The setter moved to hunt closer and flushed a rooster. She didn't flash point; there wasn't so much as a tremor in her listless flag to signal birdiness; she didn't turn to mark the bird's flight. The gunners popped away impotently, emptying their pumps, and then the light-haired man, Cindy's owner, dropped his gun and started running at the dog as she loped back to him. "Goddam you! Goddam you, Cindy! Why didn't you point that bird! Damn you! Goddam you!" he screamed. Cindy seemed unconcerned, adjusting her course to stay two steps in front of him as he ran, high-stepping through canary grass and prairie cordgrass, cursing and kicking out with his right foot. The dog never changed speeds, nor did she look back. She stayed out of his grasp, until he tripped over something unseen, a muskrat hole perhaps, or a beaver-gnawed stump, and skidded on his side in the cordgrass. He lay there for a moment, then drew his heaving body into a half-sit. Cindy loped ahead indifferently.

"Will you look at that dumbass," Gene exclaimed. Something broke inside me, the way it does in a one-time criminal, a man who committed a single act of violence and was never found out, carrying the knowledge of his deed in the back of his brain, as if it were in a sealed vial, and then in the middle of a decent, respectable life someone steps from the past into the present and knocks at his front door, and answering it the vial shatters, and his sanity splinters into glass dust. I lied, yelling "I think Gabe's on point!" and ran down to the creek, across from the man struggling for breath. He was chanting "Damn her. Damn her. Damn her," as if it were a healing mantra, and didn't notice me until I spoke, loudly, out of breath too: "Look, name your price for the dog."

He looked up, disoriented. "What? What did you say?"

"Your dog, name your price. I want her. Anything—a thousand dollars—name your price."

A bead of sweat balanced from the end of his nose, and on his right cheek, scratched by the sawtooth edge of a blade of cordgrass, pinpricks of blood welled up. Cindy materialized, trotting through the yellow, narrow-bladed grass to stop twenty feet from the man. She stood watching, showing neither fear nor curiosity, eyes indistinguishable from the black patches surrounding them. He stared at her, lifting a sleeve to catch the drop of sweat, then he fitted the bridge of his nose into the crook of his arm. His breath came in stutters, but the words were soft and distinct. "Go to hell," he said. "Just go to hell."

Cindy turned her head to me. I searched for her eyes, and found myself falling somewhere, helplessly, certain it was a place I'd never been, and that only parts of me would return.

2

UPLAND AFTERNOONS

O n this peninsula, the same water that detains the arrival of spring softens the onset of autumn. Nature hesitates before striking her match to the maples, sparking the fuse in the leaves of aspens and the needles of tamaracks. A rogue frost startles the landscape each late September, but it is almost a month before there is chill enough to stiffen the earth. By then, waxwings have stripped the chokecherries, and haws litter the ground like a child's treasure of marbles, too heavy to carry. The deformed branches of the wild crabapples still grip a few leathery fruits. Fox grapes wrinkle and granulate into tart raisins.

But the highbush cranberries are in their glory, the heavy bunches of scarlet sagging the spindly branches. I know few things for certain, but on this day at the end of October—perhaps an hour of daylight remaining, the air beginning to tighten—there will be a ruffed grouse gorging on these berries in the home covert. Earlier in the season, I took a brace of woodcock near the willow swamp that drains into Hein's Creek, but a single grouse is all this small jewel can afford. Always, it is a red-phase bird, rare among the gray *togata* subspecies that is the grouse of Wisconsin and the Lake states, and always its crop is bursting with highbush cranberries. Always, too, the sun is bleeding into the horizon, staining the hills across Kangaroo Lake, when I first hold the bird in my hands.

Afternoons. Sunsets. The images I cannot escape, the moments that have come to define what bird hunting is all about: without exception, the setting is an upland afternoon. The month might be October or January; the dogs might be my setters or George's Brittanys or Gene's German shorthairs; the game, pheasants or bobwhite or grouse; the geography, anywhere in bird country. Surely, there have been memorable mornings, wild plum thickets alive with quail, alders choked with a new fall of woodcock. There has been fast shooting, satisfying dog work, and seamless camaraderie.

Memorable, yes; but the unforgettable is confined to the afternoon. Perhaps there is too much excitement, too much anticipation, too much energy to securely frame the events of morning. In the morning, bird hunting is carnivorous, needful, atavistic. We are obsessed by goals: finding game, shooting well. We've tucked a picture of the way the day will ideally unfold in the back of our minds, like a portrait of loved ones kept in a wallet, and in the initial hours we concentrate on shaping occurrences to fit this vision, fretting when things don't go according to plan. Mornings pass in a blur of impressions; recalling them is like trying to read a reel of microfilm on fast forward.

Lunch has a mellowing effect. The simple opportunity to relax brings on a change of mood. Noon is as early as the mind's eye—or nose—can focus on sharply. I remember smells: George Boykin's Brittanys, Molly and Peaches, steaming in the back of the wagon; Bob Cowan's pungent liverwurst and onion sandwiches, vapor curling from opened thermoses of coffee and chicken bouillon, bags of oily potato chips, peeled oranges, apples, brownies. Boykin lighting a bowl of Captain Black and Cowan complaining loudly until he finds a package of Salems crushed beneath a box of #8 shot in the glove compartment.

Someone tunes in the Hawkeye game on the radio. The edge has worn off. Everyone has scratched down a bird, muscles are warm and loose, a short nap is tentatively suggested. The afternoon's hunting lacks the sense of urgency that charges the morning, but it is now we allow ourselves to step back, to appreciate the ritual and poetry of shooting. Our minds become open and accessible, fertile soil for experience to take root in memory. And there is that peculiar quality of light late in the day, a cast that, like the brush of the artist, renders the familiar fresh and new.

The home covert is not mine by title. Summer people own it, but when they board up their cottages over the Labor Day weekend, I feel proprietary. I've paced it off: the covert begins 75 yards south of my driveway. I lace on boots, hang a whistle around my neck, button my shooting vest, and snug a red feed cap ("Middlekoop Seed Corn," it reads) onto my head. When I step onto the front porch and lift a brass bell from its hook, Zack and Gabe start jumping and whining, crowding against the kennel wire. "Zack's turn today, little girl," I say to Gabe apologetically. I bell the black and white setter, heeling him to the covert. Against the low sun, I put on tinted glasses. "Whoa." Zack stops, although he can hardly contain himself, tail up, eyes wide. "All right." He streaks into the cover, and I drop 7½s into the double 20. The center of the covert is low, with clumps of marsh-grass; the bird will be near the edges, in the witch hazel and the high-bush cranberries.

The loess bluffs of western Iowa rise abruptly from the flood plain of the Missouri River, their broken terrain heartbreaking to farm. But this patchwork of poor fields, brushy draws, pockets of native prairie and timbered hillsides is home to coveys of tough, alert bob-white. It's strenuous shooting. Boykin and Cowan are among the handful of practitioners willing to leg it up and down the rough ridges and bust heavy cover behind their dogs.

There were several inches of fresh snow that January day. Bob had invited me along, and his other "guest" was Joe Miller. He had been an outstanding high school quarterback, one of the state's most highly recruited athletes. Shortly into his college career, an injury during a scrimmage literally destroyed his right knee. He never walked again without an obvious limp. As if that affliction weren't bad enough, he developed a case of chronic, unpredictable asthma.

We'd moved a huge covey—an honest 30 birds—on the Delance place, and chased the singles until noon. Joe held up well, getting his share of shots, stopping occasionally to inhale medication. That afternoon we spotted a covey feeding among sumacs on the slope above a ravine. They flushed at our approach, and, topping the hill, we gasped.

"God, it's the land of the lost!" exclaimed Cowan. The land swelled out before us in a huge bowl like a gigantic natural amphitheater, the only evidence of man's intrusion a single, fatigued fenceline. Fingers of wild plum and thumb-thick blackberry canes probed the hillsides, and it was ringed with treeless ridges where the snow had blown off to reveal the yellow loess and the golden stems of big and little bluestem. It was believable that through a warp in space we had discovered some lost cirque high in the Appalachians. Boykin's Brittanys ranged ahead, and we split up, agreeing to meet back in an hour or so.

Cowan, Boykin and I rendezvoused as planned, each of us with a quail or two in the pouch, each stunned at the wildness of the country. Joe Miller was nowhere to be seen, and we began worrying aloud that his knee had failed, or that he'd suffered a brutal attack of asthma. We hollered and yodeled; echoes were the only response.

And then we saw him, small in the distance, laboring towards us along a ridge, sun igniting the prairie grass beneath his feet, the land falling away beneath him in a vast semi-wilderness. We could only speculate on what it cost him to traverse those hundreds of yards. How could we know the magnitude of the pain in his shattered knee? The effort simply to breathe? It seemed hours before he limped up to us, tears in the corners of his eyes, and we tried to act manly, saying, "Where the hell have you been? We've been freezing our asses up here!" But the sight of Joe Miller staggering along that lonely ridge in the pure cold, in the dying light . . . Only our absurd notions of masculinity kept us from embracing him.

Zack is working the left edge—I always worry because that's where the highway comes closest to the covert—hunting around the crabapples and the dogwoods in the power line cut. I'm walking the right side, zigzagging between the juniper bushes and the balsam poplar, keeping in line with the overgrown stone fence, when the grouse starts 25 yards in front of me. I toss a feckless shotstring in its direction, and the bird angles to the southwest. I curse myself for mounting the gun poorly, too low on my shoulder. The grouse was heading for an impenetrable copse of cedars. Impossible to get a shot in there.

Cowan and Boykin introduced me to *serious* bird hunting, to using pointing dogs, to working as hard as necessary for a shot at quail, pheasant, and Hungarian partridge. They are big, powerful, athletic men. My father receives credit for teaching me gun safety, sportsmanship, and to respect the outdoors, but he and his hunting pals were dilettantes compared to Bob and George. The last time we hunted together, the day was a distillation of all our previous shoots. We started in the bottomlands, pursuing wary Huns around a 40-acre field of corn stubble and kicking pheasants out of the brush growing up in a ghost town (it's still on some maps) named Owego. Then we headed into the loess hills, moving three coveys on Beadle's farm.

But I can't remember any of the shots, nor do I enjoy the vaguest recollection of the dog work, the points and retrieves. What sticks in my mind is parking George's Suburban on a deserted county road somewhere in the hills, unfolding our knives, and cleaning the kill. We had eight bobwhite, a brace of pheasants, a single Hun, and even a jackrabbit, already in his white winter pelage, that Boykin had potted. We worked silently, hurrying in the cold. When we gutted the birds, the warm entrails steamed, their smell thick and balmy to freezing nostrils. The hearts of the birds glowed like molten iron in the final light. We saved the gizzards and the hearts and placed the cleaned game in plastic bread wrappers. The remains we tossed into roadside snow, sure fodder for scavengers. We rubbed snow on our hands to clean them, wiping them dry on our hunting pants. The sunset rouged the faces of my friends. We drove to the tavern in Moorhead, the sky blue-black by the time we got there.

I whistled to Zack, hoping he'd swing around and hunt in the direction of the grouse's flight. The home covert is probably less than a quarter-mile long from its north end to Maggie's Pool, beyond which the country changes into birdless, climax maple forest. But it possesses all the elements of classic grouse cover. There is that low stone wall, the product of some soul's labors to clear this land and grow an orchard, and there are three ancient, scarred McIntoshes, survivors of that long-ago planting. Popple attracts grouse to the edges; woodcock find soft, earthworm-rich earth beneath alders and red osiers. A narrow gravel road bisects this covert, and south of it the ground is wetter, more to the liking of 'cock, although grouse feed on the grapes twining the trees bordering the creek. And there is that tiny corner with the highbush cranberries, where I shot my first grouse on an afternoon like this, a young hen that I took fairly when she tried to rocket over my head, madly fluttering her life away in the grass edging the road as Gabe stood pop-eyed, waiting to be sent on.

The last two winters had been hard on Duke and even harder on the quail in southern Iowa. The stout German shorthair—Gene Lankford received him as a Christmas puppy from his shooting companion, Jim Allee—had spent his life pointing these birds. He'd accounted for hundreds of coveys and God only knows how many singles, and in the process became the rare animal that a man almost takes for granted. If Duke was gone for more than three or four minutes, he was locked up on point, buried in thick cover, and we'd better start looking for him. If he hunted out a cover and went on, there was no sense kicking it out further. If a covey boiled out from beneath a brush pile and Gene couldn't call Duke off point, there was a single still hunkering.

Then came the killing winters. Pheasants were spreading into that country, too, attracting more gunners and competing for habitat with the bobs. The familiar ditches and fields around Richland had been hunted hard: quail were nonexistent, pheasants ridiculously wild. Gene knew it was Duke's last season, and it angered and frustrated him to hunt his dog in birdless cover. With age and with his determination to find game, Duke had worn his muzzle to a silver patina, like a lucky coin polished by the fabric of a deep pocket. We owed him.

We were far from our usual hunting grounds, the light beginning to fail, legs aching, wills crumbling. Duke's resolve never wavered, and finally he pointed at the head of a bromegrass swale, draining from a chiseled cornfield into a timbered gully. "Hen pheasant," Gene muttered. "I ought to shoot it for him anyway." He stepped in front of the motionless dog and a bevy of quail scattered. It was a small bunch—perhaps eight birds. "We really shouldn't shoot into them," Gene said, but Duke had already nailed a single in the broken cornfield. Unashamedly, we killed three birds for the old dog. It was a decision none of us regretted.

———

Zack is hunting where I want him, but he's not making game. So that's why: the grouse is sitting in an apple tree. It flushes before I can react, power diving behind a screen of cedars, arrowing for the larger grove of evergreens where he'll surely vanish. I wave Zack into that shadowy woods, hoping for a miracle, and cut across a small clearing. In a grassy spot half the size of my living room, the grouse flushes at my feet, flies straightaway, and falls. I am unaware of having shot until the ejected hull describes its smoking arc to the earth. The grouse's wings drum the death dance; its spirit has flown. It is a young, red-phase hen, and I know by its distended crop that it has just fed on highbush cranberries. Zack materializes and sniffs the bird reverently, eyes glazed. It is time to go home.

Time to go home. I suppose that's part of it, that the final act of a day afield is the best remembered, the scene easiest to preserve in memory. Adrian Webber and I had already broken camp in the north woods of the Nicolet National Forest, vast, wild country, bird cover that takes the breath away. Despite boasting no huge bag, we were satisfied; still, we couldn't help but try one more loop before rumbling home. We turned Gabe loose, and the little black-ticked setter flashed through the aspens, tail a blur, probing deeply into the forest. We followed her far from the trailhead, straining to detect her bell. When the ringing ceased, we fought through dense spruces for what seemed minutes before finding her, pointing so intensely she looked ready to explode, tail puncturing the sky, nose high and quivering, ribcage pulsing as she drew and expelled scent. No painting, no photograph would have done it justice; there was an electricity, a drama to it that even the mind's eye can only approximate. Perhaps there is no mystery to the phenomenon of a dog pointing to a bird, but there can still be magic. It made no difference that Webber blew an easy shot at the grouse: we had witnessed a perfect point on ruffed grouse. Gabe rode between us on the front seat during the drive home, muscular body curled into a tight ball, sound asleep.

Last October Zack took the stage. Dad was along as cook, and he dropped Ade and me off at a trailhead not far from camp. We heard him skid the pickup over the gravel—he took the turn too fast—before we headed into the cover. The trail descended into the valley of a tiny, tea-colored brook, one of the hundreds that lace the Nicolet. The sun was dangerously low in the treetops, and the lengthening shadows cooled the autumn air. We missed Zack's bell, and then we glimpsed him far to our right, feathery flat outstretched, his classic, black eye-patched English setter head bent slightly to his left. It was the dream tableau of the woodcock hunter: late afternoon, English setter pointing in the damp earth beside a pure, north country steam, shooters approaching cautiously, double guns at the ready. A Pleissner watercolor come to life. And then the 'cock twittered up from the shadows, caught in a shaft of light, and the shot was still echoing in some hollow of the brain when I knelt to gather the bird.

Gabe has worked herself into a state by the time I kennel Zack, so I let her draw a warm muzzleful of grouse scent before walking down to the lake. I sit on a flat rock that slopes into the water, admiring the bird's subtle plumage, spreading its fan, smoothing its feathers a final time. A flock of bufflehead storm in from the north, screaming low over the wavelets before rising and fading from sight. I slit open the grouse's crop, and the cranberries spill into the transparent water, each one phosphorescing in the amber sunlight. I fancy that the pink hue of its flesh is from the berries. I cut into the gizzard, fold back the lobes with my thumbs, and find the pulp of crushed cranberry meat; lifted to my nose, it smells sweet and clean. I pull the tiny heart away from the chest wall, amazed as always at how small an organ it is. The rest of the entrails are food for minnows and crayfish. I place the heart and gizzard in the body cavity, clean the bloodied blade of my knife, and wash my hands in the frigid water. The sun is gone. It is no longer afternoon, but evening.

3

BLOOD

―――――――――

Walt Woodlee was the middleman in a transaction between an Alabama dog trader and a client in Sioux Falls who was in the market for a fully trained setter male that he could hunt off foot or from a pickup truck. The trader had driven to Walt's camp near West Point, Mississippi, to deliver a prospect: a high-tailed, solid white four-year-old named Duke that he claimed was steady to wing and shot, backed on sight, and retrieved to hand. A fancy, four-figure price had been quoted, and Walt was going to make sure the dog lived up to its billing before any money changed hands. "There's always a coupl'a coveys hangs out around a pecan grove I know,"

Walt said as we climbed into his Chevy truck. "Let's see how this Duke dog handles hisself."

And Walt wanted to show me more of the ground he trained bird dogs on. He was preparing my setter bitch for the spring Derbies on the Midwest field trial circuit. Not that I needed persuading that he had all the territory he needed, because if a man cantered a Tennessee Walker out of Walt's camp, accompanied by the cacophony a string of eager pointers and setters create when they're being left behind, rode past Mr. Earl's miserable company of hogs, skirted the edge of the pines blanketing a gentle ridge, and stood up in the stirrups, there wasn't a scrap of land within 180 degrees of vision that Walt wasn't welcome to train on and hunt. To the west, the terrain fell away in a crazy quilt: black patches of plowed gumbo beanfields and gray-green swatches of timber, stitched together uncertainly by creeks, drainage ditches, and fencelines. The foreground immediately north was dominated by the Baptist Church, rising like the chords of a spiritual above the rundown homes, cluttered yards and chicken coops of the families that comprised its congregation, spaced along the gravel road leading to Alternate Highway 45; farther north, on a clear day the eye might catch a gleam from the proud columns of the Lenoire Plantation's antebellum manor house. Casting east, ropes of smoke coiled from woodstoves in the hamlet of Prairie, a surreal contrast to the towering outlines of gas well derricks that studded the horizon like a version of the future. For public relations purposes, Walt allowed he'd lined up 12,000 acres of prime bobwhite country, but the true acreage seemed to include most of Clay and Monroe Counties.

Walt braked at the corner across from the highway store between

West Point and the Prairie turnoff—a good place to stop for a tin of sardines, a carton of soda crackers, and a Coke after a morning's quail hunt—and dipped a wad of Red Man. He situated his chew, gunned the Chevy through a left turn, and headed north on Alternate 45. We weren't a hundred yards up the road when he asked "Remember that setter I was tellin' you about? That one Randy Downs done some winnin' with."

"That one you traded the pointer bitch for? You were really high on the dog. 'This setter's got some wins in him' you said."

"He did. That's his carcass in the ditch," he said gesturing towards a bit of white-and-orange fur visible in the deep grass on the right hand side of the highway. "I was workin' him off horseback one mornin' there at the end of January. He popped into the woods and never came out. I rode all over the country lookin'. He must've run a deer and just got flat-ass lost. Found him there a coupl'a days later. Wasn't nothin' I could do, so I just took my collar off him. Hell, wasn't no sense gettin' all upset. I had me a pointer Derby once that was winnin' everything in sight. I turned down $5,000 for that dog, and before he turned two he dropped dead in his kennel. You just got to keep movin'.

"I got me some pups outta that setter, though. Man over in Alabama bred a nice tri-colored bitch to him, and I went over and bought the whole litter. Eight of 'em. With that hot blood from their daddy—man, he was so intense he 'bout *glowed*—they should fly when they're growed. Tell you what, when we get back to camp, why don't you pick yourself out a couple? I'll give 'em to ya."

"Julie'll brain me if I bring home another dog," I said.

"Suit yourself," Walt said.

Two weeks later, after we'd grabbed a nap early Friday evening, we drove south from Illinois in the dead of the night, humming past jackknifed semis surprised by March snow in Arkansas. At daybreak, we were looking over the puppies as they gamboled about Walt's camp. Julie had hurried out of the house when I'd come home from my previous trip, peering in the back of the station wagon, explaining that she guessed I'd be carrying more dogs than I left with. "I kind of had my heart set on a new puppy," she pouted.

The first two cuts were relatively painless. We wanted a female, eliminating half the litter, and two of the bitches sported unappealing chestnut markings. That left one with orange eye patches, and a slightly larger pup with a tan-trimmed black patch over the left eye, a pink splash on her nose, and a tail that curled over her back like an elkhound's. We chuckled as they clumsily explored this new world, their attention distracted by everything from ants to blowing leaves to petrified horse manure. Julie and I handled the pups, running our fingers along their backs and hips, checking their teeth, noticing the spring of their ribcages, the taper of their fuzzy muzzles, the tightness of their paws. We picked them up with two hands around their middles and held them squirming in front of our faces. The tri-colored puppy had the darker eyes, and, to our mind, the more engaging personality. And when we held her close, breathing in the sweet, unmistakable odor of puppy, it was mingled with another thick, musky scent. "She smells like a chicken," Julie exclaimed, and I took the word of a woman who had spent a goodly share of her girlhood on her grandparents' farm.

"Why don't you take 'em both?" Walt urged. He had a vested interest in reducing his puppy inventory: his tiny sleeping quarters were separated from the puppy pen by only a thin sheet of corrugated metal. But it had been sheer luck that we'd found a landlord who'd let us keep dogs (he was an old Missouri quail hunter). The tri-colored pup with the curled tail ("That'll straighten out purty as you please," Walt assured us), the pink blotch on her nose, and the smell of poultry became a member of the family. Over 450 miles of highway gave us plenty of time to discuss names. The one we agreed upon was Maggie.

And so we executed the initial steps in what was to be an impassioned tango. Maggie was utterly carefree; fear, caution, moderation, and restraint were strangers to her. From the beginning, she tormented Zack, two years her elder, who exhibited the patience of a saint while her needle-like puppy teeth chewed his silky ears into wet, matted messes; while she tugged on his tail as if she were a wrangler fighting to tame a mustang; when she nipped at the tendons in the back of his legs, virtually incapacitating him. I will never know how he managed not to squash her during their incessant wrestling matches, or what inner angel curbed him from going beyond the tender removal of her fierce little jaws when they were clamped on his skin. She allowed him not a moment's peace when they were in the house together, and it was when she was pursuing him after he'd escaped her grasp that her legs splayed under her on the smooth floor, straining a hock; the joint was never completely right after that, permanently enlarged, delicate and susceptible as a thoroughbred's.

In Maggie's first summer, we seized what seemed an opportunity to live a dream, abandoning our modest careers in Illinois to move to a rambling home with acreage and shoreline in Wisconsin. Mag insisted on scrambling over the slick boulders lining the lakefront, further stressing her hock until we quarantined her to the field bisected by our lane. But she loved to swim: she was the most graceful canine swimmer I ever expected to see, gliding through the water effortlessly, hardly creating a ripple, more like an otter than a dog. Swimming seemed therapeutic for her leg, and we began leading her to a sand beach where she could easily enter and exit the water.

Of course, she took a good thing too far. On a warm July afternoon, Maggie and Zack decided that the condominiums under construction on the far shore merited investigation. They were an honest quarter mile out, a pair of white bobbers on the blue waves, before I quit yelling and sprinted to the dock, jumped into the dinghy and started the sputtering Evinrude. They had already passed a pair of amazed perch fishermen anchored in the middle of the lake, swimming strongly, when I descended on them like a screaming Stuka, and abruptly hauled them over the gunwale by the collars. That was one of the few lessons either of them learned in a single session.

Walt called us from his summer digs on the South Dakota prairies to let us know how Gabe was progressing, and to inform us he'd send Maggie's papers shortly. "By the way," he said, as if it were an afterthought, "I lost all but two of that litter to Parvo. Came back from a field trial and found 'em all in bad shape. Vet couldn't save but two. Man, there was a black-headed male in that litter I had my eye on—no money could've bought him. The ones I got now I don't think that much of." The orange-marked female we'd turned down? "Dead," he said.

I spent much of the summer completing a contract in Illinois, leaving Julie to deal with the dogs. Discipline has never been her forte, and both Zack and Maggie took to extended explorations of the woods to the north and south of our meadow, heedless of her commands and entreaties. She would wait, sobbing, on the front porch swing, horrible scenarios playing across her mind until they returned, apparently guiltless, from their self-hunting binges.

Zack took the cure immediately upon my return; he knew the consequences of pushing me past the threshold of rational action. But Maggie, the habit of sneaking into the woods ingrained at an impressionable age, was wholly incorrigible. Give her as little as five yards, and she'd glance backwards once, flatten her ears, take two or three slinking steps, then streak for the timber. No known decibel level generated by human voice or Acme Thunderer caused her to break her stride. Countless times I followed her, relentless as a bounty hunter, until I tackled her and applied the lash. She was incredibly tough, in a cunning sort of way: she'd scream bloody murder during a whipping, as if the point had been made, only to jump up smiling and wagging her tail. Julie and I worked in tandem, one hiding in ambush while Maggie disobeyed the other, but this technique depended on our ability to guess exactly where she would enter the aspens, and was thus a hit-and-miss proposition. We confined her to a lead when she was let out of her kennel, but our soft hearts always gave her the benefit of the doubt after a few days, and she'd relapse at the first glimpse of freedom.

We began to wonder what it was inside that lovely skull that drove her, what fathomless desire for hunting overwhelmed her being, what irrevocable legacy of blood possessed Maggie. We began to question our ability to change her, whether there was a genuine possibility that she would respond, that some part of her would bend to our will. That she held affection for us we had no doubt: she had matured into a long-legged, well-proportioned animal, and her tail, as Walt predicted, had straightened. When Julie came home at night, Maggie would leap up to greet her, her tan-freckled paws reaching to Julie's shoulders. Julie would lean down her face, and Mag would lick her with slow, measured strokes. Maggie had claimed a foam chair as her "spot" in the house (although she preferred to climb up in our laps); she wouldn't allow either of us to pass without pawing at us, and sometimes we'd catch her watching us, unblinking, for what seemed minutes at a time, as if the predicament were reversed, and she was attempting to understand what made us tick, why we weren't content simply to let her run, to let her do what every molten fiber told her to.

When her papers arrived, we wrestled over two choices for her registered name. Devil in Disguise was an appropriate selection, but the notice of registration with the Field Dog Stud Book appeared under the name Flirtin' With Disaster.

The weeks accreted into months, and gradually the hard lessons had a cumulative effect on Maggie. Her unsanctioned forays occurred with decreasing frequency, but I was in no hurry to press her into serious field work. Zack was adjusting to the grouse woods, and in early November we brought Gabe home from the field trial circuit. The bills were piling up, and she wasn't winning. With Maggie just starting to come under control, I felt that more yard training was in order before she came unglued hunting wild birds. This puzzled my father-in-law, who informed me testily during a Thanksgiving trip to Iowa that in his opinion Maggie would make the best one of the bunch if I'd give her a chance. I tried to explain my rationale, that she was still too wild, that she needed more drilling on basic commands, but I knew he didn't buy it.

I taught Maggie *whoa* that winter, making her stand for her food until released by *all right,* and I used feeding time to accustom her to gunfire as well. I schooled her daily on *heel* and *come.* A mild February allowed me to start her in the field; she learned to run on two short whistle blasts, and to look for me when I blew a long trill. I clipped her to a check cord, working her on planted pigeons, crooning *birdsbirdsbirds* and lip-whistling the two-note bobwhite call when she acted birdy. She sometimes pointed the dizzied pigeons and sometimes didn't, but I knew it was a matter of time, and exposure to game. The raw material was there. There was a joy in the way she ran and hunted: she flew across the open, grassy fields near North Bay, stringing together cast after cast like pearls, jumping and cracking her tail, digging into the woods only to pop out ahead; I'd sing to her to let her know where I was, that she was doing it right. Watching her roam over the countryside, it was impossible not to smile.

Dreams, however, have a way of assuming their own shapes. Julie and I found ourselves in diminished circumstances, darkly second-guessing the wisdom of our move to this lonely peninsula. With unemployment above 20%, there was no work to be had. A friend mentioned that he'd heard of a man who was in the market for a setter of field trial quality. We decided that Maggie was, for a price, available.

We needed the money, but it was difficult to pursue her sale with much enthusiasm. She was family, and in the field she was getting better and better. On a cold, gray Sunday in early April, when the sandhill cranes were migrating north to the tremulous strains of their own peculiar chorus, I entered Maggie in a small field trial held near Green Bay. Her performance on that drizzly morning will always float like cream above the milk of my memories: she blazed across that muddy upland, running with amazing speed, a study in joy as she drove to hunt each patch of cover, swinging to my whistle to make certain I was still there, and I was, pulling through the mud, half-running to keep up, flushed with excitement, the judge leaning down from the saddle to whisper "That's a hell of a nice dog—I can't get over her *drive*," Maggie pointing a quail with her flag stretched skyward, and as I collared her at time overhearing one of the judges, as they rode to view the next brace, say "I guess we have our winner," and they did. An acquaintance, impressed by what he'd seen, asked what it would take to buy her. I answered "500 dollars." I had put a price on all the agony and effort, on the animal that had at last put the pieces together, her instincts and ancestry hammered and coaxed and molded into a bird dog.

But the man supposedly interested in buying her had left the trial early, before Mag's run. I spent the rest of the spring showing Maggie to him, not only during other field trials but after their completion, when the grounds were free for training. She was incomparably better than the dogs he owned at the time, and he was a well-heeled manufacturing executive, but he hemmed and hawed, not-so-subtly trying to influence my price. "She likes the woods," he'd say, and "She pounds the ground a little." His major concern was her indifference to the pigeons he planted: he questioned her pointing instinct, although he'd seen her point a semi-wild pheasant with enough style and intensity to please the most critical judge. I wouldn't back down on my price, and at last the deal fell through. "I like the dog, but I think she's going to have to be taught how to point," he said.

The weekend after he'd declined to buy her, a friend and I worked Maggie on pigeons. She pointed each bird flawlessly, as if she knew that she was no longer jeopardizing her future. I decided she was no longer for sale, at any price.

The summer was the hottest on record. I was able to train only until mid-June, but Maggie continued to improve. She channeled some of the youthful run she'd displayed into hunting the cover more thoroughly, eager to point game for the gun. I was smugly anticipating the satisfaction of shooting woodcock, grouse, and pheasant over her in the fall. I could start teaching her to retrieve then. She developed a stubborn fungus infection on the inside of her hind legs, and in addition to the prescribed ointment, we'd stake her to a long chain when the heat wasn't too oppressive, hoping sunlight would help clear up the problem. After a couple of weeks of this therapy, the circle described by the length of her chain was pocked with craters; not content merely to sun, she worked out digging post holes.

She was the implement of her own destruction. In late August, I let all three of the setters out for a romp in the cool of early evening. Maggie and Zack began a game of tag; Maggie was "it," chasing her kennelmate, when she caught her right hind leg in one of the holes she'd excavated, tearing the ligaments in the already brittle hock. I remembered how long it had taken for me to recover when I'd torn ligaments in an ankle. I wouldn't shoot any birds over Maggie that season. Disappointment clung to me like an acrid fog.

She passed the autumn—or it passed her—whining in her kennel, crying pitifully whenever I loaded Zack or Gabe in the pickup along with my gun case and shooting bag. I steeled myself to patience, determined to let her heal fully before stressing the fragile joint. It wasn't until Christmas that the hitch disappeared from her stride, and again she moved freely and gracefully.

Even in the deep snow and bitter cold of late January, there was reason for optimism. It wouldn't be that long before the snow broke, before the first hardy male woodcock returned to establish their singing fields, and I could finally concentrate on Maggie's bird work. She had her legs back. I wasn't concerned that morning when she faded from sight into the woods north of our property. She'd been cooped up for months, she was feeling good, and she'd be back after a bit. I knew about where she was, so I didn't feel compelled to wade through the snow and the brush to escort her home. I was feeling good too, looking forward to picking up college friends at the airport that afternoon. I figured Maggie would come whizzing by the window next to my desk any minute, and I'd throw on a coat, lace my boots, go outside and mock scold "Mag, where have you been," and she'd jump up on me, snowballs clumped in her feathers, and I'd take her head in my hands and roughly caress it before leading her to the kennel.

When the neighbor woman called, it was as if some catalyst had been mixed with the fluid of time, like pectin added to a simmering juice, and all motion slowed and thickened. I spread an old blanket in the back of the car, turned left at the end of our lane, and drove north on Highway 57. Her body lay in the ditch on the right hand side of the road. I read the signs in the snow that said *deer,* and saw the smear of blood on the pavement. I thought of the *Iliad,* the way the souls of the fallen heroes fled from the wounds instantly, and I hoped it had been like that for Maggie.

I drove to the end of a gravel road and carried Maggie deep into a frozen cedar swamp. I placed her under a tangled blowdown where, came spring, water would cover her, and her bones would sink, finally, into the muck. I took off her collar, kicked some snow over her, and then I lost thirty minutes of my life, the way I had when I was 13, and I'd ridden my bicycle to a park to play football. I leg tackled a kid big for his age, and his weight came down on my head, and the next thing I knew I was standing on the corner across from my house, waiting to walk my bike across Lakeport Road. I was in front of the library in Sturgeon Bay, 20 miles away, telling Julie that Maggie had been killed, blinking back tears, cursing at how unfair it was, how every goddamned cur and mongrel in the country ran loose but didn't get run over, didn't get killed by some hit-and-run sonofabitch, someone I'd kill if I ever found out, some hit-and-run sonofabitch who never slowed down, who probably saw her coming out of the woods but never slowed down, and Julie trying to soothe me, telling me there was no use crying, there was nothing we could do, maybe there was never anything we could do, we always knew it could happen, we kind of expected it, pull yourself together, we have to go to the airport, do you want me to drive.

It would make for high drama to write that I dreamed of Maggie, re-creating the event as if I had been a witness, sitting upright in sleep and screaming "No!"; it would be theatre to say I awoke to find myself sobbing, calling her name like an incantation: "Maggie, my Mag, my beautiful Maggie . . ."

But I didn't dream at all. We sat up late, drinking wine, catching up with our friends. Sleep was just that easy, frictionless lacuna, a simple absence, a perfectly white, distilled passage of time. I awoke early, long before daylight, and quietly walked downstairs. I plugged in the coffee maker. While it burped and gasped I sat in a corner of the dining room, where even in the darkness I could dimly perceive the featureless expanse of the frozen lake, its blanket of snow reflecting the dull glow of the clouds. Dawn was just a feeling, more like the slow acquisition of night vision than a true ripening of day. I could make out the skeletal birches standing on the far shoreline, the dark cedars, and the boarded-up cottages of the summer residents, people who shudder at the prospect of spending winter here, ignorant that the winters are harder than their wildest imaginings. The land rose behind them in gray masses of leafless maples. I could see above it all the ugly braid of a squall frothing in from the northwest, the first tentative flakes tumbling to earth. I rose and poured coffee, then sat back in the same chair, warming my cold hands around the hot mug.

And suddenly I could smell her, as purely as on that morning in Mississippi when I picked her up and held her in front of my face, that strange aroma that she never outgrew, that odd musk that even the sweet hay she slept in couldn't mask. I put down the coffee and stared at the palms of my hands, certain that they were the sources of her smell, the hands that had rubbed and petted and held her, the last parts of me ever to touch her. It was as if the heat from the coffee had somehow brought that residue of scent to life. I breathed deeply, trembling, not wanting the aroma to vanish, afraid I would never smell it again. I cannot say how long I stared at my hands, but when I looked up, towards the lake, I couldn't see the other side.

4

CLOSING DAY

The angry winters had punished Iowa so relentlessly that folks around Richland were coming to think of them as the norm, aching to recall what it had been to live through a lesser version. They recurred like a virus until the land lay in agony. Not that suffering was a stranger: in farm country, it has a way of entering when a man's back is turned, and when that fearful prickling licks up and down his spine, his heart stutters at the icy knowledge that what he's caught can't be cured by faith or medicine, that only the weary elapse of time will heal him, and that he'd better carry on as best he can because bad luck doesn't erase obligations. But now it seemed that the doors were flung wide open, and frigid misery stomped into every house like an unemployed relative intending to stay, a lifetime's detritus piled in the back seat of a two-tone Torino. The spindly warmth deposited by the sun in its breathless dash was sucked out of the earth the moment stars punctured darkness, and withdrawals were made from savings until dawn scaled the snow-scoured fields. Those nights, you could feel the famous prairie resilience brittle and crack like hard candy.

Yet, in my wife's family at least, a positive balance of spiritual generosity remained on account. It was a comfort to join them for the holidays, quitting urbanism and its gluey politics for one precious week of indulgence between Christmas and New Year's Day, mending whatever had frayed, and stockpiling good humor for the lean months ahead. Joy freighted the small particulars that smelled of constancy: the gritty nose of Velvet tobacco ("I promised myself when I was fourteen that one day I'd have the money to smoke nothin' but Velvet," Merle allowed) stropped along the spicy bevel of Gene's Amphora; the steaming coffee pot, kept hot from six in the morning until ten at night; the anxious rotation of aromas from Alvina's oven, cinnamon rolls to roast turkey to sour cream raisin pies, each so intense you could nearly chew it; the detergent scent of the laundry room, where Julie and I, at the bottom of the pecking order beneath her parents, her older sister Jan and brother-in-law Bruce, slept in a hide-a-bed that was impossibly small, discovering virtues in contortion. There was reassurance in the accumulation of modest graces, the predictability of Merle, at dusk, rising from his cushioned rocker for a last check of the thermometer nailed to the oak tree before drawing the linen draperies, fiddling with the vinyl-covered heating pad, and easing down to his favorite magazine, *Full Cry*. And it was always a quiet astonishment to study Mary, my tall, elegant mother-in-law, perched on a stool above the breakfast bar, focusing through her half-frames on the business of fine-cleaning the day's kill of birds, a task her pianist's hands discharged with such meticulousness—patiently excising each flattened granule of lead, every embedded feather, and any tag of ruined meat—that one might reasonably guess she were preparing entrees for Lutece rather than tomorrow's supper.

Unhappily, cleaning birds occupied less of Mary's evenings each year. The blind winters savaged without preference, sweeping our adored quail from the countryside as smartly as a croupier gathers losing bets from a gaming table. What seemed a vein of exotic proportions played out absolutely, until the only physical evidence it had ever existed were fuzzy snapshots of limit bags and the few spent, yellow hulls we'd forgotten to pocket in the excitement of a covey rise, the empties now half-hidden under matted brome. The complexion of our days afield had dried up so radically across such a narrow span of time that our reservoir of optimism was not yet drained, although the level was dangerously low.

It had been our privileged mine, this quail shooting. The fan of ground arcing south of Richland was fashioned with tilt and wrinkle enough to rescue a generous measure from the plow, and the fluency with which the soil's mysterious language translated itself into grain was expressed as plentiful leftovers for bobwhites. Within half-a-dozen miles of town, we knew sufficient bird-rich coverts to hunt wherever our fancy bent, whether for an hour or an entire day. There was no question that our dogs would make game; the sole variable lay in the gunners' abilities, in overcoming that obligatory amazement when a covey breaks cover, and rearranging the jangled faculties in time to point a shotgun. Merle himself owned two of our special places, an eighty-acre piece we called "The Y" because it bordered the Y-shaped intersection of two state highways, and a larger farm, a bobwhite *paradiso* of compact cornfields filigreed with twining, brushy ditches and spattered with grown-over pockets of uncultivated land. And there were the sprawling belts of goldenrod and ryegrass on Rosie's, the broad swath of greenbriar, blackberry, and Osage orange that began below the sad little cemetery on old lady Idy's and stretched to the section line, the unlikely-looking pastures and the reliable creek bottom that "Dirty" Keevin posted to everyone save Gene. An eight-quail limit had been a genuine possibility on any one of those parcels. Now, three hunters and four bird dogs couldn't find that first quail.

The single glimmer of light in this otherwise black scenario was the fact that the pheasant population remained healthy. Yet that too had a dark side. It had not been so long ago that this corner of Iowa was closed to pheasant hunting, and only the handful who could swing a shotgun fluidly and delighted in crisp work by pointing dogs pursued quail. But when the ringnecks established themselves, convincing the state to open the season, hunters followed in their wake the way gulls flock behind a moldboard turning earth. We thrilled at the pyrotechnic burst of feathers from a centered cockbird, especially if it was the result of a cleanly executed point and flush, but there was a decorum, a gentlemanly aspect to quail that we coveted. They defined, for us, the rules of the game, challenging while not unreasonable. For a time, we had the best of both worlds, the bobs holding their own while the pheasants multiplied, but the

number of hunters multiplied as well, and seeing a party of shooters walking one of our favored coverts instigated a kind of spiteful
disgust. "It ticks me off," Gene complained bitterly, slamming his
pipe into the heel of his hand, eyebrows arranged fiercely. "All these
people goin' through the cover with curs and feists, shootin' whatever gets up. It's no wonder the quail are gettin' wild." The pheasants
weathered the raging winters, and the state biologists admitted
under their breath that quail compete poorly with ringnecks for the
same habitat. Now that some of Iowa's densest concentrations of
pheasant were found in these counties, the sobering reality was that
the quail might never come back.

We were forced to become prospectors, assaying the weight of
every rumored seam of quail. At the Hy-Vee in Fairfield, Merle
bumped into Ronny Ray, who volunteered that the quail were thick
in the hill country southwest of town, and that Gene should stop by
his trailer one morning and he'd take him bird hunting. Gene and
Ronny Ray had run together in high school, and when Ronny Ray
tried to stick on the rodeo circuit Gene traveled with him, because
it was a good time and because Ronny Ray needed someone to
broom the dust from his ego when he got thrown. But then Gene
married and the Air Force stationed him in Bakersfield, and without Gene to pick him up when he fell Ronny Ray saddled up with a
ring of small-time cattle rustlers, with whom he galloped straight
through the gates of the penitentiary in Fort Madison.

After he served his time, Ronny Ray cozied into a life that suited
him. He sold hand-tooled leather belts and wallets to the college stu-
dents in Fairfield when the welfare check didn't cover expenses, and
autumns he hired on with a guide service in Montana, wrangling
and cooking at an elk camp. Come December, he devoted himself to

laying in a year's supply of meat. Ronny Ray's days were free because at twilight he'd sling his slug gun over one shoulder and hike to a deer blind hidden in a thumb of timber surrounded by corn. "It's just like havin' a job," he said seriously. "You have to go to work every day." Ronny Ray shared his trailer with a remarkably attractive younger woman from Arkansas who carried his baby, and her two children. He kept some milking goats in the yard. They became meat goats when the deer poaching was bad.

Ronny Ray didn't own a telephone, so Gene called Ruby, his mother, for directions. On a bright, perfect morning we found his trailer in a hollow at the bottom of a shoulderless gravel road. It was crackling cold, yet the door to the trailer was nothing more than a sheet of plexiglass stapled to a frame of one-by-twos. "County's supposed to come out and hang a real door," Ronny Ray laughed as he stepped outside. He stood five feet five on legs like a pair of parentheses. He was dark as an Indian, although as far as anyone knew his heritage was pure Anglo, and he had a way of rolling from heel to the ball of his foot when he walked that suggested athleticism. His new automatic shotgun spoke volumes about Ronny Ray's priorities.

We returned six hours, three quail, and God knows how many miles later. Ronny Ray had led us through gorgeous country, the wild, abrupt, wooded land that Iowa becomes as it nudges Missouri, a land of pale, indifferent soil and underground coal mines. We worked the edges of the irregular cornfields dictated by the broken topography, the tiny, inviting beanfields wedged between tangled ravines. Deer fled the hickories ahead of us, flowing over the sidehills and the harvested fields. We combed abandoned farmsteads in this rough country so painful to till, where agriculture meant crisis long before the two words were hitched in the vernacular. The few quail were skittery as water on smoking oil, flushing far ahead of the dogs or deploying into frightening islands of multiflora rose. The dogs were loopy from fatigue—Gene had to gather arthritic Heidi in his arms and lift her into the car—their muzzles and bellies striated with evil lacerations. Our own strength had been scattered like ashes across those endless hills. "I can't understand it," Ronny Ray apologized, shaking his brown head. "I see so many quail when I'm deer hunting." A tethered goat bleated in the maize-tinted light. At the Burger Barn in Fairfield, Gene slumped in the booth, stirring a pool of ketchup with a limp french fry. "God, I wish we could get into some quail," he said softly.

We invested our meager fund of hope in the wisdom of Merle's old friend Floyd. They spoke on the phone often, and Floyd mentioned that he'd seen several coveys, one of them made up of what he called "them big jumbo quail." Merle and Floyd had walked more miles together behind hounds running coon than either of them cared to guess. The doctors told Floyd he had a cancer, but he still pastured some beef cattle, made hay to feed them through the winter, and grew oats and corn for cash. Whenever we asked, Merle would grimace, suck air through the corner of his mouth, and say "Floyd looks bad." But that had been his reply for years, and Floyd was still kicking.

Floyd's mobile home sat atop a hill south of Ottumwa, off a serpentine dirt road that squiggled through some of the comeliest quail territory in the state, the scruffy fields bordered by gray hardwoods, weeds covering useless, rusting harrows. It might have been a sepia photograph from early in the century. Merle had to show us Floyd's; it was the kind of place you have to have a feel for to find. Baled straw insulated the foundation of the trailer, and

Floyd kept a gaunt Redbone chained to a stake out back for the rare evening he felt stout enough to hunt coon. Floyd craned his creased, warty face out the door as we pulled into the yard. "Don't you boys let them bird dogs git around that hound a'mine," he cautioned in his country drawl. "He's a mean sucker to fight." While we hunted, Merle visited with Floyd and his jolly wife, Edith, who would keep their cups filled with black coffee and, later, fix them each a cold meat sandwich and a bowl of beet pickles, and cut them a slice of yellow cake.

That day, as we hunted the fingers of cover clutching the billowing cornfields and the deep ravines fenced by briars, my English setters and Gene's German shorthairs furious to make game, the buffers of optimism finally shredded. The frustration of three years without decent quail shooting had foamed up, toxic and dreadful, inside each of us. We were helpless, trapped in a decaying spiral, pinned by the torque of circumstances we could not alter or avoid, crippled by the remembrance of that special brand of sport and what it had meant to us. When an ample covey started wild, and the befuddled dogs failed to locate the singles, that hateful bile burned in our throats until we spat it out.

"You said those birds put down in here. I can't believe the noses on these dogs are *that* poor."

"I'm sure they dropped into this field. Their wings were set when they topped the trees."

"You either saw them or you didn't."

"I watched 'em through the trees—"

"How do you know they didn't fly all the way to that ditch? Hell, they could be anywhere."

"They lit in here. They had to."

"Even if they'd set in here and run out, the dogs'd be birdy. They're not smellin' a thing. Damn it, you'd think you'd know enough to mark those birds down."

"I'm not telling you again. *This is where they went down.*"

"I don't think you have any idea where those quail flew."

We hunted until mid-afternoon, the silence interrupted only by an occasional whistle to turn a dog. The drive back to Richland took longer than any clock could measure.

If we had rubbed the nap from the whole cloth of our optimism, the anticipation of one pleasure did not erode, even if it was closing day of the bird season, and evening would witness our reluctant diaspora to the cities and jobs we suffered to pay for one week in Iowa. Attending the annual reunion dinner, like the dowry to hunt Merle's land, was a privilege conferred by marriage. Last year, the event had taken place in the restored depot in Rubio, a flat, tired burg pinched into an elbow of county blacktop in the Skunk River bottoms. It was the kind of town you had no business visiting because all the merchants had gone bust, and whatever windows not boarded over had been broken out. This year it was slated for the Lions Club hall in uptown Richland and, as our wives coordinated their culinary offerings, we dreamed of excess and buried our faces in the Sunday *Des Moines Register:* Merle read the farm page, Bruce the business section, Gene the peach-colored sports insert, and I attempted the crossword.

Inside the hall, banquet tables and metal folding chairs are arranged in orderly rows, like carefully planted crops. A photograph of President Reagan, the framed certificate of charter from the national headquarters, and an aerial view of Richland decorate the plain walls. The American flag and the state flag of Iowa flank a low proscenium abutting the far end of the building, upon which stands a portable electronic podium. At the other end of the room, the kitchen is visible through a spacious serving window.

Farming is the center of gravity around which this family orbits, and even those who have left the country for work in the Deere and Caterpillar factories are bound to it by concern and syntax. The men, looking orphaned and self-conscious in the clingy, double-knit slacks and open-collar shirts their wives buy for them, speak of late harvests, the hog market, interest rates, and, like a disease they can't shrug off, the winters. Gene pumps seldom-seen cousins for intelligence regarding quail, and the reply echoes like a lamentation: "Damn few quail left in this country."

The women crowd the kitchen, removing the Saran wrap from jello salads, warming casseroles in the ovens, portioning carrot cakes. Gossip is flimsily camouflaged under the rubric of news. The usual run of extramarital affairs, illegitimate births, and pending divorces is reported. Rumors of an interracial marriage circulate, as does talk that someone's son is employed as a hairdresser in Iowa City.

Julie re-introduces me to the assorted "relations," who promptly forget my name for another year, as I do theirs. The locus of attention is Goldie, Merle's mother, my wife's great-grandmother. All queue to greet the matriarch, one of her daughters (herself a woman of considerable age) bent at her ear, tracing the lineage of each descendant more than two generations distant. Great-Grandma reacts tepidly to Julie, who tells me, "She's never liked Jan or me. She thinks we're too skinny." The single absence worthy of note is that of Julie's uncle, Merle's younger son and farming partner, who has trailered his monstrous, futuristic combines and four-wheel drive tractors to Blossom, Texas, to perform custom fieldwork, hoping to relax the grinding debt owed on the machines.

I am here for the food, and help myself to seconds of everything. The serving table sags beneath a dizzying galaxy of glazed hams, pungent meat loaves, bubbling crocks of baked beans, narcotic potato salads, and dozens of proprietary recipes. Desserts—steaming apple pies, pumpkin pies smothered by Matterhorns of whipped cream, dark, inscrutable fudges—ooze calories. After dinner, the men light pipes, sip black coffee (cream users are considered pariahs), and deal cards for games of pitch. Older women identify the leftovers and dutifully clean up. Girls marry young in this family, and now they bottle feed their babies with the hands that shook pom-poms a year ago. Ambulatory children race and whoop out of sheer, shameless exuberance. Behind their shouts, behind the laughter of the men and the murmurs of the women hums the energy of common strengths.

I struggle to break the food-induced torpor that glazes my will as if it were a soft sweet roll, stagger to my feet, and tap Bruce on the shoulder. It's two in the afternoon, and the season closes at 4:30. Bruce groans and stubs out a Camel filter. We glimpse Gene's powder-blue sweater among a knot of card players.

"C'mon Gene. Last call for bird huntin'."

"You go on ahead."

"You're kidding."

"Nah, Heidi's pretty well stove up, and Gretel's pads are bleeding again. Think I'll stay here and catch up. You two go ahead. Ought to be pheasants on the Y."

Of course, we knew the excuses were just that. Gretel had slipped pads before, and Heidi's age had shown the past two seasons. The crux of it was that bird hunting, like all affairs of passion precarious and fragile, a high wire tensed between expectation and reality, had exacted a toll on Gene these recent seasons, and for the first time he couldn't imagine a payback that would cover the potential losses. The unrequited promise of those beautiful, bosomy hills at Ronny Ray's and Floyd's had exhausted his desire.

Bruce and I lurched out of the Lions hall, squinting in the sudden flood of sunlight, economizing our movements in the shocking cold. Christmas lights still ringed the town square, and a decorated aisle led to the gazebo where Santa Claus held forth. We walked quickly past the businesses that coughed along like black-lunged miners: the cafe where Mary had waitressed as a teenager, the locker that displayed its name in masking tape letters in the window, the grocery with its electric Sprite sign, the dress shop where those pretty cheerleaders were fitted for wedding gowns.

The Y lay two miles east of Richland. An 80-acre rectangle in the plat book, it swelled and heaved, its black soil cinched from sagging by a girdle of terraces, the twin-lobed cornfield cleft by a trough-like waterway that drained into a silty, meandering creek. The cover on both banks of the creek described a scalloped, woven edge where it met the cultivated ground; pheasants and, in the past, quail could sneak out of hiding, stuff their crops with waste corn, and sift back into the vegetation without attracting predators. Even after the cruelest winters, roosters were heard gathering their harems on the Y like noisy sheiks. It was a bone of contention between Merle and us that he refused to post it, despite the truth that every local who owned a shotgun hunted there. "It wouldn't be right," he argued. "I hunt all over this country myself, so it wouldn't do to post my own land."

Merle always left several acres in grass hard by the highway. "Them birds need a place to nest," he'd say. We pulled off there, unsleeved our guns, and clipped a lead on Zack, my setter just shy of his second birthday. We were discussing strategy when a metallic honk turned our head in time to see a hulking olive sedan braking hard, fishtailing onto the shoulder. Cranking down his window, the man on the passenger side beckoned us over. He wore a Jones cap that seemed small and lost on top of a massive, crew-cut head, and his jowly face was reddened by fractional pink filaments that wanted to crawl out of his skin. Zack jerked forward, jumping up to sniff the car's occupants, and the man cuffed him down with the solid backside of his wrist.

"That's wasn't called for," I said, frowning.

He appeared not to hear me, resting an arm along the car door. His hand was meaty, thick-fingered, and yellowed sclera surrounded corneas that swam with an opaque blue. He seemed the kind of man used to giving orders and seeing them carried out. "You boys have permission to hunt this land?" The driver, a younger, slighter man wearing mirrored sunglasses, flicked a butt out his window and folded his arms on the steering wheel.

"Yeah."

"Who gave it to you?"

"Who's asking?" I snapped.

"Listen, junior nimrod, I'll kick your . . . to Muscatine." Those pink filaments dilated, darkening into scarlet.

Bruce piped up. "You mad that we got here before you? Merle happens to be our wives' grandfather, you fat-faced—"

"Sheee*yit*," he cackled. "Merle may own this ground on paper, but the way that kid of his goes through money, it might as well be the bank's right now." He made a clucking laugh, and the other man grinned stupidly. We'd heard the rumors, at Idy's estate auction and at the Deere dealer out on the highway, the mean, ignorant spittle of people with nothing left in their lives except the sowing of wild tales. "And teach that dog some manners," he spat, rolling up the window as they left, spraying gravel on my station wagon.

In memory, it survives as a dreamscape, those 80 acres, those final two hours of the season. Perhaps it was the psychological residue or the adrenalin rush from that unnerving encounter, perhaps, the dazed euphoria lingering from dinner. Or maybe it was the quality of light, the way the sun played across the fields, gilding the cut cornstalks and the flat blades of canary grass, finally, after the bad winters, soothing the wounded earth. I would think it some sorcery of the mind, but it was a hallucination Bruce shared, and I recall it perfectly, although the images shimmer as in mirage, the actions half-speed and soft focused. There was no reason for Zack, a reckless, unpolished setter, to perform as he did, floating from point to point, pinning cockbirds that, having been hunted virtually every day for two months, by rights should have flushed wild or slinked to safety on foot; no reason for him to hold his quivering stature for minutes, buried in heavy cover until we found him, the black-spurred rooster crowing out of the canes where Zack told us he crouched, a clattering kaleidoscope of feathers. There was no explanation for the number of pheasants on this 80, when it was the hardest-hunted acreage in Keokuk County, and there was posted land, *de facto* refuges, to the east and north. What made us hunt with special care, stumbling across plowed ground to leverage spooky birds into holding, taking time to explore tiny islands of cover, to zigzag with agonizing slowness in case Zack missed a bird? What magic, when we found Zack curled in a horseshoe, pointing on a flat bench above the creek, summoned a small, priceless covey of quail to materialize from beneath a canopy of brittle vines, birds we harbored no hope of discovering, and what compelled us not to shoot, even when Zack nailed each single as squarely as a carpenter drives spikes? What alignment of stars and planets, what attitude of sun and moon, what reconciliation or forgiveness caused three cockbirds to feed in the picked corn next to the car, sliding into the cover to roost just as we returned, just as the season closed and we snugged the shells into our vests, just in time for Zack to break heel and stiffen into point, the copper roosters melting into the sunset as it spread across the terraced hillside? If, in this time, such a thing as augury can exist, there were promises enough in this land and in these birds to invest the future with certainties rather than dreams.

The word came down a few weeks later, on a January afternoon when the sky was girding for blizzard. The ugly rumors were true, but not even Merle knew it until the banks and the co-ops and the implement dealers began calling, clarifying the depth of debt his younger son had incurred. Merle had co-signed open-ended notes that had been drawn on until repayment was a fiction; the creditors would hold a land auction to recover their losses. This was not Hollywood, these were not highlights from the evening news. Merle had worked a lifetime to own his farms free and clear, and now he had to hire out as field help at $4 an hour just to make ends meet, just as he had when he and Alvina were starting out, and Gene was wearing diapers.

The family dinner didn't come off this year. Great-Grandma died, and no one really felt like it. The winter was reasonable, but the quail remain more vivid in memory than in fact. A sportscaster from one of the Des Moines stations did a special on the pheasant hunting, and now there are more gunners than ever. We are in need of new land to hunt. We have heard good things about Kansas, but we wonder what it will cost to believe them.

5

HEART OF THE SANDHILLS, SOUL OF THE PRAIRIE

Leaving Iowa, driving west on U.S. 20, the land by degrees assumes a wild aspect, like the face of a man gone too long without human contact, unshaven and feral about the eyes. Although the tokens of civilization are never wholly absent: faintly menacing, the long, centipedal irrigators crawl around proboscises sunk deep into the Ogallala aquifer, bringing the land within their considerable radii of influence to an unnatural state of verdancy, the frilly green like costume jewelry against the temperate bosom of the Sandhills. At 55 miles per hour, agriculture itself appears in the condensed version, the Midwestern-generic corn and soybeans petering out to dryland small grains, in turn giving up to hayland, until at last grazing is all the land will tolerate; this is the east-to-west spectrum of 120 miles.

Even when it shakes free and becomes a country all of horizons, suffocating in its vastness, in its harrowing, aimless sweep, a man may still take comfort in barbed wire. In the Sandhills, the fence-maker's art achieves its definitive form, the galvanized extrusions humming like harp strings in the enduring wind, the gates mysteries of leverage that a scrawny child can pop open if he knows where to apply his shoulder, that a weight lifter could damage himself on if he doesn't. There is economy in a good, tight fence: after all, it is not as if one can walk out after supper with a fencer's tool on his belt and a coil of wire in his hand to mend a break or cinch a sag, not where the ranches might be twenty miles apart, and a section of fence won't be ridden once a year. Cattle wander bravely across the sere range, clinging to the meadows where grass grows more prosperously than in the scruffy hills proper. But the herds are scattered: one may travel miles without sign of animal life, other than wheeling buteos, to top another unremarkable swell and start at the sight of a brown whorl of beeves, dumb senses recharged by this rupture in the terrible, treeless sameness.

Most find it taxing simply to itemize a single reason to visit this place. Mine is straightforward: I come to hunt prairie chickens and sharp-tailed grouse, and to assuage an aching loss. My home state,

Iowa, was the heart of the tallgrass prairie, a sea of head-high big bluestem and seed-heavy Indian grass, lacy switchgrass and nodding wild rye, delicate side-oats grama and peevish needle-and-thread. Trees were confined to watercourses and to rare archipelagos surrounded by oceans of grass. The prairie chicken was the perfect, pulsing soul of this landscape, a species evolved to flourish in big country, a lover of grasses with a neurotic antipathy toward trees. In the 1880's, when Iowa was momentarily poised at a rough equilibrium between cultivated cropland and unbroken, native prairie, the chicken population exploded to levels never to be remotely paralleled. Living was easy: at dawn and dusk, the birds left their roosts in undisturbed grassland to gorge in the grainfields. For a time, market hunters cashed in spectacularly, shipping chickens back east by the barrel, fated for the toniest restaurants.

But as the balance tilted in favor of tilled land, the prairie chicken in Iowa began its irresistible decline. The season was closed permanently in 1916, and in 1955—the year before I was born—the last of the state's chickens "marched into the unknown," as Aldo Leopold wrote of their demise elsewhere. Of course, the ring-necked pheasant closed ranks behind its departing relative, its appearance coinciding with dissemination of the radical idea that sport hunting should be practiced not only by the privileged. An eminently sporty and egalitarian bird, the pheasant blinded Iowans to the desperation of the prairie chicken. The historical record reveals scant notice of its passing.

Thus did my Iowan forefathers impoverish the land in the name of enriching it, the glinting steel of the plow rending the prairie, leaving in its wake the state where the tall corn grows, the nation's breadbasket. I harbor no illusion that there might have been another history, more benign and forward-looking, because that is a history we cannot yet write ourselves.

This knowledge, it is true, jumped me only after I became aware that Iowa was not always cornfields and hog lots. I spent a summer working as a technician for the Fish & Wildlife Service out of Madison, South Dakota, where in the course of protecting nesting cover for dabbling ducks I learned to identify the native grasses. (Imagine my horror when I was informed that the ubiquitous bromegrass, which I had always assumed represented a semblance of the native prairie, had been introduced during the Dust Bowl days.) I was taught how rare and fragile native prairie is, and I began to search it out. I came to the dismal realization that the best places to identify big bluestem, Indian grass, switchgrass, and the other native species were abandoned railroad right-of-ways, scraps of earth untouched by plows. The awful dimensions of the change, in hardly more than a century, rocked me. Would the pioneers buried atop the bluffs even recognize this place? I began to reflect on the prairie chicken. I had no quarrel with pheasants: in biological parlance, they had simply occupied a vacated ecological niche. They had also been the source of much sincerely gratifying sport. But it was ironic to consider that where the prairie chicken had risen to its high-water mark as a species, the only game birds that could now survive—with the exception of bobwhite quail in the state's southern third—were the pheasant and the Hungarian partridge, Eurasian immigrants.

At last, married and working in southern Illinois, I begged time off to hunt the Sandhills over the mid-September chicken opener. Bob Cowan and I crammed dogs, food, dog food, and shooting paraphernalia into my station wagon, and the two of us left Friday;

George Boykin and Jerry Woolridge were to arrive Saturday afternoon. The first hundred miles passed in a blur. When the landscape opened and the familiar vanished, I knew we had entered the Sandhills. For a moment, I was possessed by the exhilaration that attends any new and longed-for experience. But then I began to feel uneasy, small and a little afraid, the self-importance sucked out of me by this alien vastness. This is how it is in chicken country: the pioneering Europeans, emerging from the eastern woodlands, had no memory, personal or racial, they could summon to prop their confidence when faced with the limitless, fearful prospect of the prairie. If there is solace in open spaces, so is there dread. Nothing in my past prepared me for the Sandhills. My heart fluttered like the wings of a stunned bird.

Our destination is the isolated (a word the Sandhills bleed of meaning) ranch of Keith and Dorothy Barthel, in southwestern Holt County. Amelia, which consists of little more than a post office, is the closest name on the map; the nearest town of any significance, O'Neill, lies forty miles north. If there is serious shopping to be done, the Barthels travel to Grand Island, 120 miles one way. The Barthels are in the business of raising replacement cattle, which they graze on a couple thousand acres of meadow (tiny by Sandhills standards) before selling to feeders who fatten them on grain and "supplements" in preparation for market. George Boykin claims he and Dave Adam were scouting chicken territory when they broke down within sight of the Barthel ranch. The Barthels not only helped them repair the truck, they invited them to stay for dinner and sleep over in the bunkhouse. Lloyd Hardy, who no longer hunts because of a bum foot, swears he first made the Barthel's acquaintance and introduced them to the rest. Regardless, the Barthels, who scratch a spare living from this arid, unforgiving country, are hospitable as the Bedu of the Sahara, who would slaughter their only camel in order that passersby might feast.

This analogy can be extended. The Barthel ranch, in common with all Sandhills operations, is an oasis of self-sufficiency. If something breaks, they fix it themselves. They don't pick up groceries, they lay in supplies. They raise their own milk cows and laying hens. Boykin, Cowan, and Woolridge make a point, each visit, of presenting them with some modern convenience, an electric razor for Keith, an automatic can opener for Dorothy, a coffee maker (this was a purely selfish gift: the hunters from the city cannot do without coffee, and the Barthels do not use caffeine), a Fry Baby, anything to insulate them a little from bleakness, to provide a spongy layer of comfort. They bring food, too, canned hams and frozen turkeys.

The Barthels accept these tokens gratefully, if not with any overt enthusiasm. Especially Dorothy. They are fundamentalist Christians, and when Dorothy is not working in the kitchen, around the house, or at ranch chores, she works at religion. Hers is a doctrine that apparently does not allow for humor. She seems never to smile, or for that matter to change her severe, purposeful expression at all. On the other hand, Keith—short, barrel-chested, crew-cut—enjoys a laugh, and one surmises he would be even more jocular if Dorothy weren't so disapproving. The hunters bought Keith a green-checked, Western-style shirt from Stockyards Clothing in Sioux City, and while it fit amply through the chest and shoulders, he couldn't have snapped the top button on a bet. "Where'd you get that thick neck," asked Cowan, and we all chuckled.

Kerry, their youngest son, lives at home when he is not attending a Christian high school for the hearing-impaired in Central City. Another son, Wes, in his early twenties, lives in what was once a bunkhouse with his demure wife, Bethel, and two preschool-age children. Wes and Keith have entered into a partnership on the ranch. Wes has volunteered to guide us tomorrow after the morning chores. An older son, Alan, works on a huge spread in Colorado. I learn later that the Barthels have a fourth son: he rebelled, disavowing his parents' beliefs, and they no longer speak of him or claim him in any fashion. Their only daughter drowned while a young girl, and the grief lingers, incurable if not by itself mortal.

Cowan and I arrive in time for a late lunch of something deep-fried until unidentifiable. I have been warned that Dorothy's cooking is glamourless, and I feel strangely apprehensive about the rubberized mystery on my fork. Yes: Wes, smirking behind his black, semi-handlebar mustache, informs me, after I've dutifully cleaned my plate, "We castrated some calves this morning." My stomach rolls once, but I stand my ground. "Oh yeah? I've always wanted to try mountain oysters." Wes seems intent on revealing me as a sissified city boy, a college-educated weenie.

Keith asks what I do, and when I reply that I do environmental studies for a regional planning commission, Wes unholsters a stare and snaps "Shoot him." "Environmental" is an obscenity among these people, a word they equate with the meddlesome, standard-issue bureaucrats from Lincoln who would stop them from selling raw milk to a few neighboring ranch families. Dorothy then inquires as to the church of my choice. I answer "Methodist," and am immensely relieved that this satisfies her, as I have not been inside a church since my wedding. When they discover that my wife is in

Sioux City, they insist I phone to persuade her to drive out with Boykin and Woolridge. Their generosity is unfathomable until one steps back and assesses the choking loneliness of life in the Sandhills. However diffident they appear, they hunger for visitors. The twice-yearly visits of the hunters are looked forward to like religious holidays. They are, in the Barthel's world of wide horizons and diminished possibilities, a permissible excess, a furtive jig-step in the regimentation of ranch and church, the social highlights of the entire calendar.

In the morning, after a forgettable breakfast, Cowan collars his Brittany, Buck, I round up setters Zack and Gabe, and fifty yards from the house we begin hunting. It is a good morning for bird shooting: temperatures in the fifties, partly sunny, a light westerly breeze. We work a wide meadow, the dogs casting ahead boldly, hoping to find chickens that have flown down from roosts deep in the hills. Failing, we angle into the hills proper, dipping into miniature coulees, puffing up dry slopes tufted with little bluestem. There is an anxious moment when Gabe hurries towards us, hacking and thrashing her head violently. She has tried to tear several pods of ball cactus from her hind leg, and now a jaw-breaker-sized sphere is planted in the roof of her mouth. With Cowan holding her body between his legs and prying open her jaws, I gingerly disengage the cactus. Gabe shakes all over and sprints off to see what Buck and Zack are up to. The experience rattled us more than it did her.

Occasionally, when traversing a hilltop, we spy a jeep or pickup in the shimmering distance, bristling with gun barrels. It seems this is the favored approach to bird hunting in the Sandhills, road hunting off-road. No doubt some of these practitioners shoot from their perches, but the ticket is to spot a covey of grouse or a flock of chickens on the ground, dismount, and hurl a salvo of automatic shotgun fire at the flush. Given the sheer magnitude of the country, this method makes a certain sense. Its sporting qualities, however, leave much to be desired. The sight is remindful of television footage depicting maneuvers in a Middle Eastern war. This is the way we will hunt in the afternoon.

Toward mid-morning, a trio of chickens flush wild above us as we ease downslope. Cowan shoots to no effect; he stands between me and the birds, so I have no shot. That is my introduction to prairie chicken hunting. We move no more birds. Interest and energy wane. The dogs are visibly fatigued, stopping often to bite sand burrs from between their pads. We have covered several miles in a wavy semi-circle south of the ranch, and we have seen three birds. I blink sweat out of my eyes, and I try to purge dismay from my gut.

Julie has arrived with Boykin and Woolridge. Dorothy is already ordering her about the kitchen as if she had been raised there. My wife was brought up in a home that made a fetish of cleanliness, and I can see her recoil from the pitchers of room-temperature milk and cream, the butter melting in the dish. For some reason, the Barthels do not believe in refrigerating milk products. Boykin's wife, a refined, elegant woman from New York, accompanied him once to the Barthel ranch. She summarized her reaction in two words: "Never again." Now George has to concoct excuses for her refusal to return. The Barthels take nothing for granted: their orientation is painfully utilitarian. To embrace anything fancy, or even plainly unnecessary, would be to admit a ruinous optimism that might distract them from matters of pure survival. In a less jaundiced, more hopeful era, the Barthels might have been called the salt of the earth.

Of the afternoon hunt, five of us in Wes's serviceable green pickup, there is little to tell. The heat, the interminable bouncing over the indistinguishable hills, Wes cackling as the Cornhuskers shelled the Hawkeyes: I was stupefied, conscious only in a fuzzy, unfocussed way. We started several flocks of chickens, which flew beyond the limits of vision. From a Sandhills promontory, the eye can see forever, but forever is not big enough to hold a flock of chickens with reason to move. We potted a few doves flying in and out of the cottonwoods bordering a pond. We topped a rise, sighted a half-dozen bird heads peering about stupidly, like tourists, and dropped four sharptails, in a blaze of fire, when they flushed underfoot. The big excitement came when Wes roared blindly up one side of a hill only to jam the brake pedal to the floor. The truck was poised at the brink of a great, gaping gash where a rolling slope should have been. Such phenomena are named blowouts, and they occur when vegetation loses its tenuous, stabilizing grasp on the restless sand. Given an inch, the chiseling wind can carve grotesque moonscapes.

Do not be deceived: The Sandhills are not comprised of loam with a little sand thrown in. Except for a discontinuous film of organic matter, they are pure sand, fine, abrasive stuff deposited by incessant winds 10,000 years ago, 9,000 square miles of it. The Barthels insist that all footwear be removed before entering their house. Otherwise, the tracked-in sand would shred their carpets like crushed glass. The harshness of the environment disguises its fragility. The soil and vegetation of the Sandhills have evolved symbiotically—side-by-side, if you will—reaching a precarious equipoise. Over-grazing, as during the Thirties, invited massive blowouts, as does center-pivot irrigation in the Eighties. The land, formed under conditions of semi-aridity, simply sloughs away when bombarded by an excess of water. Revegetation can take decades. In the Sandhills, wounds heal slowly.

At the head of the long meadow where Cowan and I started the day, Kerry dropped us off before driving ahead to the ranch house. A single chicken flushes forty yards ahead, at the break between meadow and hill. I know my bounds, as well as those of my shotgun, and hold fire. Stridently, Wes calls "That bird was in range!" I shrug, and he shakes his head. A few rods beyond, another single rises. Wes drops it with an expert, long-range crossing shot. Then we are done. Twilight infuses an even more urgent loneliness.

Sunday morning, the Barthels attend church in Burwell, 30 miles south. Keith wears his new shirt, and Kerry remembers to hang his shotgun on the rack in the pickup truck, in case they spot any birds. He has already accounted for a goodly share of grouse and chicken this September, despite the season being officially but a day old. In the Sandhills, shooting game is regarded an inalienable right, not a privilege. The neckties in Lincoln who set the seasons and limits exert negligible authority over the ranch families. The prevailing attitude is that the game found on their land is as much their property as livestock, and they should be able to harvest it at their pleasure. But they see no correlation between land use and game populations. Their view is simple: if game birds are scarce, it's because hawks and other predators are not. The omnipresence, throughout the American west, of rifles racked in pickup cabs has been reported so relentlessly that it has become trivialized. The mortal ramifications of this fact, especially for coyotes and other "varmints," have, as a consequence, paled.

We cast the dogs in a broad meadow east of the ranch, where the Barthels cut wild hay. Our start was late—we dawdled unaccountably over breakfast—and the chamois shirt congeals to my back in a matter of minutes. The chickens have dawdled, too. By rights they should not still be here in the middle of the morning, but we move several fine flocks when the meadow bends west, bunches of eight to ten birds. All flush out of range, and it would take the eyesight of a peregrine to follow their flight to its conclusion. One moment the air is empty, the next it is threshed by the curving wings of chickens, looking absurdly long compared to the compressed cylinder of body as they sail straight away, beating surely, gliding, beating again, and gone. Once more, the dizzying stillness.

And my own stunned confusion, now that the hunt is over. What was it, really, that I had expected? Had I bargained for anything like this? I knew only that somehow I thought it would be easier, not in the sense that bird hunting is ever truly easy, but that if certain conditions of skill and persistence are met, opportunities for satisfaction arise. In the Sandhills, the rules changed. Was luck all-important, and had I been flatly unlucky? Had I set too much store in the tales of Cowan and Boykin? (I should have known better.) But they had been hunting here for years, and were not the types to return did they not fully expect some tangible gratification. The trip had been memorable, shockingly so, but for reasons I could not have imagined: the Barthels sweating to wring a livelihood from this spindly grassland, aspirations dried to the bone, making grand gestures of hospitality to literal strangers; hunters mounted on four-wheel drives roaming over the hills like bands of guerrillas; Wes's thinly-veiled baiting; the almost nauseating emptiness of the Sandhills. I fretted over these questions for a few weeks. Then the pheasant season opened in Iowa. I reoriented myself to the joyfully familiar. It was as if I had been marooned. On opening day, I shot beautifully.

I didn't think much about chickens, or the Sandhills, for a time. But then, four years later, I began planning to return. I guess it was because time had softened that gritty memory of failure, and because of a funky, mischievous optimism that whispered "This time, Tom, things will be better." I began to rationalize that first trip as purely exploratory. I had gotten the lay of the land. Now, I could get down to some serious hunting. It became a mission. I envisioned the Sandhills themselves as more adaptable, my dogs older and wiser. My plan was to work public land around Valentine, farther west than I had been previously, camping and hunting on my own, then rendezvous with Boykin (the others couldn't make it) at the Barthel's. (The partnership had been dissolved; Wes had moved to Colorado.)

It was a good plan on paper. But driving west, when the limits evaporated, when all became sand and grass and wire, that formless apprehension struck, leaving me breathless as if body punched. Nothing had changed; if anything, the omens had darkened. I had driven into the middle of a preposterous heat wave. The sole radio signal that came in clearly originated from the Rosebud Indian Reservation in South Dakota, where the jock reported record highs in every direction: nothing less than 90, a few topping the century. I fought to keep good thoughts, grappling to persuade myself it wouldn't be as bad farther west, as the altitude crept up. I could concentrate on hunting early and late, when it wasn't killing hot.

Just outside town, a billboard announces "Welcome to Valentine, the HEART of the Sandhills." When I worked for the Fish & Wildlife Service, I roomed with the Assistant Manager of the Wetlands District. In his early thirties, he held an M.S. in Wildlife Management from Ohio State. His first job with the Service was a post at the Valentine National Wildlife Refuge. He and his wife, a bright, pretty, ambitious woman with a degree in anthropology, were practically newlyweds when they moved to the Sandhills. Whatever parts of them had dovetailed, whatever it was that fitted them together, the uncaring wind of the Sandhills polished smooth, until there was nothing between them to hang a love on, nothing, when they tried to stay a couple, that would catch up and hold. She left to pursue her doctorate at UCLA. He went antelope hunting.

Downtown, the bank marquee reads 98 degrees. Immersion in outdoor magazines while an impressionable lad has left me with a moronic faith in The Myth of the Knowledgeable Local, usually portrayed as a tight-lipped merchant who is transformed into the ideal of loquacity when casual-sounding questions are accompanied by some meaningful purchase. I step into a hardware store to buy a license, which I need, and a box of shells, which I don't. A broadside near the door alerts interested parties that an auction of surplus buffalo is to be called next week on the Fort Niobrara National Wildlife Refuge. The clerk offers vague and unreliable information (he is obviously not a Knowledgeable Local), and points me to a canoe outfitter three blocks down and a block west.

A stack of evilly dented aluminum canoes marks the outfitter's shop, which doubles, I find, as a liquor store. Judging from the contents of the interior, booze is responsible for the bulk of the income. A pleasant woman greets me with the disclaimer that she is just filling in for the proprietor, who has a dentist's appointment. Her advice is to drive to the Merritt Dam, 26 miles southwest, where she's sure there is a campground, and also a general store/tackle shop.

On the way to Merritt, the road dives into the valley of the Niobrara River, a precious seam of conventional beauty in a land that is otherwise an acquired taste at best. Here, nature dares again to be profligate, yielding to a hedonism of trees, a luxuriance of grasses it does not permit elsewhere in the Sandhills. The valley contains a confusion of botanical systems: the naturalist David Quammen calls it "a situation of exceptional biological interactions, an ecumenical biotic forum unmatched anywhere in the country." Predictably, that pernicious consortium, the Bureau of Reclamation and the Army Corps of Engineers, has for decades cast lustful and rapacious leers at the Niobrara, justifying their carnal desire for a dam by alleging benefits in the form of irrigation water to increase corn production. This in a state already gagging on too much corn, in a land that tends to vanish when irrigated. Logic, sadly, cannot be trusted to arbitrate matters involving BuRec and the Corps.

The Merritt Dam, on a tributary of the Niobrara, the Snake, created a several-thousand-acre impoundment, and, after stocking with the traditional Midwestern gamefish and a prolific forage fish called a gizzard shad, some of the hottest walleye action in Nebraska. At the general store/tackle shop, a man is intent on covering every square inch of a banquet table with Shad Raps, popular walleye lures of Finnish manufacture. He works his way to where I am standing and stares at my hand, which is occupying empty space on the table, until I remove it. He fills the space with Shad Raps.

"Where can I find some decent bird hunting around here?" I ask politely.

"Grouse?" he asks back, still arranging Shad Raps.

I nod. "Hills," he says, jerking his head unspecifically. I have been driving all day, my body chemistry reacts wretchedly to heat, and when I let the dogs out to stretch their legs, they collected sand burrs like gleaners harvesting grain. I refuse to have to buy something from this man to determine if he is Knowledgeable.

"*Where* in the hills?" I counter, irritated.

He completes his display of Finnish lures. "If you can get on private land, you're in like Flynn," he says. It is apparently lost on him that had I access to such land, I wouldn't be asking in the first place. "Course, you don't want to hunt without permission. Some of these ranchers get pretty irate."

"What about public land?" I prompt.

"There's the refuge, and then there's McKelvie."

"Which is better?"

"Same," he says. "McKelvie's closer. There's a hundred and fifteen thousand acres of public land. Take the road back across the dam, then follow it north into the hills. There's a campsite. You'll see signs. It's fifteen miles or so."

"Forest" is a comical euphemism in the Sandhills. The Samuel R. McKelvie National Forest is all grass and emptiness, save for the willows and cottonwoods near the sloughs and the ponderosa pines that anchor an occasional hillside. The appearance of the campground buoys my spirits: shaded by towering pines, scrupulously maintained, and, I am pleased to discover, free. A grill and a redwood picnic table grace each site. I stake the dogs in the shade, pitch my tent, and walk to the pump to fetch water. A homely but hopeful-looking young woman is having trouble pumping with one hand and holding a narrow-necked jug with the other, so I volunteer to pump while she holds. She is traveling with her two children and her boyfriend, although she cannot seem to articulate why they are camping here, or what might be the purpose and destination of the trip. She tells me she plans to fry hamburgers for their supper, but she can't find her spatula. I tell her she can use mine if she needs to.

An abstract of feathers and undigested rose hips beneath the pump shows that a grouse was cleaned here. Rose hips are the sharptail's staple food throughout much of its western range, and this is primarily sharptail country, too far west and too arid for chickens. The sharptail remains an important game bird across the Great Plains and the Prairie Provinces of Canada because its habitat is not so profitably transfigured by agriculture as is the prairie chicken's. Northern populations of sharptails run afoul of forestry practices that discourage open, successional brushlands in favor of conifer plantations, but elsewhere the bird is relatively stable. The wisdom of the pioneers held that while the prairie chicken advanced with the plow, the sharptail retreated before it. They could not know that the plow would drive the chicken into oblivion in what had been the heart of its range.

Towards nightfall, the air cools perceptibly. I loose the dogs for a run north of the campground, but it is still hot by their standards, and in a moment they are lathered and gasping, rib cages heaving as they slump among the radial yucca and the golden little bluestem. I sleep fitfully, as always during first nights in camp, wake early, and fire up the Coleman stove, boiling water for coffee, frying bacon and scrambled eggs. Breakfast is the high point of the morning, because by the time I arrive at the place I want to hunt, the perimeters of a long slough nestled beneath unusually fecund-looking hills, it cannot be less than 80. And the sun is just fractionally above the horizon. We circumnavigate the slough, disturb a flock of blue-winged teal along with scattered doves, then head for the hills. The dogs act birdy briefly near a marsh edge, but it proves a false alarm. After describing a wide, looping arc across the fruitless hills, the dazed setters stagger for shade beneath the car, and gulp water by the quart. The heat is plainly ridiculous. I fear for the health of the dogs.

In an almighty hurry, I break camp, crank the air conditioner up full blast, and race out of the Sandhills with my tail between my legs. I call George Boykin once I reach Sioux City, and he is genuinely relieved that he's no longer obligated to show up at the Barthel's. I gather my fractured wits for a day, then leave for home in Wisconsin where the season has opened on woodcock and ruffed grouse, reasonable, generous birds that inhabit cool, accessible country, places with beginnings and ends.

If not a peace, exactly, I believe I've achieved a kind of fidgety truce with the Sandhills. Of course, it's a perfectly one-sided arrangement. The Sandhills are neither hostile nor personal, just hugely indifferent, and they shrugged off my clumsy wanting like any other selfish dalliance. Come as a wrestler, come as a lover: change, or the Sandhills will scour your spirit until it is colorless and reduced to its adamant germ. A man should approach the Sandhills expecting nothing, and be appreciative of the flintiest grace. The Barthels, I think, understand this in a clear way that language could only make hazy. Even the corn farmers understand they are on borrowed time, that they can mine a cash crop for a while with a monsoon of irrigation and a blizzard of fertilizer, but one morning they'll wake to a cleansing wind, and their fields will have just blown away.

I realize, too, that were the Sandhills less difficult, less heartbreaking, the prairie chicken would be real only in memory, as it is in Iowa. And I should not have expected the bird to be any different than the country it inhabits. Before, it was not enough for me simply to know that a place exists where chickens—and sharptails— survive. Now, it is, and there is comfort in the knowledge.

The conservationist Paul Olson is fond of remarking "Poverty and chickens go together." He means human poverty. In a place like the Sandhills, chickens and sharptails are the very fat of the land.

6

THIS PENINSULA

———————

Come October, the woods go fragrant of Margaux and truffles and cider. Grapes hang heavy and sensuous from tangled vines; wafers of translucent gold, the aspen leaves rustle like rice paper in wind tinted by winter. By day, the Canadas ride that wind, and the peregrine on passage. But at night, when the breeze turns gentle and cool as a mother's breath when she blows through her baby's fine hair, it buoys the woodcock up from the alders and carries them across the water to this peninsula. Some of these nights, when the sky is an embroidery of stars and the moon has absorbed the colors of sunset, you can almost feel the woodcock moving through the air, like spirits that can't be touched or seen, and sense them drifting down to earth.

When William Harnden Foster wrote about "the bayberry pastures and the junipers, where the alder runs continue down from the birch side hills that are dotted with white pines and cedars, and here and there is found a wild apple tree in the corner of an ancient stone wall with blackberry vines and bullbriers tangled together beneath . . . ," he was describing the New England that he knew and adored. But he could just as well have been painting a word picture of this peninsula, for it is a lozenge of land quarried from New England and transported to Wisconsin: tidy villages poised at the confluence of earth and water; orchards, sugarbushes, and dairy farms sectioned by stone fences; a rugged, glacier-sculpted country broken into fields and woodlots. The people, too, possess Yankee virtues: independence, self-reliance, resilience of spirit. It bears scant resemblance to the Wisconsin of deep, vast forests that most bird hunters see in their mind's eye, where trees cover entire counties, and logging trails wind for miles through the shadowed timber. Instead, it is a place of discrete, intimately-knowable coverts: old fields, robbed of their fertility, giving way to popple; islands of mixed timber surrounded by grassy meadows; strips of dogwood and alder paralleling tiny streams; the edges of cedar swamps. Again, it summons the words of Foster; "Nothing suits the grouse better and no place makes more pleasing and romantic hunting country than the grown-up farm lands, the abandoned apple orchards and the big pastures that have long since gone back to birch, juniper, and white pine."

A million tourists a year visit here. They come for the water and the beaches, the fishing and sailing, parks, camping, hiking, shopping, festivals, theater, and simply to get away. As nearly as I can figure, none of them come to hunt grouse or woodcock. And of the 25,000 people who live here year-'round, maybe a half-dozen do so. Most of the locals wouldn't know a woodcock from a woodpecker, and a "partridge" is the bird that scares the hell out of you when you're deer hunting. For all its considerable charms, the peninsula boasts no tradition of bird hunting. What this means, in practical terms, is that I don't share my coverts with anyone.

I moved here six year ago from Illinois, an unpleasant state that seemed to have more bird dogs than birds, and where every autumn morning the vehicles back up a quarter-mile or more at the entrances to the public hunting areas. Pheasant and quail and the fertile farms of Iowa were what I knew; grouse and woodcock were names attached to pictures. A relative informed me that the peninsula had "no hunting to speak of," but then I chanced to read in the county newspaper of a local man who could be contacted for Ruffed Grouse Society banquet tickets. His name was Ken Ridderikhoff, and when he discovered that I too fancied English setters—and that I could talk dogs—he volunteered to show me the ropes. He taught me what grouse and woodcock cover looks like, shared a covert or two, and became a good friend. Of course, he played it cagey for awhile; the first time he took me to his premier covert, which lay generally due west of his home, he followed a twisting, circuitous route that would have befuddled a cartographer. A grouse hunter, after all, can never be too careful.

Ken's extreme prudence was not really necessary. I've always taken a dim view of "sportsmen" who cash in greedily on the kindness of others, and I wanted to pioneer my own coverts. My "work" at the time consisted of renovating the old house we'd occupied, painting and wallpapering and staining and patching in order to open in the spring as a modest bed and breakfast. I'd quit early in the afternoon, smell of turpentine on my hands, and go hunting. The pickup I'd inherited was silly with rust—I had to bolt a piece of plywood over a dangerous hole in the floorboards—but I reasoned that if I ever got it irretrievably marooned in some swamp, I could leave it there without suffering any financial loss.

This is how I began to know the peninsula, its backroads, the character of the land and its people. I came face-to-face with the stern, private, Scandinavian farmers whose ancestors had settled this spine of rock, tendering my request to hunt "partridge" in their woods. They looked at me hard with those polar eyes, as if assessing the purity of my intentions, then shrugged and said, "Go ahead." I didn't know what I was doing, really, and in fact I know now that many of those woodlots were poor cover. But I followed my belled setters through them all: the barren climax maples; the clutching cedars; the ankle-deep swamps. Gradually, I learned that grouse preferred the popple and the dogwood and the highbush cranberries, and the dogs learned too where to focus their energy. I remember becoming disoriented in a strange woods late in the day, and feeling my way out by keeping the sound of Lake Michigan's surf at my back. I remember the giddy elation of the rare moments when a grouse fell at my shot, how it felt almost heroic to hang the bird from a nail on the front porch, knowing my wife would see it there in the yellow light when she came home through the November darkness. And I remember awakening to this fact: these coverts were *mine,* in all their stone-fenced, apple-treed, classic beauty, mine in which to forge my own traditions and cast my own memories.

These memories run deep. That first season, I began hunting too late to catch the woodcock before they left for Louisiana. But I made up for it the following year. I was indoctrinated in the rank, sweaty, mosquito-ridden, miserable joy that is September woodcock hunting, when the green woods swallow a pointing dog, and you see one 'cock for every five you hear. It was exciting, if frustrating, sport. I considered it a form of dues-paying, and as September elapsed and the leaves resigned, the gunning turned to poetry: the setters cut the cover to ribbons; the birds materialized cleanly against the impressionistic background of the woods; and the gun seemed to mount and fire of its own accord.

The shooting has never been less than beautiful since. From opening day until early November, there are no birdless coverts here. All of them—from a swath of alders no wider than a sidewalk to a willow slough in the middle of a hayfield—hold woodcock, the local birds freshened by a steady flow of migrants from points north. Indeed, the woodcock hunting is far more reliable than the grouse shooting, which is affected by peninsular vagaries of climate and geography that throw the usual population cycles out of synch.

A very few people know how good this woodcock gunning is. One of my favorite coverts, believe it or not, is a public hunting area. Across six seasons, I can count the number of other hunters I've met there on one hand. I mentioned the superb hunting to the man charged with managing the area for the DNR. "Keep it to yourself," he hissed. "That's one of the best coverts around, and no one knows about it."

But I confess to falling from grace. In need of coin and credibility as a budding writer, I sold an explicit where-to-go article about the peninsula's woodcock hunting to a national magazine. I sang like a canary, naming names, giving dates, details, and directions. Mildly horrified at what I'd done, I awaited the consequences. There were none. It was as if some convivial god had erased the memories of every eager sportsman who'd read the piece, or caused their eyes to move across the page without recognizing the words. I, and my proprietary coverts, were saved.

There was even an unexpected bonus. A man called Steve Gordon phoned, out of the ether, to say he'd enjoyed the article, and to inform me that he did some guiding for woodcock on the island. This island sprawls six miles off the tip of the peninsula, separated by a strait the French explorers named Porte des Mortes—Death's Door—for its malicious reefs and currents. Steve invited me to shoot with him, and a tradition began. Every October, I board the car ferry along with the tourists, the lumber and fuel oil trucks, and the other purveyors who service the several hundred permanent residents. The ferry thrums past the lighthouses and the Coast Guard station, past the squat tugs of the commercial fisherman and their convoys of gulls, over the shipwrecks known and not. Steve meets me at the dock in his battered blue Jeep, its interior a chaos of dogs, shells, and guns, and the day is ours. The cover has that classic quality of the peninsula's—there are the same borders of stone and clearings returning to popple and apples underpinned by bracken— but on the island the feel of hunting in the wake of the departed is even more palpable. Most of the farms are truly abandoned: lilacs obscure the slumping farmsteads; grape vines cover the fences; the pastures have gone wild and disheveled. The Icelandics who settled this place a century ago, the Bjarnarsons and Gunnlagssons and the rest, work regular jobs, and the land lies idle. Woodcock are the primary beneficiaries. (In case you're wondering, Steve no longer guides: he wearied of clients more interested in heavy bags than rare experiences, and now reserves the hunting for himself, his son Matt, and a handful of supremely fortunate friends.)

For my part, I share my special places with only one other gunner. Terry Barker—veterinarian and bon vivant—shows up on a mid-October weekend for our annual ritual of hunting and feasting. Our wives adopt a "boys will be boys" attitude, unsheathe their credit cards, and go shopping. A mixture of intensity and glee describes our approach. Terry too is a lover of tradition, with his orange and white English setters and sidelock doubles, and he invariably insists on what he calls "the obligatory pictures of birds, dogs, and guns against the stone wall." We make good partners because our abilities with a shotgun are about equal, the advantage swinging year-to-year on a pendulum of mediocrity. Evenings, we clean our kill with the sun bleeding into the horizon, always with a bright blue can of Point beer within reach.

Then, again to quote Terry, we "partake of the charred flesh of dead animals." Most recently, this meant prairie chicken breasts flamed in brandy. We drink excessively of a variety of spirits, eat like orgiastic Romans, and quote at length from Guy de la Valdene, patron saint of profligate woodcock hunters. Although we would prefer to settle down to a B-movie in which Sybil Danning removes her clothes, we instead defer to our wives and fall asleep halfway through some chestnut starring Cary Grant. They wake us up when it's over, and steer us into bed. In the morning, like the song says, we get up and do it again, Amen.

As in most vacation regions, the locals regard the tourists with a certain amount of contempt—the term "drones" is often bandied about—while at the same time cheerfully accepting their money. This paradox is crystallized by a bartender of my acquaintance when he snorts, "Nothing pisses me off more than some rich kid paying for a beer with a $50 bill." On the other hand, many tourists subscribe to the "happy artisan" theory, viz., the residents of the peninsula (especially the northern, more "touristy" portion) live idyllic, uncomplicated existences, whistling while they work, as it were. The quintessential expression of this belief was uttered by a woman dining at a restaurant where a waitress-friend overheard her. "Oh, the local people are so colorful and rustic!" she squealed. I passed this anecdote along to Terry, who promptly began referring to us as "the colorful, rustic Davises."

One crisp afternoon, as Terry and I emerged from the popple edges of a woodcock covert, setters at heel, guns crooked in our arms, blood staining our vests and pants, a family with out-of-state plates drove past. Five heads swiveled as one to gape at us; we could see the father's mouth forming words. "'Look, children, it's some of the colorful, rustic locals we've been telling you about!,'" Terry mocked. We were probably the only hunters they had ever seen, other than Elmer Fudd, and it was impossible not to wonder if they regarded us as a quaint part of the landscape, or as a savage aberration.

But this is why I enjoy so little competition: no serious bird hunter can bring himself to believe that this playground for vacationers could possibly offer worthwhile shooting. It seems too public, too visible, too aware of itself. Until a person comes to know the peninsula's private side, it simply doesn't *feel* like bird country. You have to take the back roads, risk the narrow, tree-canopied two-tracks, query the resolute souls who wring a living from this rocky spit.

I suppose I can get a bit smug about my secret knowledge, like a kid who sits at the dinner table carrying a frog in his pocket, without his parents suspecting a thing. There's a raw delight to it. But maybe—just maybe—others might not value this knowledge so highly. From a hard-liner's viewpoint, the grouse hunting on this peninsula is spotty. I'll hunt days without flushing one, despite a dog who is, if nothing else, a bird-finder. Oh, the grouse are here, but not in the numbers found elsewhere in Wisconsin. And although the woodcock gunning is excellent, it's not of the "flush-a-minute" variety, the rumors of which draw sportsmen to Michigan's Upper Peninsula the way the reports of the salmon-fly hatch draw anglers to Henry's Fork.

No: it is as a setting, an environment, that the peninsula rises above the ordinary. And increasingly, that is the component of the experience I treasure most. The peninsula is a place Pleissner might have painted, and there are moments, when the woods swirl with color and a woodcock whistles away from a setter's point, that evade the jurisdiction of time to remain immaculate and bright. I think of those clear mornings, whitewash spattered beneath the red osier, when the air goes electric, and geese trombone above. I think of the boarded-up Norwegian farm house, its rusting blue pump still tapping a spring of sweet water, and the nearby edges where in May I hunt morels, and in October I shoot woodcock. I think of working the alders along streams alive with salmon, and of their furious, doomed purpose. I hear the melody of brass bells underscored by the ancient resonance of Lake Michigan's surf. I hear the north wind high in the popples; I see the late sun lick the maple leaves and the burnished apples with its tongue of fire.

It is among these places, these images and perceptions, that my setters and I learned the mysterious language of grouse and wood-cock. They foam with memories of shots made and missed, points that set the blood humming in my ears. On this peninsula, an intri-cate fabric of satisfactions, the threads of which cannot all be fol-lowed, was loomed.

Every bird hunter, I hope, is fortunate enough to have his own peninsula.

7

EMMY'S PHEASANTS

When I was growing up in Iowa, a man appeared at our back porch once a year, always on a dreamlike summer evening, selling salve door-to-door. It came in a flat, round tin, like shoe polish, except the edges were rounded. There was writing on the lid, but I don't know that I ever read it. Dad would buy a tin or two, paying all of a dollar, while I stood behind him, hearing the stranger ask if he'd like to try his fine salve, watching Dad fish into his pocket for the money. "This is the best salve," he'd say, as he dipped the palp of his index finger into the balm, drew back his lips,

spread the salve over them, and moved them across one an-
other, working it in. It made his lips shine and catch the
light. Then he'd hold out the open tin to me. It felt wonder-
ful, slick and cool and soothing, and it smelled like nothing
else, not like menthol or camphor, just itself. And because of
what Dad said, and the way he said it, I imagined the salve
had special properties, powers beyond the merely obvious. It
seemed like something I should tell people about, because it
would make them feel better. We never knew the name of the
man who sold it, or where he was from, and when he
stopped coming, we had no source for the salve.

The door swung open some time in the night, and let
November in. Its hands pressed against my chest; cold in-
vaded bone. I shuddered awake, to see the eastern horizon beginning to clarify, the sky starting to go blue, detaching from the dark
earth. No wind, no sound, no sense of movement, as if the image
were a bubble trapped in glass. Some moments passed before I realized that I was not looking through a window, but directly into the
urgent birth of an Iowa dawn. I creaked down from the bunk, shiv-
ering, to pull the door shut.

The cold clutched at me like a beggar as I crawled back into the
sleeping bag. I lay awake, alert to the wind's first stirrings, eyes adjusting to the gathering volume of light. I had begun to dress when
Denver knocked. "Tom?" he queried. "Telephone—it's your wife."
There was no good reason for her to call at 7:00 in the morning, unless it was bad news. I hurried out of the trailer, squinting in the
sudden flow of light, and crossed the frosted lawn to the farmhouse.

Gladys plugged in the percolator with one hand, and held out the phone with the other. "What's wrong?" I asked nervously.

"I just wanted to wish you a happy birthday before you went hunting," she said, brightly. So it was my birthday. I'd forgotten.

Hunting Iowa over Thanksgiving week is as necessary to me as breathing. It is what I do. My glib, make-conversation response to the question "Why?" is that it coincides with the nine-day, blaze orange *danse macabre* known as the Wisconsin deer season, and only a fool would risk his life, and his dogs', to hunt grouse then. Of course, that's the smallest part of it: the larger reasons have to do with continuity and renewal, with the need to return to the birds, places, and people who shaped my perceptions and attitudes, the irrevocable influences that made me a hunter. The memories occasioned by familiar farms—even by the gravel roads that lead to them—are precious as the game they hold; the daily preparations, from meals to choosing cover to caring for dogs to cleaning birds, assume a heightened, ceremonial quality, like ritual. And I crave the light of the late, Iowa afternoon, when it falls over the cornfields and creek bottoms with a final surge of intensity, the land seeming to rise up to meet it, their joining brilliant and palpable as hammered gold.

According to the biologists, it promised to be the finest year in a decade. Pheasants were up nearly 40% statewide, while the quail population had increased a staggering 108%. I should have been wildly, unconditionally excited about the prospects for good shooting. But without Gene, a piece of the mosaic that makes up hunting in Iowa was missing. Gene, who asked every season which barrel of his over/under he should fire first. Gene, who was invariably lighting his pipe whenever an unpointed cockbird decided to flush.

Gene, cynical, stubborn, and bitching. Gene, whose daughter I'd married. A drunk had roared through two stop signs, T-boning Mary and him in their station wagon. They were folded inside the wreckage like origami, and had to be cut free. The helicopter probably saved Mary's life; conscious but delirious, Gene kept asking the nurses where his shoes were. A Peoria hospital became their summer home. Yet even with a steel halo screwed into his skull to keep his cracked neck immobile, and his right arm so weak after shoulder surgery he could barely lift it, Gene vowed to be in the field come November. Vowed, that is, until Mary wisely revealed his fevered plan to one of the troupe of doctors, who fixed him with a hypodermic stare and said, "Don't even *think* about it." This season, Gene's hunting would occur only in the bird-rich fields of the imagination. The coverts we'd shared would feel strange, a little empty, without him.

It was a season of loss and change in another way as well. A shoulder injury, its exact cause a mystery, had forced Gabe, my setter female, into early retirement. I would miss her boundless spirit, but I could not help thinking that it was perhaps a blessing in disguise. The anguish she had inflicted upon me over the course of her career was more than a sane man would have tolerated. Gabe was like an athlete of extraordinary physical gifts who couldn't mentally stay in the game. What legs she had: from a standing start, she could jump up and look me straight in the eye. When she hit scent, running flat out, the impact was like two trains colliding. You could almost *hear* it. It took your breath away to watch her make game, and no dog was more stylish in motion. Her heart, too, was huge: she was tough as clear hickory, stoic in the face of pain, and affectionate to the point of being bothersome.

Unfortunately, Gabe could get lost in the same room with you. Her directional control was faulty. It functioned properly about one-third of the time, which meant that two-thirds of the time she was AWOL, and I had to play MP. I am glad that I possess a highly selective memory, because now I recall only dimly the frequent rages suffered in her company, while I remember her sterling performances in minute detail. And for those, I love her.

I tried to breed Gabe, twice, shipping her at considerable cost (she was the most expensive dog I ever hope to own) first to a stud in New England, later to one in Michigan. Both were handsome dogs of regal lineage and impeccable credentials. Unimpressed, Gabe wanted to tear their slobbering faces off. The owners of both males went out of their way to have veterinarians perform artificial inseminations; she conceived only upon the second breeding, and nine weeks later Terry, my veterinarian and hunting partner, delivered via Caesarian section (while I observed) a single pup which did not live. He sewed her up and that was the end of it. Whatever her blood might have brought to the breed, for better or worse, would remain locked inside her genes.

With Zack, my other setter and primary gun dog, growing long of tooth, a new puppy remained a priority. The man who introduced me to grouse and woodcock when I moved to Wisconsin, Ken Ridderikhoff, owned a tri-colored setter bitch I admired terribly, one of those rare naturals that did it all—and did it right—from the beginning. I prevailed upon Ken to breed Tara to a champion standing at stud in Oklahoma. In return for paying the stud fee, I received pick of the litter. Tara whelped five healthy, tricolored girls. I liked the pup that carried the highest tail; my wife mooned over the one with "the sweetest face." Luckily, the same puppy met both specifications. Emmylou, a.k.a. Grievous Angel, came home in April. She began as the most irresistible ball of fur and mischief I've ever seen, and matured into a fetching, leggy debutante, fast and classy, but still with the devil in her eyes.

This was now my complement of dogs: Zack, the eight-year-old veteran of the bird hunting wars, and Emmy, nine months, unlettered, undisciplined, an unknown quantity. I expected nothing of her; it was to be, for Emmy, one of those famous "learning experiences." To shoot a bird over her point, or even to see her point and hold, would be cream gravy.

Our first morning, the wind keened out of the north like a polished steel blade, carving away what little warmth the November sun could muster. Clouds scudded low against a cold blue sky. We were four: Terry, whom I'd followed to Mingo, his home town, and the site of what Iowans have come to call "MingoGate," a nasty scandal involving a state legislator, an exotic dancer, and bad timing; Denver, Terry's father, a weathered and lean retired farmer with the watchful aspect of a hawk, a man who'd faced cancer and beaten it; Steve, a friend and expert pheasant hunter from St. Paul; and myself. Wild flushes, predictable in such wind, were the sole rewards for our setters' early efforts. Then, a rooster offered me an easy chance, cackling out of the east fork of a ditch draining a cornfield. I missed resoundingly with the right barrel. The second shot nicked him, and the cockbird hit the stubble running. I gave chase, gasping glassy shards of air, only to see the bird slither through a fence and disappear. Dogs and men searched fruitlessly. Wounded game haunts me; how could I fail on such a wide-open, close-range opportunity? My bitter feeling didn't improve when, a few minutes later, I scratched another rooster. To my relief, the dogs were on hand to corral the wounded bird.

A birthday cake—the doing of Sally, Terry's petite, thoughtful wife—waited for me back at the house. That kindness mellowed my outlook considerably. After eating too much lunch, as hunters will, it was a struggle to get moving again. We resisted the temptation of comfortable chairs and the inevitable naps to strike out once more, working in a wide arc west and south, over country Denver still owned. The dogs performed admirably, enduring the evil briars of a grown-over pasture sloping to a teardrop-shaped pond, quartering dutifully through strips of thick switchgrass that followed the contours of a sidehill, weaving in and out of the brittle canes guarding the edges of cut corn. Several superb points on hens were tendered, but the cockbirds had gone underground. A covey of quail flushed wild from a vine-tangled fence corner; the singles, as seems the norm these days, vanished utterly. We trudged up to the farmyard, across the plowed field that had guided my eye to the horizon, with scarcely an hour of daylight left.

I kenneled a weary Zack and called on Emmy, all energy and anticipation. North of the house, past the rutted dirt road and the sagging barn that was now home to raccoons, the land spread and tilted to a creek bottom, fingers of cover spliced throughout. We split up, and soon I heard a single, authoritative report from Steve's direction. Then, to the west, two shots from Terry. I am convinced there is magic in the air of late afternoon, sorcery in the light: the unexpected, the undreamt of happens too often then to be assigned to coincidence. Watching Emmy, as the shadows lengthened and the wind stilled, I marveled at her fervor, her pure, thoughtless desire, the uncut joy she showed for the hunt. She slashed the cover like a knife-fighter, white flag her weapon, moving with speed and acceleration that brought shivers of excitement to my skin. Emmy was revealing her character, forged of breeding and instinct, and I was mesmerized.

When she pointed along a brushy edge, leaning into the scent like a ski jumper, my native skepticism argued that she was sight-pointing the ground sparrows that flitted among the stalks of rye-grass. But then a volley of songbirds flew out over the cut corn, and Emmy didn't even blink. She cat-footed several paces, stiff-legged, head high, and swelled into another point. It was the real thing: a cockbird exploded skyward, the orange sun igniting his plumage. I swung smoothly, fired, and he fell hard in the golden stubble, killed cleanly. Emmy was on him in an instant, her muzzle buried in those molten feathers, filling her senses with that narcotic aroma. Her first pheasant, the bird I consider the most difficult of all for a pointing dog to handle properly, and she couldn't have done it more expertly. I remembered again that it was my birthday. I held the rooster by the legs, index finger curled beneath the curved spurs, carrying it like the trophy it was. Emmy hunted furiously, all the way home.

We drove south the next day, after an uneventful morning hunt, to Davis County. I'd finished the previous season there with a double on quail over Zack's point, and earlier that fall Don had written, "I've never seen the like of it for quail this year . . . big coveys, too." A lifelong friend of Gene's, the accident had so shaken him that he became physically ill. I was gladdened when he wrote to say that he and Betty still expected me to come and bird hunt, Gene's absence notwithstanding.

But those are the kind of people they are. They live closer to the bone than anyone I know, surviving almost literally off the land, yet the example of their generosity shames me. They own virtually nothing except their tiny, cluttered trailer, some livestock, and a few acres of thin, indifferent soil. I believe they would sell it all if a friend were in need. I brought a pair of hunting chaps for Don, brass bells for Betty's goats, and a pink sweatshirt for Kim, their beautiful child, a four-year old with a serious expression who, last season, told Gene her favorite things to eat were "squirrel and quail." Had I given them the Taj Mahal, they couldn't have been more thankful. "You'll never know how much we appreciate all this," Don said. I wished I could do more.

The afternoon of our arrival, the hunting looked to live up to its billing. Don took us to a parcel enrolled in the government's "set-aside" program—one of dozens in this, Iowa's poorest county—where foxtail commanded fields that last year had been corn. Steve took a cockbird pointed by Spook, his outstanding young white-and-orange setter, at the head of a weedy draw; Terry and I collaborated on a rooster that Zack not only nailed squarely, but on one of his rare whims, chose to retrieve. The dogs made disappointing contact with two fencerow coveys, milling around indecisively until the bobs' nerves broke, but at least we knew there were quail to be had.

That evening, Don and Betty insisted we join them for the Thanksgiving pot luck at the Evangelical church in Savannah, a wide spot in the highway as it rolls into Missouri. In the huddled basement of the small, white frame building, the evangelist blessed the hams and casseroles, the scalloped potatoes and creamed corn, the pumpkin pie and the berry cobbler. The members of the congregation, most of whom have little in the way of material things, joined him in giving fervent thanks for what they do possess: family, friends, the adamant bonds of the spirit. We were greeted warmly, like old friends, by men wearing long sideburns, western shirts, and cowboy boots. The women responsible for the food—

young mothers, sturdy matrons—encouraged us to return for seconds and thirds (as if we needed prompting); the men talked hunting and wished us luck with the birds. "Good year for quail," they agreed.

But things turned bad for us. The next day was like an illustration from a calendar: an immaculate sky, the landscape all gold and wine and chocolate. Birds should have been on the edges—"moving," as old-timers say—but in a full morning of diligent hunting, over big, woolly country that Don knew held multiple coveys, we saw exactly one quail. Not one covey: one quail. In the afternoon, combing a gorgeous piece of ground where last season we'd chased four coveys, we startled one scroungy bevy, too small to shoot into or pursue. The only genuine excitement came when Spook pointed in a bottomland forty grown to foxtail. My first impression was of an enormous cock pheasant; then the bird resolved into a turkey, the field erupting as fifteen more took wing. "Davis County quail," Don joked ruefully.

The rains came that evening, the cold November kind that define misery. Not of a mood to further erode our crumbling psyches, we said our goodbyes to Don and Betty in the morning, grimly noting a covey gritting on the highway shoulder as we turned down the gravel road to their trailer. Don made copious, unnecessary apologies for the poor shooting, as if he were personally responsible for the caprice of gamebirds, and pleaded with us to return next season. "Maybe if you came down opening weekend?" he suggested. He stood in the rain as we drove away, waving hard, like a man trying to flag someone down.

Now on my own, I headed east, through the abysmal rain, to Richland. Merle and Alvina had lunch waiting, cheese soup ("Gene and Mary like this recipe," Alvina offered), sandwiches, the finest home-baked molasses cookies in the world, and coffee, always coffee. I'd hoped to hunt some of the old spots, the places Gene had introduced me to when I was still just a persistent boyfriend whom he grudgingly tolerated. But there was no sense to it in this rain, no sense heaping discomfort on disappointment. The trip was in decaying orbit, like so many of my recent excursions to Iowa: the satisfactions of place and people still intact, still profoundly gratifying, but the promise of great sport unfulfilled. An icy emptiness yawned in my chest; when I breathed, it seemed the air rushed in raw and cold, and gave my blood no nourishment.

The rain abated at last. It was the day before Thanksgiving; I had time for a hunt before I was due at Mary and Gene's, in central Illinois. Doran's place was on the way, out in that fertile plain near Wayland.

I don't know why, exactly, I chose Emmy and left Zack howling in the back of the truck. Doran's farm is the most reliable producer of birds I've ever gunned; the cover is magnificent, and he rarely allows hunting. Zack would surely point pheasants there, very likely quail as well; on the basis of a single rooster, I had no right to expect anything from Emmy. Perhaps my need to take game had weakened, and I had become resigned and accepting. Or perhaps I simply rationalized that Emmy would profit more from the experience, regardless of its content, than I would from killing a bird or two.

I could walk that comely farm with my eyes closed, so engraved on my memory are its wrinkles and contours: the lush canary grass along the creek, the log where I cross it, the grassy swales that funnel runoff from the cornfields, the timbered ditches reaching up the gentle hillside, the abandoned pasture grown to blackberry and greenbriar. I have thought and dreamed and written of it in the dozen years since Gene and I first made it ours in the way bird hunters do, owning it more intimately than by title. I have been haunted by what I have seen there, and I have been thrilled to the very marrow. And what Emmy did on that gray afternoon, when the wind had winter on its breath, was like salvation, a return to grace, the finding of something feared lost. She hunted as if on the end of a string, as if I could communicate with her by the force of will alone. Her fire, her elan, her searing love for the hunt shone in every crack of her tail. When she busted a brace of cockbirds, hitting scent too fast to stop, I just smiled; when she danced into a point in the crackling grass below a terrace, and a rooster materialized only to fall at my unconscious shot, I felt I was being pulled by some delicious gravity I could not resist. She pointed again at the top of a ditch, cutting a glance at me as I stepped in. A cock flushed out the far side, sailing downhill to the creek, but another burst into the open, quartering away low and quick. It is a shot I never make, yet this bird crumpled as if it was what he was born for.

Emmy's eyes blazed, fueled by all the noble setters whose blood had been mingled to make her. She summoned ghosts: I could see Duke, Gene's great and trusted German shorthair, as he relentlessly made game in these same draws; I imagined Heidi, Duke's bracemate, proudly presenting another bird to her master. We looped back down the creek, Emmy's pace never relaxing. Beneath a blowdown, she found the last pheasant.

And then I was walking to the truck in the gathering darkness, the third and final rooster dangling from my right hand. I balanced the double on my left shoulder, holding it by the muzzles. Emmy, of course, could not know what she had accomplished, or that the hunt was over. I whistled her in, ran my hands along her fine head and down her silken ears, and looked deep into those eyes the color of flame-streaked walnut. I did not know what to say; I felt as if we were still strangers, still with much to learn of the other's quirks and rhythms, but that with time it would all come clear. I kenneled Emmy and lay her pheasants carefully in the bed of the pickup. I wasn't going to clean them yet.

I wanted Gene to see them.

8

THE PRACTICE

Hunting pheasant in Iowa is as close to the practice of religion as anything I do. It is a collection of beliefs and values and wisdom, cemented by tradition and grounded in faith, that I inherited from my father. He, in turn, inherited it from his father, who, as one of the first generation to hunt pheasant in Iowa, established its doctrines and principles. Example: until the birds and guns are cleaned, no one eats, drinks, or otherwise enjoys himself. Example: It's better to be lucky than good.

I grew up within the rituals and sacraments of pheasant hunting, and because of that, because I can't step outside, it's hard for me to articulate its subtle shades and colors. In his beautiful novel, *Spartina*, John Casey distills the essence of this dilemma: "You only saw it whole if you were a ways off; you only felt it if you were inside it." I can't see it whole from where I stand—but at least I can try to describe how it feels.

Eleven months of the year, the Palmer House is just another truck stop on Highway 20. But come November, it is where the pheasant hunters of Sioux City gather for breakfast, and is therefore sanctified. They—we—begin to arrive at about 5:30, the stars still glittering icily, the air sharp as glass. We're bleary-eyed and thick-tongued, moving clumsily in our longjohns and canvas pants and wool shirts, surrounded by a fog that only massive doses of caffeine can burn off. The last duck hunters are leaving then, hastily paying their bills and grabbing an emergency ration of candy bars before heading for their blinds in the Missouri River bottoms. By 6:00, the parking lot is bumper-to-bumper with station wagons, Suburbans ("The Cadillac of the Prairies") and their kin. Each carries a similar cargo of cased shotguns, military-surplus ammo boxes, coolers, shooting bags, sack lunches, and, most important of all, dogs. They eye us suspiciously from battered Kennel-Aires: Labs, German shorthairs, and Brittanies mostly, along with a smattering of setters, springers, and goldens. Their breath condenses against the windows.

Inside, the restaurant is a swirling collage of tan and green and blaze orange. Cigarette smoke clings to the ceiling. Waitresses bustle between the kitchen and their tables, balancing enormous platters of cakes, eggs, sausages, and hash browns, filling thermoses with high-octane coffee. They are unflappable, these women, in their prim smocks and stretch pants. Nothing fazes them, not a hungry long-haul trucker or a pheasant hunter in a hurry. They are all members of that nebulous middle age, and they all have names like Mildred or Shirley or Gladys, good, solid names you don't hear anymore in this era of Heathers and Tiffanys.

Except for the conversation at your own table, the talk around you fuses into an unintelligible din. But then, round and distinct as an Alleluia, a name rises above the clamor, a name that you recognize. Its sound penetrates to the remotest corners of your soul. You hear it not because it is spoken loudly, but because it is freighted with the meaning of place. A few minutes later, your ear cuts another name from the confusion, and another. *Climbing Hill, Castana, Little Sioux, Soldier, Holly Springs:* any of the farm towns cradled in the fertile swelling bosom of the country, towns with red brick banks, white-frame houses, high-steepled churches, and formica-countered cafes where a piece of sour cream raisin pie is a wedge of heaven. Some pheasant hunter, you know, has invested his faith in the land around that town, just as you had once, and would again. Before I could appreciate the poetry of the names themselves, they were already magical. And when they were spoken by the congregation at the Palmer House, they became invocations. They conjured particular fields and fence rows, certain birds and chances that were utterly individual and unmistakable, the fingerprints of a hunter's memory. They conjured possibilities, too, for fast shooting and heavy bags, for new farms tangled with cover. The names of these towns were fuel for a combustible imagination.

And although the flash point now is a little higher, they still are. Mention any of these places, and my mind's eye travels there, back to the rustling cornfields and the marshy draws and the creeks edged with briars, back to the cockbirds exploding in front of a set-ter, back to the smell of mud and powder and wet fur, back to the rolling gravel roads that stretch forever, back to the delicious weari-ness that overcomes you after a day of walking the hills, back to that sunset like no other. This is how pheasant hunting feels.

9

In Peshtigo Country

We knew our destination by name only. It was a camp-ground deep in the northern Wisconsin forest. According to the literature supplied by the Forest Service, a network of hunter walking trails, seeded to clover and closed to vehicles, lay nearby, across the Peshtigo River. *Peshtigo:* whatever it meant, the sound of it was irresistibly romantic. We imagined a country seething with grouse and woodcock, a land of unbroken timber inhabited only by the spirits of voyageurs and lumberjacks.

Other than a few books, records, and articles of clothing, I carried my worldly belongings with me: three English setters, two shotguns, a good flyrod, camera gear, camping equipment, and related paraphernalia. If anything, Adrian's material worth was less than mine. I owned the white-over-rust pickup, too, not in much better shape then than it was when I sold it, two years later, for $150, cap included. The speedometer was the single gauge that worked. Because the gas gauge didn't, and because the tank was known to leak, we gave our business in tiny increments to numerous filling stations, just to be safe.

We topped it off in Wabeno, left the highway, and struck out over the backroads. The moon had not yet risen. Our world compressed to the cone of vision defined by the headlights. We worried the map like a pair of terriers, as if we believed it was holding out, not telling us all that it could.

Then, out of the blackness, a sign appeared. We followed its arrow into the deserted campground. As we approached sight number 5, the moon emerged, spilling platinum across the lake. The water bore its precious weight, a necklace across the breast of a dark-skinned woman. The headlights limned a neat stack of split wood standing next to the fire pit; we assumed this was Forest Service s.o.p., only to discover later it was the largesse of the previous occupants. A flock of geese beat skyward as we stepped from the truck. We fancied we could see them moving against the stars—we couldn't, really—and their music filled the night, crowding out the sound of our own breathing. As if in response, a pack of coyotes began howling somewhere to the north, songs rising from those tilted muzzles like messages aimed at space, but only us to hear them. The Coleman lantern flared, then steadied. Adrian built a fire. We washed cheese-and-onion sandwiches down with Hamm's beer, and watched the sparks ascend and vanish.

That was our introduction to the Peshtigo country. Strictly by the calendar, it wasn't that long ago. To Adrian and myself, hunting grouse and woodcock there has come to seem like something we've done forever, the intersection at which our lives have been aimed since I was a kid skipping school to chase pheasants in Iowa, and Ade was a lad in the west of England, casting nets for hake and plaice into the Irish Sea. We've exchanged the impoverished freedom of unemployment for the encumbered security of regular paychecks, but we manage, every October, to return.

There is no single reason why. We return for the birds: for the secretive woodcock, birds whose presence might never be revealed save for the miraculous nose of a setter, birds that appear and disappear as quickly and magically as the gold in the leaves of an aspen; for the grouse, maddening and adored, birds that almost combust with life, as if all the energy of the forest were somehow channelled into their being. We return for the coverts, for the memories we've cached of points and shots, for the promises they keep and the ones they break. We return for the fragments that compose camp life: the split-body sensation of being toasted on one side by the fire, and frozen on the other by twenty-degree air; the comforting, gaseous hiss of the Coleman; the sight of Zack, an old bear of a setter, ritualistically wetting down every bush within a fifty-foot radius of the tent; the delicious agony in shedding the cocoon-like warmth of a sleeping bag to face the frigid morning; Ade finding his contact lenses frozen in their solution; wolfing eggs and sausage as fast as the heavy skillet can fry them; brewing tea in a cold rain and cupping our numb hands around the mugs; watching the sun burn the mists off the lake.

And we return simply for the feel of this wild and lonely country. It is like a coat slipped over our shoulders when we're not looking: suddenly, it is just there. It is hidden in those endless timbered ridges, in those valleys dense with shadows, in the cool air that collects in the swamps. It is in the murmur of the alder-canopied creeks, the clean-edged track of a whitetailed buck, in the pure, brilliant sky. Mysterious, arterial, the Peshtigo is a presence at the heart of it all, the key to the soul of the country.

If the fabric of hunting the Peshtigo remains the same, its texture changes from year-to-year. The first trip was marked by revelations, both personal and objective in nature. Objectively, we discovered that a lot of the designated hunter walking trails wind through birdless, mature forest, but that there are still miles and miles of trails that penetrate likely cover. Personally, I discovered that, in an expansive outdoor setting, it is easy to confuse intoxication with euphoria. Ade and I started the cocktail hour with beer, then switched to Dewar's after supper. When the Dewar's ran out, we switched back to beer. We philosophized by the fire, devouring Snickers bars at a terrific rate, and generally felt, well, euphoric. This is all so great, we kept telling each other. Great, just great.

I awoke with a hangover the size of Vermont. My brain pressed so urgently against my eyes that they were in danger of being ejected like spent shells. I almost blacked out when I touched off my shotgun, and the shriek of a dog whistle was like a spike being driven through my ears. Adrian, who I swear was weaned on hard cider, suffered no ill effects whatsoever. He missed every bird he fired at that morning, while I killed a limit of woodcock.

I do not prescribe a hangover as a shooting-slump remedy, although I was tempted to try it two years later. I arrived a half-day before Adrian, in time to check out a choice bit of woodcock cover wedged between a road and a bend in the river. Zack struck point immediately, and I tumbled a left-crossing 'cock. "This is going to be good," I thought smugly. It might have been for someone else, but it wasn't for me. Zack pointed woodcock after woodcock, and I missed the hell out of all of them. I should have had a limit in fifteen minutes. Instead, I limited out on frustration, despair, and anguish, none of which can be glazed with wild grape jelly and served over wild rice. I pledged my eternal gratitude to Zack for not lifting his leg on me. The Peshtigo is always beautiful, but not always kind.

This was also the year for the infamous "hash grays." Adrian's wife, Janelle, had decided to come along, and one evening she cheerfully announced that hash browns were on the dinner menu. While I heated oil in the skillet, she shredded the potatoes. Outwardly, they appeared to be normal, everyday spuds. In fact, they were the Potatoes From Another Planet. A blow torch wouldn't have turned them brown. We cooked them, and cooked them, and cooked them some more. Nothing happened. Finally, they went all gray and rubbery. None of us had the stomach to taste them. We offered the hash grays to the dogs, who looked at us with expressions that said, "You've *got* to be kidding." In retrospect, we probably could have made a fortune if we'd sold them to Goodyear.

In 1987, our trip to the Peshtigo coincided with four inches of snow and a high pressure system direct from the Arctic Circle. Other than an evening spent clinging to the side of New Hampshire's Mount Washington, I've never been so cold for so long as I was the two nights we shivered away in camp. Adrian's contact lenses froze solid. The water in the dogs' bucket froze solid. The campground pump froze solid. Ade rigged a tarp to trap extra heat from the fire, and we edged as close as we dared to the flames, bundled up and hunched over like ice fishermen. Intermittently, one of us would cry, "Safari!" through chattering teeth, in reference to the name of the low-rent—but warm—motel in Wabeno. We persevered. It helped to have Zack sleeping between us in the tent: it was like having a fur rug to snuggle against.

Given the conditions, the hunting was remarkably good. The woodcock were still present in decent numbers, and we couldn't walk to the campground privy without flushing grouse—literally. In a new covert just over the hill from camp, Ade made one of the most spectacular shots on grouse I'll ever see. Zack pointed on a gentle slope clustered with young aspens. While Ade stayed below on the path, I slithered in to flush. The grouse must have run. It lifted far ahead, and I turned to watch it sail over the spindly trees, safely out of range. Then Ade's little SKB barked spitefully. The grouse cartwheeled into the snow, stone dead. I was stunned. "You got it! You got it!" I hollered, crashing through the underbrush. Ade just stood there regarding his shotgun with the same kind of wide-eyed amazement the Indians must have displayed when they first witnessed the magical power of the whiteman's thundersticks. The Red gods had smiled upon him. In the Peshtigo country, they often do.

As much as it belongs to us, the Peshtigo belongs to the setters. And as intimately as we think we know it, they know it even better. Maggie, loving, incorrigible, doomed Maggie, made that first trip, never to return. Gabe, now retired, would take your breath away when she pointed, leaning into the scent as if it were a gale, tail kissing the sky. She made her share of game, and although we spent as much time hunting for her as we did for birds—gunning behind Gabe was always an adventure in geography—we have nothing but fond memories of her performances. Emmy's debut could not have been less auspicious: her inaugural morning in camp, she wandered off, became disoriented, and got lost. We burned up the forest roads frantically searching. Another hunter found her eight miles to the southwest, scared but unhurt, and after phoning my wife (thank God she accepted a collect call from a stranger), he contacted the Forest Service in Laona. The Samaritan delivered Emmy safe and sound, and refused my offer of a "finder's fee." It was here, a year later, that Emmy came into her own as a woodcock dog, striking point after point literally within sight of the river.

And then there is Zack. He's made every trip: Adrian still laughs over waking in the tent to the sight of Zack peering down on him like a jowly vulture. I cannot imagine hunting the Peshtigo country without this hard-headed old setter. His bell plays the musical score that accompanies our days in the woods. How many times have Ade and I strained to hear that copper bell as it faded in and out, only to be galvanized into action by the *beep-beep-beep* of his Tracker? How many times have we fought through the hazel and the black-berries and the balsams, losing our hats, to find him on point, head high, nose drinking scent, the bird mesmerized? We've played out hundreds of these small, tense dramas, each as luminous and finely-crafted as a scene by Truffaut. In a very real sense, Zack is the agent responsible for revealing the secrets of the Peshtigo to us. Through him, we see beyond the surface, and into its reclusive, en-thralling soul.

I was told just the other day that one of the Ojibway meanings of *Peshtigo* is "wild goose." Thinking back to that first trip, when a flock of Canadas rose honking into the moonlight as we made camp, I understand now that the meaning has been plain all along.

10

HYPNOTIZED

She was a bandy-legged, whiskery-chinned, low-to-the-ground English setter. Her big eyes were a deep, lustrous brown, and she had a black patch around the left one that made her look a little bit like Petey, the friendly mutt that tagged along with Alfalfa, Buckwheat, and the rest of the Rascals. Like Petey, too, she was alert, inquisitive, and ready for everything. But this girl's name was Gabe. In the Field Dog Stud Book, she was registered as Got Me Hypnotized, after the old Fleetwood Mac song: *Seems like a dream . . . Got me hypnotized.* Her pedigree sparkled with the stars of setterdom. Wiregrass Thor, a dog many observers felt deserved to be crowned National Champion in 1977, was her daddy; the immortal Johnny Crockett, who won the National in 1970 (the last setter to do so), was her maternal grandsire.

The instant I saw the litter advertised in *The American Field*, I knew it was the one. For years, since I'd been a kid, the idea of owning a field trial setter had smouldered in the back of my mind. The exploits of the great setters of the past thrilled me to the marrow; their names—Tony Boy, Sioux, Prince Rodney, Mississippi Zev— were the wings of my imagination. I wanted a setter worthy of its blood, a dog with presence and fire and unforgettable style. Grandiose expectations, but why not?

Of course, it didn't quite work out according to plan. With dogs, it seldom does. If you factored in the probability, even inevitability, of heartbreak right from the beginning, you might never take the chance. And you'd miss it all. In retrospect, I see that it was a wild, romantic notion, that I had no business buying a dog bred to run, that owning a field trial setter was just a young man's dream. But I'll tell you this: my life would be impoverished, deeply so, if Gabe had never entered it. Yes, she exacted a toll of disappointment, frustration, and sadness, but she also gave a priceless measure of joy. I carry my memories of Gabe like pearls, strung on the incandescent filament of her spirit . . .

"Lessee who she can hypnotize," drawled Walt Woodlee. Gabe had spent the summer under Walt's tutelage on the South Dakota prairies, and now she was ready to strut her stuff in her first derby stake. It wasn't a big trial, but several hard-riding pros were competing, along with some tough amateurs. My wife Julie and I rode the dog wagon, just behind the mounted handlers and judges. Gabe broke away in a blur, the way she always did. You could see the surprise register in the eyes of her bracemate, a leggy pointer, as she flew over the hill. The other derbies had trouble finding birds, but not Gabe: she pointed pheasants twice with high style and acceptable manners. Gabe gave it everything she had—again, as always—but the day had turned warm, and she couldn't maintain her furious pace. Her range shortened considerably in the final minutes. The judges admired her heart, but they couldn't use her.

Still, I was ecstatic. Gabe's performance had been all that I had a right to expect. What I remember best, though, is not Gabe's race, or even the flush of pride when one of the other pros approached us to say, "That's an awfully nice little setter you've got there." As Walt cantered his Tennessee Walker back to the dog wagon at the end of the heat, heeling Gabe on a long rope, the driver stopped to open a box for her. "Won't be needin' that," Walt allowed. He dismounted, said, "C'mon, l'il sweetheart," scooped Gabe up in his big hands, and set her in my wife's lap for the trip back to the clubhouse. "Right here's where she'll be ridin'." Julie hugged Gabe, and they both beamed. It was hard to tell who was happier.

That winter, Walt took his string to Mississippi, where he steadied Gabe to wing and shot on wild quail. Some dogs fold under the pressure of "breaking;" one of the reasons pointers are favored by field trialers is that they can "take it" better than setters. Gabe broke beautifully, without losing an ounce of her style, confidence, or enthusiasm. "First time I saw her," Walt confessed, "I said to myself, 'She'll never take breakin'. Well, I found out just how tough she is. She never even whimpered."

Gabe was at her best in Mississippi. If she was bred for anything, it was Southern quail hunting. She loved to tour those birdy bean-field edges, head high, tail cracking, and when she caught the scent of a covey, it was as if lightning had struck. She seemed to throw sparks. Gabe also loved the omnipresent Mississippi mud, in which she wallowed to her heart's content.

Riding beside Walt through those hallowed fields, listening to him sing Gabe down the briary hedgerows and the tangled creek bottoms, watching her fade from sight only to re-appear, a white blaze crossing to the front: I felt as if I were part of one of the grandest traditions in American sport. I felt as if I were no longer outside looking in, that instead I had been admitted into an envied company, a company ungoverned by mortality. Nash Buckingham was there, and Jim Avent, and Wonsover and Turnto and Sport's Peerless Pride, and all the souls, living and dead, human and canine, that had shaped both the breed and the sport. And the key, the password that opened the door, was the gritty little setter who kept us tall in the saddle when she ran.

Walt's monthly training reports were models of verbal economy. He'd scrawl a couple sentences across the bill, mostly variations on the theme, "Gabe is lookin' good." The second summer Gabe spent in South Dakota, I stopped by Walt's place enroute to a Canadian fishing trip. I delivered a blueberry pie Julie baked for him, and we put Gabe through her paces. One mellow evening, she got too close to a running pheasant and forgot her manners. Walt just laughed. When his statement arrived, it contained the following report:

Hi Tom
I got Gabe broke again
How was the fishing trip
My pie is all gone.
Walt

Gabe never made much of a splash on the field trial circuit, although I'm convinced that Walt extracted every bit of her potential. She placed a time or two in small stakes, and showed impressively in several others. She had all the class any judge could ask for, but her range, by horseback standards, was moderate. Plus, she got so wound up before running that she'd practically hyperventilate, and unless there was plenty of water on the course to keep her cool, she'd be gasping fifteen minutes into the heat. Even though she wasn't winning, I felt a sense of satisfaction just knowing that she was on the circuit, doing her best, carrying the flag of the setter cause. I wanted to keep trying, but we moved from southern Illinois to northern Wisconsin. The move involved a career change: from having one to not. Despite Walt's ridiculously low rate, we couldn't afford it. Regretfully, I brought Gabe home.

Years later, during a period when Walt was down on his luck, I tried to apologize, over a few beers, for pulling Gabe from his string. "Mister Tom," he said, "I never had a dog I liked better'n Gabe. But I think we took her about as far in field trials as she was ever gonna go."

My efforts to re-cast Gabe into a walking gun dog were, in all candor, marginally successful. She was more dog than I could handle, especially in the tight cover of the grouse woods. Someone more skilled, I'm sure, could have engineered the transition, but I pretty much made a hash of things. Walt once told me, "You couldn't lose Gabe if you tried." Lord knows I didn't try; it just happened. For a while, I suspected she was running deer, but gradually I realized that she was just self-hunting and ignoring the hell out of me. There was no doubt that Gabe was capable of brilliance; when she chose to handle, we enjoyed splendid hunts. Like the little girl in the story, when Gabe was good, she was very good—but when she was bad, she was very, *very* bad.

Trouble was, I couldn't stay mad at her. She had a way of canting her muzzle downward, looking up as if she was peering over a pair of half-frames, and coquettishly batting her eyes that melted whatever iciness had formed at the edges of my heart. I'd say, "Gabe, what's wrong with you?" and when I knelt to pet her, she'd press against me with the top of her head, like a butting goat.

Where the country was big enough to hold her, Gabe shined. She was a superb Hungarian partridge dog; I only wish I could have given her more opportunities to work them. Every November, a group of sportsmen in northeastern Wisconsin get together for a semi-organized Hun shoot. Teams of hunters canvass the stubble-fields in search of partridge. Then, come evening, they all repair to a nearby restaurant for gratuitous drinking, gluttonous feasting, and shameless lie-telling. A few days before the first such shoot I was invited to attend, Gabe somehow tore a hole the size of a fifty-cent piece in her shoulder. A pendulous flap of skin dangled from the wound like the petal of an iris. It wasn't serious, but I decided the prudent move would be not to take her to the Hun hunt. My friend Terry Barker, DVM, convinced me otherwise. "Gabe's the dog we need," he argued. "If her sutures break, I'll just re-sew them."

Terry's advice proved sage. Fifteen minutes into the hunt, we scrambled up a rise in a picked cornfield to spy Gabe on a sky-kissing point. The two other gunners in our party—their names are forever condemned to perfidy—who should have closed in from the left, didn't take a step. We waved, desperately trying to get their attention, but they were preoccupied with personal matters of pressing urgency. Terry and I walked in anyway. The covey flushed at forty yards, offering obscenely difficult targets that we both missed. If the other guns had been in position—but why speculate? As Terry so eloquently put it that night at the banquet, "They were standing there with their penises in their hands!"

And yes, Terry did have to repair Gabe's stitches. The operating table was the bed in his guest room. Terry insists he administered an anaesthetic. This reconciles perfectly with my memory of the event: he was indeed well-anaesthetized by the time we got back to his house (the Dinkel-Acker was flowing freely). In any case, Gabe, who was absolutely indifferent to pain, sat stoically throughout the procedure.

Gabe didn't do anything half-assed. When she walked, she sashayed. When she wagged her tail, her whole body shimmied. When she showed affection, she lavished it with frantic licks and persistent nudges. And when another dog, male or female, got a little too intimate, Gabe didn't growl; she was transformed into a 35-pound buzzsaw. She wouldn't tolerate any crap from her fellow canines, and she never backed down.

Predictably, she carried this radical attitude to extremes, and against the wrong opponent. Gabe may not have been a field trial champion, but she was the undisputed title-holder for most porcupine quills in a single dog at one time. She returned from a foray into the woods near my home looking like a canine pin cushion. After a refrain of emphatic "Oh, *shits!*" I bundled her into the pickup and sped to Terry's clinic. He was flabbergasted. "Are you sure that's Gabe?" he laughed. "She looks like a German wirehair!" The two of us spent a solid hour-and-a-half, non-stop, plucking quills. Then, for another half-hour, Terry worked on her mouth, gums, and tongue. We pulled five hundred quills if we pulled one.

Months later, buried quills were still emerging from Gabe's flews, muzzle, and head. She never again attacked a porcupine; my guess is that she simply never *found* another one.

It is tempting to write of the bad times, to jerk tears and rend hearts. But that wouldn't be right; it wouldn't be Gabe. There are too many maudlin stories about dogs that died, and this is about a dog who lived. Gabe could be contrite, bewildered, she could be hurting, but a fierce exuberance always surrounded her, like a shimmering nimbus. You could see it when she was a pint-sized puppy, tirelessly coursing meadowlarks across the vast waving meadows of the Nebraska Sandhills; you could see it at a field trial when she outraced her bracemate to the horizon; you could see it when she struck point, so suddenly and intensely that she, not the bird, seemed about to explode.

There was a sound Gabe made. She would stretch her neck, tilt her muzzle, purse her lips, and out would come something like *roo-roo-roo!* Sometimes, it was a greeting; sometimes, it meant she wanted attention. And sometimes, she did it because she sensed that I was down, and she knew that a *roo* would unfailingly cheer me up.

I hear her, still. It seems like a dream.

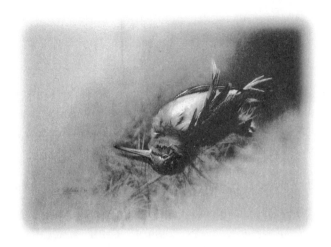

11

WOODCOCK CAMP
REVISITED

To those of us who adore woodcock gunning above all other sporting pursuits, the year naturally cleaves into two portions: October (i.e., woodcock season), and not-October. And among the few things I know for certain is this: October is too short. There should be a way to steal some days from a month with precious little to recommend it—March, for example—and perform a graft. It seems like a classic win-win deal: less of March to endure, more of October to enjoy. Politicians, take note.

Alas, I fear that this is just one of those pipe dreams brought on by the doldrums of not-October. Besides, woodcock operate on a calendar that is encoded into their very being, not printed on glossy stock beneath a photograph of Cindy Crawford. What matters, finally, is the purity of our devotion. To hunt as hard and as often and as well as possible, to make the most of the opportunities afforded us: this is a credo worthy of the bird. The measure of the honor we accord the woodcock is the level of intensity we bring to its pursuit. It should, to paraphrase Yeats, be nothing less than passionate.

So when my friend Andy "Bwana" Cook schedules the early October "Woodcock Weekend" hunt at his place, Andy's Acres, up in the sticks of northern Wisconsin, it is as if a binding contract has been signed. The dates are held in inviolable trust; only death, or the reasonable equivalent thereof, could force my absence. I commit for the duration, which generally means arriving Thursday afternoon (in time for a couple hours' gunning) and breaking camp Tuesday at dusk. This Thursday–Tuesday "weekend" is a sure-fire way to stretch October, although it depends heavily on an understanding family and a sympathetic employer. The sport is never less than memorable—Bwana's ability to correctly estimate the peak of the flight is uncanny—and the camaraderie is as mellow as good whiskey. There's an old saying that the quality of a sportsman's character is inversely proportional to the size of the quarry he prefers. Judging by the company that assembles for Woodcock Weekend, I think there's a germ of truth in that.

You have to be looking for Andy's place to find it. Set atop a modest escarpment that falls away to the north and west, it was originally a farmstead—in a part of the world where the thin, rocky soil yields a crop grudgingly, and the threat of frost is ever-present. One of the outbuildings is a small, dilapidated milking parlor. To the delight of an increasing flock of wild turkeys, not to mention migratory Canada geese, a neighbor still rents some of the land for corn and hay. Deer browse on apples, literally in the back yard; about every other year, a kamikaze grouse crashes through a window.

The single-story house is comfortable and deceptively spacious. Last autumn, for example, it easily accommodated six hunters (a venture capitalist, an attorney, a manufacturing representative, a veterinarian, an artist, and a writer) and seven dogs (three English setters, a pointer, two yellow labs, and a golden). Territorial disputes were kept to a minimum. The kitchen boasts most of the modern conveniences. Prints adorn the walls of the living room, which are also festooned with antlers taken during the annual November deer camp (they're handy for hanging wet chaps, brush pants, vests, etc.). Stacks of outdoor magazines crowd the shelves and table tops. There's even a screened-in back porch for storing coolers and feeding dogs. Short of a heat-and-humidity controlled gun room—I'll have to talk to Bwana about that—the place offers all the amenities a humble woodcock hunter could ask for. We eat like kings—massive T-bones, fresh-baked pies, cold-smoked salmon—sleep like logs, hunt like fools, and, in our spare moments, fashion creative solutions to such vexing problems as crime, overpopulation, government spending, and the intractability of the opposite sex. The hell with Robert Bly and all this drum-beating, chest-pounding, soul-baring "wild man" crap. We know who we are, and what we're about.

Everyone pulls his weight around camp, cleaning birds, cooking, doing dishes, providing comic relief. Actually, I don't recall Erik or

Donny doing any cooking, but they instinctively volunteer for the dishwashing detail. My culinary domain includes the grill and the cast-iron skillet (frying bacon is a secret fetish of mine), while Bwana mans the saucepans, stockpots, and oven. His spaghetti and meatballs is to die for. We expect no more of Terry than preparing the occasional hors d'oeuvre, but then, we take shameful advantage of his veterinary acumen. And I have to confess to foisting my grouse off on Terry because, despite my enormous admiration for the species, I simply hate to clean them. The fact of the matter is that grouse stink to high heaven. This is never mentioned in the literature; it would be like accusing a saint of flatulence.

Plus, Terry can clean a grouse, or any other gamebird, without getting so much as a speck of blood on his hands. In contrast, I look like some miscreant in the throes of being tarred-and-feathered. Terry attributes his fastidiousness to his surgical skill; I claim he's made a pact with the devil.

Erik and I dutifully clip the wings from our woodcock and deposit them in the envelopes provided by the Fish & Wildlife Service. Our ostensible reason for doing this is to advance the cause of science, and to foster sound wildlife management. It would be nearer the truth, however, to say that we do it in order to peruse the statistics we're sent in return, and congratulate ourselves on how resoundingly above average we are.

But sport, finally, is our *raison d'etre*. And for the kind of woodcock shooting we find among those glorious popple hillsides, I'd gladly sleep on the ground and eat cold pork-and-beans. Hell, I have. Not that long ago, when I began hunting the Wisconsin northwoods with Adrian Webber (this was before Adrian got into more politically correct activities like sea kayaking and mountain biking), we operated out of a tent pitched not far, as the crow flies, from Andy's Acres. There were lots of suppers catered by Dinty Moore, a lot of teeth-chattering, muscle-cramping nights under the cold, glittering stars. But those makeshift woodcock camps had a satisfying, close-to-the-bone feel, a sense of intimacy and rightness. It seemed like the proper way to learn the lay of the land, to become attuned to the rhythms of the birds. And at night, huddled close to the dancing flames, the solitude was as big as the country. It inspired reverence. How could I help but fall in love with this mysterious, ephemeral bird, when it inhabits such grand places?

I wouldn't trade those experiences for any quotient of wealth or fame. They are woven into the minor tapestry that is my life, and they've supplied nourishing fodder for my writing. Indeed, one of the first hunting stories I ever wrote was entitled "Woodcock Camp." I dug it out recently, having not read it in years. (Contrary to popular belief, writers do not remember every word they put down, which explains why they repeat themselves so relentlessly.) All things considered, it struck me as a pretty decent piece. I particularly like this passage:

> By the warm light of the lantern, we built a fire, set up the tent, and attended to the other rituals of establishing camp. We fed and watered the dogs, pulled up stout maple logs for chairs, then washed down the last of the cheese-and-onion sandwiches with bottles of cold beer . . .
>
> "We were as alone as we cared to be, talking of woodcock until frost crystallized on the downed leaves and forced us into mummy bags. An English setter lay between us, radiating heat, redolent of the sweet hay that was his normal

bedding, but sleep came hard—the way it does when some-thing good is coming with the morning.

This hasn't really changed, although woodcock camp now fea-tures a roof, central heating, and indoor plumbing. I still crawl into the same sleeping bag (Bwana furnishes bunks, but not linens), an English setter still curls at my side, and sleep still comes hard. The day's events, the points and flushes and shots, demand to be relived; the anticipation of tomorrow tingles like a mild electrical current.

And then, suddenly, it's dawn, the gray light filtering through the blinds, the smell of coffee brewing, the sound of canine toenails clicking on the kitchen floor. Chances are that Donny has already left for a short run—this, for him, translates into five miles or so. Erik is also a runner, which means that when the two of them are paired up in the woods, as they usually are, the other members of their squad are in for some serious aerobic exercise. Donny and Erik are famous for setting what some could call a "brisk" pace. Others have been known to call it murderous.

It has always struck me as ironic, if not a little ludicrous, that to hunt a six-ounce bird in the approved manner you need an ab-solutely staggering quantity of equipment. Dogs and dog-related paraphernalia (crates, bells, beepers, whistles, leads, dishes, ad.inf.); guns, extra guns, gun cleaning tools, and box after box of shells; clothing, including footwear, for every conceivable mutation of weather; food, drink, and refrigerated containers for same; maps and compasses; knives and shears; and, last but hardly least, a capa-cious four-wheel drive. That we cheerfully go to the trouble (and considerable expense) of amassing this "machine" testifies to the power of the woodcock's spell. It also explains why we never seem able to get by with fewer than three vehicles. There's just too much *stuff*. In reference to another irresistible six-ounce gamebird, Havilah Babcock observed that he didn't want shoot an elephant. Well, when we stream out of Andy's driveway en route to the woodcock coverts, Troopers and Four-Runners bristling with materiel, the procession looks for all the world like an African safari.

Andy and Erik, who by dint of familiarity with the terrain serve as co-huntmasters, believe strongly in the rule stating that the harder a spot is to get to, the better it will be. In other words, we do a lot of rock-hopping and creeping along in low gear down abandoned logging roads before the caravan grinds to a halt. But you only have to scan the cover to know that the journey was worth it: the broomstick popple stretches as far as the eye can see, its golden leaves shimmering hypnotically. While we employ a variety of strategies, the usual approach is to split into two groups, flushers and pointers, and head in opposite directions. Over the long haul, both teams seem to enjoy the same level of action. It always gladdens my heart to hear the other guys shooting in the distance, because there is no substitute on this earth for the thrill of getting into birds.

Oh, and we do get into birds. There may be places where the shooting is faster, but I doubt that it is better anywhere. The widely-traveled Peter Corbin, who attended the 1991 renewal of Woodcock Weekend—his print, "October Afternoon," is the fruit of that trip—called it the best woodcock hunting he's ever seen. Anyone of moderate competence with a shotgun should be able to scratch down his complement of birds. You don't even necessarily need a dog: a couple of years ago, when Bwana and I went left, up a gentle rise, my headstrong old setter, Zack, went right, down the slope—and never the twain did meet. We killed a half-dozen 'cock on what was essentially a stroll through the autumn woods. A chastened Zack was waiting for us back at the truck.

Having become accustomed to Zack's peregrinations, I knew he'd return. This was not the case when Erik lost April, his indefatigable golden retriever. In reality, April wasn't lost at all. When Peter and I started shooting on the flank of the ridge, we unwittingly tolled her in. You have to understand that April is a veritable Hoover: If a bird falls anywhere within her ken, she's there to pick it up. She responds to the sound of gunplay as gleefully as schoolchildren respond to the recess bell. April also has the endearing habit of barking when she encounters a grouse in a tree—sort of a vocal "point."

Anyway, assuming that Erik had deduced what happened, we hunted our way back to the vehicles, April and Peter's excellent yellow Lab, Chelsea, quartering busily ahead. We waited ten, twenty, thirty minutes . . . and finally Donny crested the hill, striding hurriedly through the sweet fern.

"Have you seen April?"

"She's right here—she came into us as soon as we started shooting. We thought you knew."

"No—the last time we saw her, she was heading in the other direction. She must have cut back behind us. We've been searching for over an hour. God, Erik's just frantic."

With that, Donny fired three quick shots. This volley informed Erik that April had been found, but it didn't tell him what condition she was in. As far as he knew, she could have a muzzleful of porcupine quills, a broken leg—or worse. Erik is sort of gaunt and haunted-looking, no doubt a subconscious reflection of his choice of career (lawyer). But when he hove into sight on the trail, his face was a furrowed mask of worry. The expression of relief that replaced it when an unscathed April bounded up to greet him spoke volumes about the bond between a bird gunner and his gun dog.

Erik and I get a kick out of composing bad prose in the worst tradition of cliché-ridden outdoor writing. For example, "The trusty smokepole delivered its death-dealing message, and the lonely hills reverberated at the thunderous echo of its mighty report." It gives us something to do while we're pondering our next move over sharp cheese, smoked sausage, tart apples, and Snickers bars. I prompt a flurry of grimaces and choking noises from the peanut gallery when I produce a bottle of Green River pop to wash everything down. It's so bad, it's good. It looks and tastes just like the lime phosphates I used to order at the soda fountain in Mikkelsen's Pharmacy (oooh, that Lynn Mikkelsen, she was loaded for bear), and the only place I've ever seen it for sale is the grocery store in Goodman, a logging town we pass through on the way to Andy's Acres. Ah, the fringe benefits of going to woodcock camp!

For the most part, we shoot barely well enough to avoid embarrassing ourselves. And, fortunately, the abundance of birds gives us plenty of opportunities for redemption when our marksmanship temporarily goes "into the toilet," as Bwana likes to say. Last year, Peter couldn't get into the groove. Instead of boom-"Fetch!" we'd hear boomboom, followed by a muttered oath. He was spraying an obscene amount of lead across the landscape, to no perceivable effect. In common with most people of extreme accomplishment, Peter is a perfectionist, so this run of buzzard's luck started to gnaw on his psyche. I knew he was desperate when he confessed to studying the way Erik and I handle our "smokepoles" in an attempt to determine what he was doing wrong. Holding me up as a model of shotgunning skill is about like holding Roseanne Barr up as the epitome of feminine grace. Two days, three boxes of shells, and a change of guns later, Peter smoothed out the kinks.

(Actually, in a twisted sort of way, it was delightful to see Peter brought down to earth, where we mortals reside. He's just so damn good at everything. I mean, fly-fishing with the man is humiliating—he throws a hundred feet of line as casually as most of us throw thirty.)

However, the direst missing streak in the annals of Woodcock Weekend belongs to Bwana. It was a crisp, sunny morning; I'd decided to tote a camera instead of a twenty-bore and let Andy defend our honor. Emmy, my sprightly setter, whipped into point straight out of the gate, and the action over the next couple hours was frenetic. The woodcock had arrived en masse. I don't think we went more than five minutes without a point. Bwana nailed two 'cock— and then fell headfirst into the shitter. Having been there myself, more times than I care to recall, I empathized completely. He couldn't connect to save his soul, although he did bag at least one trophy sapling. I got some good pictures, though, before he walked up to me, tersely said, "Here," and handed me his Ruger, along with the few shells he'd conserved.

That was the same morning that Babe, Terry's lean little setter, showed at a tender five months of age that she had the makings of an exceptional woodcock dog. Not only did she point a number of birds with style and authority, she held staunch while Terry flushed them. Needless to say, her precocity rocketed him to cloud nine. Babe has gone on to fulfill her early promise, although it was soon discovered that gutting the birds she retrieved was superfluous.

Think of hitting an open tube of toothpaste with a sledgehammer, and you'll get the picture. While cleaning out his vest at the end of a recent season, Terry's fingers detected a hard and shriveled object. It proved to be a desiccated woodcock heart, extruded by the crushing pressure of Babe's jaws. She is currently taking the cure under the supervision of professional trainer Bob Olson. Bob is also trying to put a handle on my supercharged pointer, Traveler, so that when I say, "I think I'll run Traveler," it doesn't precipitate a mass defection to the flushing-dog team.

There's more, much more, I could talk about: the point Emmy made on a grouse that, by all rights, should have been unapproachable; the way Popper, Bwana's stocky yellow Lab, snorts and snuffles when she scents a bird; Erik and Andy's frequent communication breakdowns regarding where each plans to hunt ("You said the *south* side of Buck Hill." "No, I said the *east* side of the Mac . . ."); scrambling out of the trucks, at dusk, to flush woodcock that refuse to budge from the road; grilling T-bones while a fine snow sifts down; stepping over comatose dogs to get seconds from the kitchen; Peter holding a woodcock in his left hand, looking at it through an artist's eyes, and sketching it with his right; checking the thermometer a final time ("Twenty-nine . . .") before turning in, and finding that Emmy is already fast asleep on the bunk.

October is too short.

12

LOST IN THE 20TH CENTURY

If you were tilted in that direction already, like Van Gogh, perhaps, sunset on the prairies would drive you mad. It is too
much for the mind to comprehend. The colors swirl and mutate impossibly (even Vincent himself could not have painted them); the
grasses pulse like charged filaments; the astonished sky expands.
You feel yourself diminishing uncontrollably, as if the inventory of
your soul, your very being, is escaping your grasp. Once beyond
your reach, it joins those distant stars said to be hurtling toward the
rubbery walls of the universe.

Such are the thoughts that occur to a nervous system careening on truck stop coffee, and a brain soggy from interstate driving. The pickup is loaded, pointing west. South Dakota, Nebraska maybe: wherever the thunderheads were stacked miles high, and lightning cracked them as if they were brimming ewers. The grass will be good there, the big bluestem pooling its maroon in the meadows, the grama gone yellow against the smooth-backed hills. This is where the birds will be, the prairie chickens and the sharp-tailed grouse, in a place that hasn't changed, a place that cattle and plows and combines haven't used up.

I go as much for the country as for the birds. It's a long trip. Zack will sprawl on the seat beside me, his back paws twitching against my leg and his weary muzzle wedged between the backrest and the door. A cache of Emmylou Harris cassettes will be scattered on top of the dashboard, except for the one in the tape player, with the volume cranked. Her voice reminds me of the faces of Depression-era women frozen in time by Dorothea Lange's photographs. I imagine them, thirty going on eternal, singing to their brave children, their voices clear, proud, and whetted by the gritty stone of despair. They went west too, these women, hearts half-filled with hope, half-filled with dread. The way their husbands talked, a better life was something they would simply find, like a lost calf, or an arrowhead.

So it's a dangerous enterprise, heading west with something in mind, something related to expectations. I know: I've gone chicken hunting with great ones and watched them shatter; I've gone with none and seen the prairies alive with birds, shot them, cradled them in my hand and stroked their soft barred breasts with the backs of my fingers. The survivor's attitude is just to go, and take what comes.

This much I'm sure of: It'll just be the setters and me, eating, sleeping, and hunting out of a tent pitched on the brink of nowhere. Coffee in the morning, sour mash at night. Great looping fervent casts, the dogs tacking upwind like sloops, grass parting in their wakes, their flags like burgees snapping in the wind. Zack will make game first, standing like a monument, and Em will honor instantly, crouched low in front, brown eyes riveted on her kennelmate. Chickens in the air, reports that barely scratch the overwhelming silence, a bird on the ground, setter muzzles whuffing the feathers. Naps in the warm afternoon, and books that can stand the weather: Kittredge, McGuane.

My camp will not be high, but it will be plenty lonesome. If all goes according to plan, the view will encompass no man-made objects whatsoever, other than the tent and the pickup. On second thought, I'd be willing to grant an exception for an abandoned ranch house, curtains still moving behind dark windows, especially one with a creaky windmill off to the side, a windmill that stood up to blizzards and droughts, and accomplished a quantity of work that couldn't be measured. That would seem right, a kind of lighthouse on this sea of grass.

I want to do it the way my friend Jon does, remote and self-sufficient, far from artifice and close to the honest bone. He makes his grouse camp up on the Missouri Coteau, not far from the Canadian border. Like me, Jon runs English setters, but he doesn't tote a shotgun. Instead, he carries a falcon on his fist. It's been said that flying hawks at prairie grouse is the ultimate expression of this ancient sport, the pinnacle of achievement for the falconer. Whether this is true, I'm not prepared to say. But I do know that when one of Jon's birds kills a sharptail—waiting on until the flock rises, then folding its wings, compressing its feathers and stooping, air shriek-ing through its bells—the moment is luminous. Later, Jon will grill the wine-red breast of the grouse over an open fire, just as the Bedouin falconers of Arabia might roast a bustard, their hooded sakers solemn as statuary. There is a continuum of tradition here, atavistic, pure, and unencumbered by existential baggage. The at-traction is powerful. This is the way men should hunt; gun or fal-con, it makes no difference.

Ideally, my camp will be as far removed from fences as possible, but this desire may not be realistic. I'll be hunting public land, the primary use of which seems to be the fattening of private cattle. Cattle translate into barbed wire. As I understand it, grazing rights to the public domain are leased under the same brand of sweetheart arrangements that make it cheaper for lumber companies to log the national forests than to harvest timber from their own stands. This land is your land, this land is my land, but no one consulted us when our elected stewards bent over and squealed for the pleasure of cattle interests. I say: Save a prairie chicken, declare open season on range beef.

Obviously, I've been reading far too much Ed Abbey lately.

In fact, it would be easy to recite chapter and verse about the mis-treatment these birds have received—particularly the prairie chicken—at the hands of man. For a time in the late 19th century, when the original tallgrass prairies were only partially broken by the plow, chickens were fabulously abundant. There was still enough good grass for nesting, brooding the chicks, and roosting, and, in the form of corn, barley, rye and other cultivated grains, a literal glut of food. It has even been suggested that the decimation of the bison had a salubrious effect on the chicken populations because it left the prairies undisturbed by large herbivores. But cattle soon replaced buffalo, and the inexorable plow left little native sod unturned. As early as the 1920s, one eminent ornithologist would lament that only the passenger pigeon had suffered a crueler fate in the face of "civilization" than the prairie chicken.

They are anachronisms, these grouse of the prairies, living out on the edge of things, where it's too dry to plant and too big to graze to the nub. Perhaps this is why the idea of hunting them is so compelling: Clearly, they do not belong here, in 1990, but to an older era, an era of sod huts and horse-drawn plows, of shocked corn and steam engines, black-powder shotguns and dogs that point with low tails, gunners wearing ties, waxed mustaches, and bowler hats. Think Currier & Ives.

I wonder if I belong there, too. My mother, who puts much stock in such matters, tells me that in a former life I was a genteel sportsman of southern extraction—Virginian, probably—who cottoned to English setters, upland bird hunting, and fast women. If she is correct, the timing would have been right: I envision a Butleresque version of myself clacking west in a handsomely-appointed railroad car, enroute to the prairies for a week of shooting, happily relieving Yankees of their bankrolls in friendly games of poker, each garnered pot a sweet, symbolic act of revenge for the lost war.

Profoundly suspicious of the impulse to assign tidy answers to questions beginning with "Why?" I like Mom's explanation as well as any. And I can't help thinking, whenever I watch a flock of chickens sail out of sight, as they inevitably do, that the reason they disappear has nothing to do with distance, or with the limitations of the human eye. The reason they fly so far, the reason they vanish, is that they are searching for a flaw in the fabric of time, a rent that will ferry them back to the 19th century. They are not looking for a better place; they are looking for a better time.

But enough of metaphysics. The best populations of prairie chickens anywhere occur in Kansas, which also boasts the largest harvest. Statistics, however, lie. The season in Kansas doesn't open until November; by then, the birds have aggregated into extensive flocks, and their nerves are cocked against a hair-trigger. A hunter on foot with a dog has about as much chance of getting close to them as a naked and raving lunatic has of dodging Michael Jackson's bodyguards and getting autographed on the tush. It ain't going to happen. The deal in Kansas is to pass shoot in the afternoons when the chickens are trading between feeding areas (cornfields, mostly) and roosts. It's a little like dove shooting, but colder; very sporty and undeniably effective.

Trouble is, it doesn't appeal to me in the least. I have this perverse need to feel that I've earned my birds, a need that can be satisfied only by walking them up (this ethos applies to all gamebirds except quail, but as John Madson put it, you don't hunt quail, you hunt for the dog that is hunting for the quail). The choice, then, is between the grasslands of central South Dakota, below Pierre, and the eastern half of the Nebraska Sandhills. I generally lean toward Dakota, simply because it has less cactus and is therefore kinder to the dogs. The seasons in both states open in mid-September, when the birds still play fair. Actually, early-season grouse and chickens can be ridiculously easy, especially if they're hunkered down in sloughgrass or other heavy cover. They flush literally off your toe, are casual about getting up to speed, and once the flight plan is established, they don't deviate. In other words, they fly straight and slow (although they are burners at terminal velocity, as any falconer who has watched one pull away from a peregrine will attest).

You almost feel a twinge of guilt at shooting such agreeable birds. Don't worry; they'll soon extract their own peculiar toll, which you'll pay for in the currency of out-of-range flushes, long and staggeringly difficult shots, legs alchemized into lead, and dead-on-your-feet exhaustion. Some number-cruncher once calculated that in a thin year the average chicken/sharptail hunter walks seven miles per bird. That's 21 miles for a three-bird limit, Dr. Einstein. Even in a good year, the distance between birds is measured in miles. This is not a sport for the infirm of body or the weak of heart.

Nor is it a game for soft, short-winded canines. Prairie hunting demands everything a bird dog has to give, and then some. A poorly-conditioned animal will soon be dragging its sorry ass; after a few days of this, you and your dog(s) both will be broken and pathetic. I remember checking on Zack in his truck kennel a couple days into a chicken hunt, just to see how the old boy was doing. A knuckle tapped on the window provoked no response. I called his name; no sign of life. A wave of anxiety crested in my stomach. "Zack!" I cried, rapping furiously on the glass. With excruciating effort, he cracked one eye, a gesture that said, "Let me lie, you pestiferous son of a bitch!"

While September has its virtues, I'll trade its easy marks for the educated birds of October. By then, the frosts will be visiting regularly, and the colors of the prairie will have mellowed to ocher, burnt sienna, and apricot, all streaming beneath a china sky. Besides, the scars incurred on that September trip to the Sandhills a while back remain vivid and painful to the touch. After 850 miles on the road, we—the setters and I—landed in Hell's Kitchen. The heat was ludicrous; I'm talking a hundred degrees. I tried to hunt at dawn, hoping to take advantage of the cool dew, and I damn near killed my dogs. It was the most outrageously ill-fated expedition of my career; there's not even a close second. It reminded me of the Custer joke: Corporal—looks like a pin cushion, so many arrows sticking out of his hide—crawls up to Custer at the Little Big Horn. "General," he gasps, "I've got some good news, and I've got some bad news."

"Tell me the bad news first," Custer orders.

"The bad news is that all our ammunition's gone, most of the horses are four hooves up, we can't run, we can't hide, and after we're dead the Sioux women will cut off our balls."

"What's the good news?"

"We won't have to ride back through Nebraska."

Whether I wind up in Nebraska or South Dakota, the shooting will be mixed, chickens and sharptails both. There are subtle differences in each bird's habitat preferences—sharptails gravitate more to brush than chickens; conversely, chickens do better in straight, undiluted grass—but for all practical purposes you're hunting the same bird. As if to prove the point, they commonly interbreed, and often as not you'll see both species in the same flock. Short course in identification: The birds with the white undersides and the spiky tails are sharptails, the ones that are dark all over and have rounded tails are chickens. The respective DNRs do not ask you to distinguish them on the wing: To the warden, they're both "grouse," and you're allowed three a day.

I confess to a weakness for prairie chickens. They're rarer, for one thing, and, to paraphrase Marlowe, I'm fascinated by their "tragical history." They strike a resonant chord in my soul. In the Sandhills, they'll tell you that chickens are wilder than grouse, but in South Dakota they claim that the opposite is true. What is for certain is that they both adore wide horizons, they both tend to flush "out there," and they fly forever, alternately beating their wings and gliding. Because they are muscled for long flights, their breast is profusely supplied with blood vessels. The meat is dark red, almost purple, the color of Pommard. It is incomparably tender and intensely flavorful: Imagine the finest tournedos of beef, prepared very rare, and you'll have an approximate idea of the taste. Eating the flesh of chickens or sharptails is an event—or should be. Parisians would beg, even weep, for such a delicacy.

It would be preposterous to advocate strategies for hunting these birds. The first bit of advice I received on the subject is still the sagest: "Keep walking—you can get well in a hurry." You need good grass, of course, which is one of those commodities you learn to recognize without being able to define precisely, like style or beauty. An upwind approach will get you closer, and be a huge help to your dog. Use enough gun: nothing less than an ounce of sixes. Some sportsmen like to work the meadows early and late, and concentrate on high ground during the day. Another variation is to hunt the grass in the morning, hit the sloughs and thickets when the heat is on, and then return to the grass just before sunset. Patches of wild rose and buffalo berry are always worth a look. Frankly, I'm convinced that chickens and sharptails operate on a totally random schedule, like wealthy eccentrics. So, I just keep walking.

That man I saw in South Dakota had it right. It was just he, his merry-gaited springer, and prairie enough to swallow them whole. I waved as I passed in the truck; he smiled and nodded. It sounds

hopelessly cliché, but he carried a Parker. Hours later, I found myself passing by again. His car hadn't moved, but now there were
dishes of food and water resting in the shade of the rear bumper.
Suddenly, I had a clear picture of them: the man stretched out on
the grass, hands clasped behind his head, cap pulled over his eyes,
legs crossed at the ankle; the spaniel curled at his side, the curve of
its back fitting into the hollow above the man's hip. When the
shadow of a marsh hawk brushed over them, the dog came alert,
and the man, without knowing it, laid a reassuring hand on its
flank. No, I couldn't really see them, in a physical sense: They were
somewhere out on the billowing prairie, searching for birds, waiting
for their chance, for the simple opportunity, knowing the rest would
take care of itself. I could see this man because I knew his mind. It
was the same as my own.

Her voice sustains me, it lifts me up. We roll across the sand counties, thick with deer, of central Wisconsin, then enter the Coulee
Country. The glaciers swerved when they got here, leaving the earth
squeezed tight into ridges and valleys, like the bellows of an accor-
dion. We bridge the Mississippi, climb the limestone bluffs of eastern Minnesota, top out on the vast tilled plain that stretches all the
way to the Missouri. Stultifying, the land too clean, too polished to
hold its soil. Dirty clouds curl up from the fields. A cock pheasant
peeking from the brome is a revelation; a covey of Hungarian partridge gritting on the parallel gravel road a miracle. At Heron Lake,
a pang of sadness for the great flocks of canvasbacks that once rafted
there, gorging on wild celery. Gone, to come no more.

My mind races ahead. I won't stop until I catch it, at a place where
the land heaves itself up in broad, tan hills, only to fall away in blue
vistas that undulate beyond a man's reckoning; a place where I can

hunt all day and never retrace my steps, where the setters and I finally merge with the rhythms of the country, becoming as much a part of that music as the white-rumped pronghorns, the twitchy-eared jackrabbits, and the wheeling falcons, following the grouse and the chickens like partners in a dance, a dance that began before any of us were born.

13

THE PROMISE

The covey caught me off guard. But then, quail always do. You're never ready for them, really; the flush always comes a step sooner, or a step later, than you anticipate, and it always turns you into a skin-wrapped bag of jello.

This particular bevy, however, surprised me because I was in the remotest hinterlands of bobwhite range. In fact, I was in the heart of the heart of pheasant country; the broad, November-bleak Missouri River bottoms of southeastern South Dakota, to be precise. They don't kill enough quail in South Dakota to set a decent first course at a middle-sized family picnic.

So when I circled a cattail-rimmed slough to find Traveler standing solid in a flat of chest-high scrub, bobs were the furthest thing from my mind. Truth to tell, I wasn't expecting a flush, period. We hadn't been able to get close to a hen all day, much less a rooster that had been dodging lead for a full month. Everywhere I looked in the soft, loamy sand, there were pheasant tracks; with hundreds, even thousands of acres of unbroken cover to vanish in, why fly? It was like trying to arrest a pickpocket in the slums of Calcutta.

Anyway, I rather casually slid in front of Traveler's point, and nearly filled my pants when the quail boiled up all around me. It wasn't a big covey; maybe half-a-dozen birds. My first shot was essentially an involuntary spasm. The second shot never happened; I'd recently acquired the lovely old 16-gauge Fox CE, and its double triggers remained a mystery to me. I just kept reefing on the trigger I'd already pulled, wondering why the hell the gun wasn't going bang.

Luckily, I was able to mark the birds down. They pitched into a grove of tall, beamy cottonwoods about 150 yards to the north, and by the time I crossed the flat and scrambled up an embankment overgrown with briars, Traveler had already made game. A single rocketed out of a frost-browned tuft of ryegrass, but the Fox seemed to react of its own accord, the way a finely crafted shotgun is supposed to.

It was an event of sorts: the handsome little bob was the first wild quail I'd killed over Traveler. You have to understand that, to me, Traveler is not simply a pointer. He's an Elhew pointer, a dog I'd dreamed of owning since I was a kid, and I used to spend hours staring at the Elhew Kennels ads in *Sports Afield*, letting my imagination put me there in the photos, hunting behind Jungle, Zeus and Marksman, each a National Champion. They were the hero dogs of my youth. A quarter-century later, their royal blood coursed in Traveler's veins, and this knowledge gave me immense pleasure.

And it was the first quail I'd ever taken with the Fox—although there's no telling how many the gun itself had accounted for since it was shipped from the Philadelphia factory, circa 1914. It had obviously seen its share of honest use. The 28-inch, Krupp steel tubes had been reblued at least once, and the slim, graceful frame, with its elegant "spearpoint" cheek panels, had lost all but a trace of its case coloring. But the whimsical gamescene engraving—a brace of quail on one side, a pair of woodcock on the other, a setter underneath—still exuded nostalgic charm, and the semi-pistol grip stock not only boasted remarkably "modern" dimensions, but French walnut of uncommon figure, complexity and richness, the kind of wood that turns the heads of the dead.

To shoot over an Elhew pointer with a Fox gun: it was the ultimate fantasy, fulfilled. And yet as I held the quail in my hand, pensively stroking the perfect feathers of its breast with the backs of my knuckles, none of this occurred to me. I was thinking about a gruff old sonofabitch half-a-continent away, a man in whose company I'd spent a few hours the previous winter. For all I knew, he was dead; he'd made it clear, without the slightest trace of self-pity, that he wouldn't be around much longer. I'd promised him something, and as I saw it, my obligation was binding, and irrevocable.

The Eastern Shore of Chesapeake Bay is the cradle of American waterfowling tradition. It conjures a tapestry of images: hard-bitten market gunners and their businesslike retrievers, dogs bred not only to brave the roughest, coldest seas, but to be unconditionally loyal to their masters and profoundly suspicious of everybody else; the colorful "baymen" whose occupations—boatbuilder, guide, oyster-man, crabber—changed with the tides and with the seasons; famous decoy-makers like the country-smart Ward Brothers; rafts of canvasbacks, redheads and bluebills that covered the water like a vast, billowing blanket; the skies alive with skeins of gabbling Canada geese, trading between the winter wheatfields and the secluded marshes; countless gunner's dawns, each dense with anticipation and excitement.

None of this was lost on me as I sat on the hood of my rental car, watching the sunset from a deserted beach on Tilghman Island. It was an oddly mild evening in late February; I was comfortable wearing just a light fleece jacket. The next morning, I'd arranged an interview with a man in nearby Easton who was a close friend and frequent hunting companion of the celebrated wildlife artist, Richard Bishop. I'd been warned that Jim Hornor could be a tough customer, and I learned it for myself when I called him from Wisconsin to solicit some information for an article. "If you want me to talk about Dick Bishop," he growled, "you'll have to see me in person. I'll be goddamned if I'm going to tell you anything over the phone." His voice sounded exactly like Ralph Bellamy's.

It was a quiet, serene sunset; no solar fireworks, no dazzling ribbons of colors. Out of nowhere—I swear this is true—a handsome golden retriever materialized, carrying a piece of driftwood. He stood next to the car, slowing wagging his thickly feathered tail, staring at me, until I swung down, took the stick from his mouth, and lobbed it into the lapping waters of the bay. Swimming smoothly, the golden executed a confident retrieve-to-hand. We kept up the game for several minutes. Then, like a kid who knows intuitively when it's time to leave the playground and get home for supper, the dog trotted jauntily down the road, still holding the stick.

I smiled, took a deep breath of salt-scented air, and for the first time in weeks felt my soul go calm. My wife had moved out a month earlier. She announced she was leaving the day I got back from a quail hunting trip to Texas; in fact, she'd lined up a rental condo during my absence. It was kind of like flushing a covey; I knew in my heart it was bound to happen, but I still wasn't altogether prepared when it did. The long and short of it is that the shit had been hitting the fan pretty emphatically, and now, finally, some small measure of optimism had gained a toehold. When I found a seafood restaurant in St. Michael that was running a special on raw oysters, which I adore (a dollar-a-dozen with any entrée), it was clear that things were definitely looking up.

After waking to the soft clamor of geese, I took a walk through the narrow, Sunday-sleepy streets of Easton. The simple, clean-lined colonial architecture reminded me of Cape Cod. Standing in front of Albright's Gun Shop, I peered longingly at the rack of fine doubles inside. The Parkers, with their trademark "eyeball" hingepin, were easy to identify, like drake pintails. A letter from Gene Hill was part of the window display.

Jim Hornor's directions led me to a spacious, immaculately land-scaped retirement village, its attractive bungalows clustered at the ends of the cul-de-sacs that branched from the main road. I approached a man sitting outside, next to his front door. His legs were crossed; he was smoking a cigarette and gazing straight ahead.

"Mr. Hornor?" I inquired.

"Mr. Davis?" He was bald except for a prickly looking white fringe above the ears, and he wore a foam neck brace covered with ribbed beige cloth, the aftermath of recent surgery, that extended from his collarbone to the bottom of his jaw. His mottled, inelastic skin stretched tightly over a frame that seemed to be collapsing under the pressure. There was scarcely any flesh left on the man. A portion of his shin was visible below his trousers, and the leading edge of the bone was as sharply defined as the bit of an axe. But he had an alert, hawkish expression, distinguished by eyes that were shockingly blue, yet strangely opaque.

"I've gone blind, you know." It was as if he were answering the unspoken question in my mind. "I'm pretty well broken down, too. It's a good thing you caught me when you did, because I won't be here six months from now."

He rose stiffly, flicked away his cigarette butt, and beckoned me inside where Mrs. Hornor, a slight, birdlike woman who addressed her husband as "Thee," greeted me. An original Richard Bishop oil, *Pintails in the Snow,* hung on one wall of the living room. Audubon's print of ruffed grouse—the genuine article, not a mass-produced copy—adorned another, along with Bishop's series of decorative sporting dog plates. "When we lived in Philadelphia," Mrs. Hornor volunteered, "we had much more art. We simply didn't have room for it all when we moved down here."

Before us, on a low, rectangular coffee table, Mrs. Hornor had set out the three Bishop books, as well as various memorabilia and correspondence. Jim Hornor set the tone of the interview immediately. Referring to one of the books, he declared, "That's the goddamnedest assortment of hot air I've ever read in my life. I'm not going to contribute to anything like that. If you want a bunch of hot air to fill your article, you can do it yourself."

He paused to catch his breath, then resumed his tirade. "Everyone who's written about Bishop has exaggerated to beat hell. He was just a perfectly normal, nice fellow who did the best he could. He was very talented, he was a hell of a good shot . . . and he did not suffer fools gladly."

With that, Hornor reached down to the coffee table, and felt through the documents there until his fingers identified what he was looking for, a two-page typed manuscript with numerous hand-written corrections. "If you think any of this might be helpful," he offered, "you have my permission to use it." Untitled and undated, it was inscribed "James C. Hornor copyright." I quickly skimmed the introductory paragraphs:

"The worthy G.P. who had the privilege of administering a hearty smack to the glowing buttocks of one Richard E. Bishop on May 30th, 1887, probably did not realize that he was launching into this world a Cornell graduate, an engineer, an author, an outstanding bird photographer, a fine artist, a world traveler, and first and last, a most competent gunner . . .

"As Dick was my senior by some twenty-two years, unfortunately our paths did not cross until the mid-1930s. But shortly thereafter, we saw much of each other in the course of the years, gunned waterfowl, grouse, doves, woodcock, snipe and pheasants together, and also cavorted about in sundry retriever and springer spaniel field trials as 'Official Guns.'

"Dick shot his way through the declining years of the Golden Age of American gunning, in a period which produced such greats as Colonel Hal Sheldon, Nash Buckingham, Captain Charles Askins Sr.,

Horatio Bigelow, Captain Paul Curtis, and Charles Biddle, all of whom he knew, and like them, he was a dedicated conservationist . . ."

As the interview unfolded, it began to assume a shape and life of its own. The talk of Bishop's art would surface briefly, only to be submerged by recollections of Bishop the sportsman. Hornor spoke of Bishop's love for the Santee Club in South Carolina ("It boasted the finest duck hunting in the East, and the most distinguished membership in North America"); his frugal insistence on shooting a Model 21 instead of a London "Best" ("Of all things—he might as well have had a goddamn popgun"); the fact that he never owned a hunting dog ("He didn't have to—his friends owned some of the best dogs in the country"). There was the time Bishop was dragooned into judging a retriever trial, and caused an uproar by placing a dog that had committed a flagrant breach of etiquette. "You can't place that dog," protested the field trial chairman, who was among Bishop's closest friends. "You've got to go by the book!"

"The hell with the book!" Bishop stormed. "You told me to pick the dog I like, and this is it!" A full year of silence went by before the two friends deigned to speak to each other again.

Many of Hornor's fondest memories of Bishop were rooted in their experiences serving as guns at field trials. "The two of us killed 111 pheasants in one afternoon at a spaniel trial," he recalled. "I was never so goddamn tired in my life." On another occasion, at the posh Tuxedo Club in upstate New York, Bishop was Captain of the guns for a springer stake of national significance. One of his charges, a veteran of the legendary World War I fighter squadron, the Lafayette Escadrille, kept shooting his birds the instant they became airborne. "Look, Charlie," Bishop rebuked, "you've got to let the birds get out farther."

"Goddamn it, Bishop," snapped the crusty old ace, "I've been shooting for the pot all my life, and I'm too damn old to change!"

Hornor laughed until the tears trickled down his cheeks. He wiped his eyes with the back of a hand, and shook his head. "There aren't the field shots in this country that there used to be," he mused. I mentioned Nash Buckingham in that context, and Hornor laughed again.

"I knew Buck rather well," he elaborated. "He talked just the way he wrote. You had the feeling that ninety percent of what he said was hot air—but he was still a delight to listen to. He never learned to drive a car, you know. He lived as if the world hadn't changed in a hundred years.

"Buck could sure throw it, I'll tell you that."

By now, Hornor had warmed to the task. And he understood that I was a kindred spirit, that what he was telling me had resonance far beyond its utility as mere fodder for a story. He had opened the door to a vanished world, a world that not only teemed with game, but in which sportsmen were larger-than-life. They moved freely; they were welcomed everywhere, and the respect they displayed was repaid in kind. They shot the finest guns ever made over the grandest dogs ever bred, not for appearance's sake, but simply because that was how it was done. Compared to the optimism and abundance of that era—it ended, I suppose, with the assassination of Kennedy, the dis-illusion of Vietnam, and America's general loss of innocence—our modern age seems hopelessly cynical and impoverished.

But for a few hours that morning in Maryland, I was transported back. I hung on Hornor's every word, and in the presence of an au-dience the memories flowed, like tributaries mingling their waters to form a broad river. He spoke of the many dogs he'd owned—pointers, setters, spaniels—of grouse and woodcock hunting in the Poconos, of gunning waterfowl up and down the Eastern seaboard. He confessed that he preferred woodcock to grouse on the table (as do I), and he lamented the fact that today's dogs don't seem to have the brains their forebears did.

"I gunned wherever I could," he reminisced. "I hunted ptarmigan in Norway, and I made eleven trips to Scotland to shoot red grouse. Scottish grouse are not to be compared with bobwhite quail, however. The bobwhite quail's the greatest gamebird God ever made, in my opinion.

"I owned the best upland gun you ever saw in your life. It was a 5-pound, 11-ounce Purdey 12-bore, with no choke in either barrel. It knew when a bird got up—I didn't have to do anything. It was so light that I over-controlled it at first, so I had those haughty boys on Audley Street lift the rib and put a half-ounce of lead under the muzzle. That cured it. I had three Purdeys, all of them stocked exactly alike. It broke my heart to give them up, I'll tell you that."

Abruptly, Hornor called to his wife in the kitchen. "What time is it?" he asked.

"About 11:30," she replied.

"Time for a drink," he concluded. "How about a Bloody Mary?"

Mrs. Hornor's recipe for Bloody Marys involved dropping several ice cubes into a Bishop-designed cocktail glass, filling it two-thirds full of vodka, and then slightly discoloring it with tomato juice. Drinks in hand, Jim and I stepped outside, where he lit a cigarette. "She won't let me smoke in the house anymore," he grumbled. I learned that he had been in the commercial real estate business in Philadelphia, and that later he'd dabbled as a dealer in high-grade guns. For a time, Hornor had even been on the Board of Directors of Holland & Holland. "When Chanel bought the company," he chuckled, "we joked that with every gun you got a flask of Number 5."

After a traditional Eastern Shore lunch—crab cakes, fresh asparagus and strawberries sprinkled with sugar—I made the mistake, over coffee, of professing my admiration for the Fox shotgun. A look of disgust passed over Hornor's face. "My boy," he chided, "you've gotten off the track somewhere. Ansley Fox was a womanizer!"

"What does that have to do with making shotguns?"

Hornor dismissed me with a scowl and a wave of the hand, and muttered something derogatory about the Fox barrels. In his estimation, only the classic London marques—Purdey, Boss, Woodward, Churchill, H&H, etc.—were worthy of discussion, although he grudgingly admitted that, in a pinch, it might be possible to make do with a Lefever.

The conversation continued to roam, like a big-going pointer on the Canadian prairies. It ran from Hungarian partridge shooting on Prince Edward Island ("The fellow who introduced the birds there discovered that they weren't getting the right kind of grit, so he had six boatloads of crushed granite brought in from England") to "body-booting" in Chesapeake Bay (It's a form of idiot's delight— you kill ducks, but it's an asinine way to do it"). As a teenager, Hornor had spent a summer canoeing the maze-like Lake of the Woods country of northwestern Ontario, the same country that I knew intimately. And whatever lingering doubts he entertained about my character—in addition to the Fox debacle, I'd been berated for failing to satisfactorily explain the difference between "slip" and "nonslip" retrievers—were dispelled when it turned out that we had both graduated from the same small college, he with the class of '33, myself with the class of '79.

With Hornor's permission, I perused the bookshelves in his study while he went outside for another cigarette. "My library isn't what it used to be," he said, apologetically. "I donated most of my books to the Academy of Natural Science in Philadelphia." But the few dozen he'd kept were gems, a selection of rare titles that any collector—indeed, any literate sportsman—would sell his soul for. The first edition of *New England Grouse Shooting*, by William Harnden Foster. *National Field Trial Champions*, by William Brown and Nash Buckingham. *Stag Shooting in Scotland*. Many Derrydales. I wanted to hold them all in my hands, heft their weight, feel the texture of the covers, smell the pages. I wanted to make their magic mine, but the surfeit of choices left me paralyzed. I couldn't decide which volume to open first.

Movement at the periphery of vision interrupted my reverie. Mrs. Hornor was standing in the doorway. "You can't imagine," she said softly, "how difficult it's been for Jim to lose his sight. To not be able to read, or shoot, or hunt . . ."

Her voice trailed off, and she turned and walked back towards the kitchen. I said nothing, but I was convinced that she was wrong. I *could* imagine it. I could imagine it because those same things mattered to me, deeply, and the thought of losing them was unbearable. To be left with nothing but memories . . . it was a chilling prospect. At least Jim Hornor had saved a lot of them; more, by far, than most men. Whether or not it was enough to live on was a question only he could answer.

I repaired to the living room, and started to read his little memoir of Dick Bishop. "As the clear and bright January morning dawned,"

Hornor wrote, "we saw to the eastward a big rick of canvasback a mile or so away, the white backs of the drakes gleaming in the light of the rising sun. Work boats going down the river began to put these fowl up, and it seemed as if every bunch gave us a dart. Down wind they would come, outside the stools, jink as they went by at full throttle, then pull up and perform one of those magnificent pylon turns, when even at an eighth-of-a-mile's distance, one could hear the sound of their wings as if twenty yards of canvas were being torn asunder. The heads of the drakes flashed like red hot coals as they turned in the sunlight, and with black feet and paddles extended, rocking on stiff wings, in they rushed with that indefinable aura of ferocity . . ."

When Hornor returned, I could think of nothing more to ask. Later, of course, a hundred questions occurred to me. Had he known Dr. Charles Norris, the prominent Philadelphia physician and author of *Eastern Upland Shooting*, the man George Bird Evans wrote of in *Recollections of a Shooting Guest*? Did he prefer pointers to setters, or vice-versa? What about snipe shooting? I kicked myself for not thinking of these questions when I had the chance, for not tapping the irreplaceable, impossible-to-duplicate well of knowledge and experience he possessed. He had seen and done things that no man would ever see or do again. Perhaps that was his secret, his reason for keeping on; perhaps he knew how enormously fortunate he'd been, and that there was nothing about his life he would willingly change, trade or surrender. Perhaps there was nothing more he needed to see.

Hornor, too, had run out of things to say. "Most of you fellows have diarrhea with the pen anyway," he snorted. I said goodbye to Mrs. Hornor, and thanked her again for the lovely meal. "It was nice of you to come and see us," she smiled. "We don't get many visitors these days."

Jim Hornor followed me outside. The sun was still bright; the day had the aroma of spring. We shook hands, and as I began to walk towards the car his voice stopped me.

"Do me a favor, will you?"

"Sure. I'd be happy to."

"The next time you shoot a bobwhite quail, think of me."

"I'll do that."

Jim Hornor lived longer than he expected to. The six months he'd given himself stretched into three years. I have no doubt that he came to regard his longevity as a curse, especially after Mrs. Hornor passed away in the fifty-sixth year of their marriage. Nor do I harbor any doubt that when his own time came, on November 28, 1994, he welcomed it.

But death, finally, is immaterial. The only important thing is the manner in which a man lives. Jim Hornor lived richly, fully and by his own terms. He envied no one.

I think of him whenever I shoot a bobwhite quail.

14

LETTING GO

O ne was the dog I'll always follow, when the fire has burned to embers, the ice has melted in my glass, and I close my eyes to dream. The other was the dog I'll always wonder about, the dog that had it all, that might have been a champion.

They hunted together once, the 14-year-old setter and the pointer still shy of her first birthday, before I had to let them go.

It was an accident, really, the unplanned end to a sequence of events set in motion by a phone call. A casual acquaintance named Craig had decided to buy a puppy, and he wanted my input on the three breeds he was considering. I wholeheartedly endorsed his first two picks, English setter and Gordon setter, with the caveat that he should scrupulously avoid any lines tainted by show blood. But when Craig told me that the third breed he had in mind was the Weimaraner, I was, well, puzzled. Good Weimaraners are rumored to exist, but so are Bigfoot, Elvis, and affordable health care.

Craig finally admitted that getting a Weimaraner was his wife's idea. It seems she was quite taken by the breed after seeing some William Wegman photographs. While I'm sure that legitimate arguments can be mustered on the Weimaraner's behalf, its willingness to submit to indignity doesn't seem to be among them.

Anyway, I succeeded in getting Craig back on track. And we set a date to meet at a nearby shooting preserve so he could begin to develop a feel for the mechanics of gunning over pointing dogs. In particular, he was interested in seeing my fiery setter bitch, Emmylou, strut her stuff. At six-and-a-half, she was a proven commodity: bold, stylish, relentless. I was confident that she'd impress Craig and provide him with a yardstick for comparison.

We met on a raw, blustery afternoon in mid-December. Fitful volleys of snow spat down from the pewter sky; the bare-limbed maples were as solemn as orthodox saints. In the rattling chill, in the flat, featureless light, you could feel the earth sliding headlong into winter.

Craig and I parked on the north side of a stone fence while the proprietor of the shooting preserve released five pheasants in the 40-acre square to the south. An abandoned farm field, it had grown up with a good thick stand of bromegrass, dotted at random with clumps of brittle goldenrod. There were a few rows of shattered, year-old corn, too, their mouldering husks rustling dryly in the bitter wind.

All four of my dogs were in the trailer. Emmylou and Traveler, a barrel-chested pointer just entering his prime, comprised the work force. They'd hunted well all season; just a few days earlier, Em had looked especially sharp during an outing with a friend who flies falcons. "I've seen a lot of setters," he declared, "but she's one of the best." Flushed with such praise, I had little doubt that these pen-raised birds would prove easy marks, or that there'd be plenty of time to take Hannah, the darkly marked, high-strung pointer puppy, and Zack, the wise, long-since retired setter, on a leisurely stroll before dark.

I think it is safe to say that the Hebrew priests responsible for compiling the Old Testament were not pheasant hunters. But the one who wrote, "Pride goeth before destruction, and a haughty spirit before a fall," might have been. Craig and I were still fumbling with shells and gloves and whistles when I heard the unmistakable taunting klaxon of a cockbird taking wing. I looked up to see him, a daub of pigment against December's monochromatic canvas, as he disappeared into a grove of hardwoods—off the property, of course. This unscheduled departure presumably left four ringnecks in the field. Over the next couple of hours, Emmy and Traveler cut those 40 acres to ribbons. But other than a maddening series of unproductives in places where birds had clearly been (and a lofty stand on a feral cat that scampered across the road into a sagging, sway-backed barn), the only thing they had to show for their efforts was a solitary hen. And even that encounter did not end happily: Craig, unaccustomed to shooting hens, dithered for what seemed an eternity before touching off his 12-bore. Unfortunately, he did not enjoy the luxury of an eternity, as you sometimes do with slow-flying preserve birds. By the time he fired, the wind-aided hen was pushing effective range. In other words, he missed. A back-up salvo from my 20-gauge was, at that point, out of the question.

And that was that. Perhaps 45 minutes of shooting light remained, but Craig was expected home. "Tough hunting in this wind," I shrugged, a little grumpily, as we shook hands. "Hey, that's the way it goes sometimes," he cheerfully observed. "I had a lot of fun. Let's get together again, Okay?" To his credit, Craig is one of those people whose enthusiasm never seems to flag. And he did, eventually, purchase an English setter puppy.

As I was expected nowhere—the joy and curse, I suppose, of bachelorhood—I let Hannah and Zack out of the trailer. Hannah emerged in an instant, a coiled spring, while it took Zack several seconds to unfold his creaky bones, stand up, poke his head out of the fiberglass box, and wait, as if he were some sort of pampered royalty, for me to lift him down. Bits of yellow hay clung to his silky ears. He pranced around stiffly, excitedly; it had been a long time since he'd seen me carrying a shotgun, and although his body had atrophied under the insults of age, his desire burned as brightly as ever. That was why, ultimately, I'd had to retire Zack: He drove himself too hard, and even after a short hunt he'd clearly be in agony from the pain in his arthritic joints.

The north field, the one in which I was parked, had a mowed path that made a roughly circular loop. I hit the whistle to let Hannah know where I was—she'd immediately rocketed out of sight—and with Zack trundling alongside, I set off down the trail in a clockwise direction. Hannah reappeared in a matter of moments, flying across the front from my left, a black-and-white streak. She stopped, checked my whereabouts, and blazed on, tail cracking with every jump, reminding me once again that in terms of sheer natural ability, I'd never seen her equal. The lithe pointer pup hunted the country like a veteran, making wide, sweeping casts but never losing contact, putting down the kind of pattern you dream about.

I became so absorbed in her performance, in fact, that I totally forgot about Zack. We were almost back to the truck before I realized he'd been missing for several minutes. This would have been nothing out of the ordinary in the setter's prime; Zack was always a roamer. If he didn't return on his own from a long, rambling cast, you could bet the bank he was on point. But now, as I scanned the darkening field and detected no sign of movement, I felt a sharp twinge of panic. He'd been right there, trotting along with a jaunty air that belied his years, and now he was gone. It would serve no purpose to whistle; Zack had grown as deaf as the proverbial post. (This was a great source of amusement to my hunting companions, who delighted in jeering, "How can you tell? Even when he could hear, Zack didn't listen!")

All I could think was that his stout heart had finally failed. When the dog in question is 14, that is not an unreasonable assumption. Zack slept in the house on a sort of foam futon, and I knew that the morning was coming when he simply wouldn't wake up.

And then I saw him. The field sloped gently from west to east, where it flattened out before merging with a ragged swath of aspens and the occasional stark birch, its white trunk in jarring contrast to the somber purple of its branches. Just this side of the timber, a good hundred yards away, a low stone fence ran north-and-south. That's where Zack was, parallel to the wall. In the gauzy, shadowless light, his black ticking blended perfectly with the pattern of the stones. He was on point.

"My God," I said out loud. Perhaps Zack's tail was not aimed sky-ward, the way it once had been, but his intensity remained com-plete. Even in the twilight of his career, he possessed an uncanny ability to mesmerize game. It is an ability, I'm convinced, that can-not be acquired; a dog must be born with it. I could see, too, as I began to jog toward him, that his head, his beautiful, noble, know-ing head, was held high. That, to me, was Zack's signature. All of us who are favored by the company of a singular dog fall into the habit of making exaggerated claims, claims that invariably begin, "He never . . ." or, "He always . . ." I am no different, but I sincerely be-lieve that the one categorical claim I make for Zack is true. He al-ways, *always,* pointed with a high head. Whether it was a woodcock or a wild turkey, whether he'd hit the scent hard or unraveled it carefully, whether he was right on top of the bird or winding it from a distance, whether he was hunting the billowing prairies or the pinched alder bottoms, his head was always high.

Walking through the wind-bent grass, I was wading through memories. They surged around me like flood-waters. I'd been a young man when Zack entered my life, naïve, idealistic, confident. Now, although not yet old, none of the same adjectives applied. We'd covered a lot of territory together, Zack and I, and you can't do that without leaving parts of yourself behind. There are wounds that heal, and others that leave scars; mistakes that can be forgiven, and others that are irreparable. You never know, until much, much later, what you've really done, what's really become of you.

But through it all, through the odd and enigmatic permutations, Zack was the constant. He was an anchor, calm and imperturbable. And as I approached him, standing resolutely in the cold December gloaming, it became clear that this was the apex of the pyramid, that

14 years of elation, sorrow, trust, and love, along with the thousands of unremembered day-to-day transactions they implied, had intersected at this one luminous point. Zack was my tutor; what I'd known of birds and hunting was nothing compared to what he taught me. He interpreted their language in a way I could understand: the nearly lost dialect of the prairie chicken; the plainspeak of the bobwhite quail; the heavily inflected tongue of the Hungarian partridge. This fluency was his genius. The birds spoke to him, and he spoke back.

Out of the corner of my eye, I caught a flash of movement. Hannah hurtled past, only to skid to a stop when she spotted Zack. You could almost hear the squeal of tires, smell the burning rubber. She posed handsomely, even, it seemed to me, arrogantly. Already, I'd begun to wonder if Hannah, in some mysterious fashion, wasn't aware of her superiority. At just 11 months of age, she'd established her dominance over Emmy and Traveler in the kennel pecking order. She was an alpha female if there ever was one. Hannah deferred only to Zack—as, for the most part, they all did. He'd assumed something of the person of a gruff old English viscount, and the other dogs appeared to respect his standing as the lord of the manor.

Instead of the pheasant I'd anticipated, a pair of chukars, obviously left over from a previous release, blustered out of hiding. Their flight paths diverged at a 90-degree angle—very obliging of them, I thought—and I capitalized on the chance to make a classic right-and-left. The left bird nearly ricocheted off Hannah on its earthward arc; she was on it in a heartbeat. The other chukar toppled on the far side of the fence, and Zack struggled to clamber over the uneven stones for the retrieve. It took a minute or so to coax the pup to surrender her bird—she was having a grand time swaggering around with it—but at last I gently eased it from her jaws. I crossed the fence then, to find Zack with his muzzle pressed deep into the chukar's breast feathers, reverently inhaling that exquisite aroma. A bird dog with a nose full of scent must experience what a believer does when he feels his soul inhabited by the Divine. I knelt, picked up the chukar, and stroked Zack's head. "You old bear," I said, my voice cracking with emotion. Never one for maudlin displays, Zack met my gaze briefly, as if to acknowledge the gravity of the occasion, the tenure and reciprocity of our relationship. Then he sauntered off to find another bird.

The story might have ended there. But the truth is, it didn't. We made our way back to the truck, where I lifted Zack into the cab. He was laboring, limping on his spindly hind legs, and I saw no sense in pushing our luck. Hearing me, Traveler whimpered entreatingly from his box, while Emmy pawed at her door. I removed my yellow shooting glasses to wipe a smudge from one of the lenses, and was startled at how dark it had become. But there was still enough light to shoot by—as long as I wore the glasses, at least—enough time to let Hannah make a pass across the south field. There had to be a pheasant skulking somewhere in that brome.

There was. Hannah swung wide to my left, raced back across the front, and swapped ends in the blink of an eye. It was as if the scent were a snare that caught her in mid-stride; you could see her body contort, see her stiffen into a point before her feet touched the ground. I shook my head, more than a little awed. She'd nailed a rooster dead to rights. It made a terrific racket as it flushed, but Hannah stood steady to wing. This was nothing I'd taught her; it was in her genes. She broke at the shot and retrieved the gaudy package more-or-less to hand. It was a rather comical sight: Between the deep grass and the dimensions of the bird, Hannah's only distinguishable features were a pair of glittering, obsidian eyes and the bobbing tip of her tail. And no, the irony of it was not lost on me. Emmy and Traveler, the tough, hard-bitten pros, had scoured this patch and essentially come up empty; Hannah, the green, unlettered pup, produced a cockbird for the gun in roughly three minutes.

All of which made the decision to let Hannah go that much more agonizing. A breeder of golden retrievers once said something that struck me as very insightful. Describing a litter that had turned out well, she remarked, "They're good hunting dogs, and they're fun dogs to be around, too. That's not always the case."

It certainly wasn't with Hannah. As dazzling as she was in the field, I regretfully had to admit that I just didn't *like* her. There was a calculating, mercenary quality to Hannah that went beyond simple disdain; at times, a streak of meanness even manifested itself. Her personality was appealing in a superficial way, but there was no real warmth, no true affection. She made it clear that she didn't want to be my pal, the way the other dogs did. She wanted to hunt, period, and as long as I functioned as her agent, her facilitator, in this regard, she'd grudgingly tolerate me. Otherwise, Hannah seemed to take perverse glee in making my life miserable. She tormented Emmy and Traveler too, which did nothing to improve her popularity.

So I made a gift of Hannah to a friend in Texas who squeezes more bird hunting into an average year than a lot of sportsmen do in 10. She'd be perfect for him, I figured, because his dogs are more employees than they are partners, and his contact with them during the off-season is minimal. They're treated well, to be sure, but it's an impersonal, professional relationship. In other words, he wouldn't have to deal with Hannah on a daily basis the way I did.

My friend was skeptical about the whole arrangement—until he cut Hannah loose on his quail lease. In short, she knocked his socks off, pointing, backing, digging into the cover, running to the front, holding her own with older, vastly more experienced dogs, doing it all. He is convinced that I must be mentally incompetent, if not certifiably insane, to have willingly let a dog as accomplished as Hannah go. The way I look at it, we both made out.

I had to let Zack go, too, although it was not, of course, for the same reasons. His heart stayed strong, but the rest of him began to waste away. When I could see that even his spirit was faltering, that he was losing the battle to maintain his dignity, his pride, I knew that the time had come.

Zack's ashes are scattered near the crest of a south-facing slope in the Loess Hills of western Iowa, not far from a place where I once shot a double over him on bobwhite quail. The prairie plants still grow there, the bluestem, the grama, the coneflowers, the wild plum. And in the lee of a curving ridge, the wind blows softly, carrying its invisible freight of molecules, molecules that were, to Zack, as brilliant and distinct as stars.

15

ONE GROUSE

We had been hunting almost two hours. Traveler's bell had gone silent often during that span, but it had been the silence of a question waiting to be answered, not a declaration demanding action. He'd stop, I'd call his name in a level, measured tone and he'd move on, boring into the cover, re-oriented and reassured.

Then came the exception. By the emphatic way the ringing ended, the music cut short mid-note, I knew that this time Trav meant business. He was ahead and to my right, on a little half-acre knob surrounded by hummocky scrub. I had to weave through a screen of spruces to get to him, and each bough I touched showered me with last night's snow. Some of it found the back of my neck. I gasped and my entire body convulsed in a shiver.

Some of the snow also collected in the muzzles of my weathered Browning 20, the gun I carry when my intentions are deadlier than usual. And on this flawless, diamond-bright December morning, the sun shining for the first time in days, they were. I wanted to kill a grouse.

Just one. Certainly no more than that, for these late-season birds are especially precious. It is simply common sense that a ruffed grouse alive in December stands a better chance of surviving until spring—and reproducing—than a grouse alive in October. Years ago I had the privilege of engaging two eminent wildlife biologists in conversation on this topic at a cocktail party, men who had been protégés of Aldo Leopold's. They were of the unshakable opinion that Wisconsin's grouse season was too long.

"Dammit," exclaimed the older of the pair, growing so agitated he nearly spilled his Scotch, "they should close it down December first! After that you start cutting into your brood stock!"

Coming from what I considered an unimpeachable source, that statement—and the conviction with which it was uttered—impressed me deeply. Though I didn't stake out the moral high ground and hang it up entirely at the end of November, I did get into the habit of quitting for the day after bagging one or, at most, two birds—on the days I was lucky enough to bag a bird at all, that is. The grouse is a stern master anywhere, but nowhere more so than in this conifer-infested neck of the woods. A forester of broad experience once told me that in all his travels he'd never seen a place where white cedar grows in such profusion. Spruce, balsam fir and hemlock do pretty well here too, the ramifications of which should be obvious. Even under ideal conditions a flushing grouse offers the most fleeting of opportunities for a shot; throw a heavy dose of evergreens into the mix and your chances are reduced by half—at least. On a memorable end-of-December hunt a couple seasons ago I counted 13 flushes. I didn't see one bird.

I broke open the Browning, extracted the shells—seven-eighths-ounce No. 8s in the right barrel, an ounce of 7s in the left—pursed my lips and blew into the bores to clear the snow from the muzzles. Then, locked and loaded, I set off to find Traveler. The big pointer was standing in a small grove of wrist-thick popple, tail poker-straight, head bent slightly to the left, his great keg of a ribcage expanding and contracting as he drew those draughts of scent. His focus seemed to be a scraggly high-bush cranberry, the scarlet fruit of which grouse adore. It looked like a perfect spot—and it would have been, perhaps, if we'd arrived a few minutes or even seconds sooner. The fluffy new snow was filigreed with grouse tracks, but the bird that had made them was gone. Traveler's brow wrinkled in disbelief as I kicked and thrashed to no avail.

I released him from point by saying, "All right, Trav, all right, where's the bird?" He bounded forward, tail whipping madly, throwing his head in every direction as he tried to source that fugitive tendril of scent. We made a wide counterclockwise sweep, hoping to intercept the bird, but its whereabouts remained unknown. A grouse's brain may be the size of a filbert, but in a battle of wits with man and dog it is, in the vast majority of cases, severely undermatched.

Traveler continued to hunt with verve and purpose, swinging back and forth across the front like a pendulum, handling as kindly as the proverbial glove. Only rarely, when he dug far to the sides—a miner in search of ore—did I have to hit the whistle. When your taste runs to bold, ambitious, hard-driving pointers and setters, you tread a fine line. You expect them to get out and swallow sizable chunks of country, but you want them to be biddable, too. There are days when the twain do not meet, and it's tug-and-haul all the way. And there are other days, days like this one, when your dog seems to read your mind. When you think he should turn, he turns; when you think he should hunt close, he hunts close. Keith Erlandson, the Welshman who has bred and trained some of the finest springers and cockers of the modern era, likes to say that he looks for dogs that he can shoot over "without irritation." Ultimately, I think that's the kind of dog we're all looking for—provided, of course, it makes a creditable effort to produce game for the gun and isn't merely tagging along for the exercise.

As we broke into the open at an abandoned pasture, the sudden flood of sunlight was dazzling. According to the thermometer, which stood in the upper 20s, it was a cold day. But it felt warm, as if the soft blanket of snow had insulated the very air. Dark dashes rising and falling against the blue bowl of sky, a flock of pine siskins flitted overhead, their buzzing calls in counterpoint to the melodic cadence of the dog bell. Traveler popped out of the cover then, shook himself off and galloped to my side, where he leaned into my leg with his rump as if he were a hockey player dishing out a hip check. It is an endearing, if idiosyncratic, way of displaying affection; according to the man who bred Trav, his granddaddy does the same thing.

We rimmed the brushy margins of the pasture, clawed through an isthmus of alders to a large opening and cut across it via an old two-track logging road, its borders tangled with vines of bittersweet and wild grape. At one time or another I'd moved grouse all along this route: a brood of seven in the blackberry briers at the corner of the pasture; a bird in the alders that rocketed over the right shoulder of my friend George Boykin and left him shaking his head in astonishment; that grouse in the apple tree on the south side of the road—a bird whose presence I swear I *felt* before Zack, the setter, slewed into a point. As exciting—and necessary—as it is to prospect new coverts, the old familiar ones, the ones you have a history with, are best. Hunting them is like falling into the arms of a woman you love, a woman who is warm, generous, a bit mysterious and just unpredictable enough to keep you on your toes.

As Traveler and I put the sun to our backs and began to fight our way north through a claustrophobic cedar/tamarack swamp, my resolve to stop at one grouse intensified. Obviously, birds were few and far between. Love implies respect, and it was clear that the respectful thing to do would be to take my one grouse—if I could get it—and then rest this covert for the remainder of the season. I wanted to make sure that when I returned in April and May to work the dogs on spring woodcock and to pick morels that I'd feel that peculiar sensation in my breastbone, that subsonic *whump!* that precedes what the ears discern as the sound of drumming.

In nature there is a dynamic balance between predator and prey, a balance that ensures the survival of enough individuals to perpetuate the species. The human predator, on the other hand, has stepped outside the loop. He no longer has to kill to eat, and as a result enjoys the luxury of being able to pursue his quarry with ferocious single-mindedness—even past the point at which wild predators would shift their attention to other, more abundant prey.

Perhaps, as the biologists contend, grouse cannot be "shot out" as long as sufficient habitat exists. This does not, however, lead to the conclusion that they're invulnerable to hunting pressure. As the old-timers used to say, you've got to leave a few for seed—out of self-interest if not an acute sense of moral obligation. It was a rule of thumb among gentlemen quail hunters that a given covey was never to be shot down to fewer than six, or, better yet, eight birds. I apply a similar rule to my grouse coverts: If the dogs and I don't move more than a couple birds on successive hunts, it's time to pull the plug.

We passed more landmarks: the marshy cutover that had been stiff with snipe the year the beavers damned the creek and the water backed up ankle-deep around the sedge tussocks; the morass of blowdowns where Emmylou, Traveler's long-haired kennelmate, pinned six grouse dead to rights only to have Terry Barker and me each fan pathetically with both barrels; the red osier flat where I killed my first limit of woodcock over Zack on five-for-six shooting; the patch of prickly cotoneaster bushes from which I shot my one and only double on grouse. That, too, had been with Zack, on the afternoon of a day much like this. Just as I'd spied him on point a grouse had thundered out to the setter's right, too far for a shot. Zack hadn't so much as batted an eye—and he wasn't trained to be steady to wing. Knowing there had to be another bird, I'd moved up quickly, my heart pounding. I'd been wrong: There'd been *two* other birds, and they'd thumped down hard, right and left, at the double bark of my 28-gauge.

Perhaps because of their comparative rarity, perhaps because of their essential purity, perhaps because of the stark, minimalist setting, these late-season points stand out in bold relief. One of the most stunning sporting tableaux I've witnessed occurred when Terry Barker's lean little setter, Babe, found a grouse in a vaguely spooky hardwood bottom. It was a raw, gloomy kind of day; we'd slipped into the timber, more or less on spec, after canvassing a large, irregularly contoured field of corn stubble in fruitless search of Hungarian partridge. The dogs weren't belled, and just as Terry remarked that they hadn't swung past in a while we noticed Emmylou dead ahead, pointing with lofty style. As we approached her, however, we saw that she was in fact backing Willie, her fiery son, who'd established a high-stationed stand of his own. We moved up on either side, the tension almost unbearable, only to realize that Willie was honoring Babe.

For reasons I have never been able to understand, Terry decided that Babe was pointing fur, not feathers, and dropped his guard. At that instant the grouse roared out from beneath a deadfall. There are occasions in hunting when it works to your advantage to be totally unprepared, to react instinctively. This, sadly, was not one of them. But although the missed bird was soon forgotten, the image of those three setters standing like monuments will be forever engraved upon our memories.

Somewhere up ahead the bell went quiet. "Traveler," I called, thinking that he had stopped to get his bearings. "Traveler." There was no sound, only the enormous, expectant silence invoked by a dog on point. I pushed forward, and at the same moment Trav snapped into focus beneath a canopy of high-bush cranberries, the tip of his tail raw and bloody. I caught the briefest glimpse of a grouse as it lifted far in front and angled off deep to our right. "Whoa, Trav," I cautioned, looping in front of his stand in case a sleeper lingered.

There was something different about this place, something that took me a moment to put my finger on. The ground was green. The forest floor was carpeted with delicate maidenhair ferns no more than three or four inches tall. They had no business being so audaciously alive in December, so vibrantly colorful—but there they were. Then, as I looked more carefully, I saw why. The entire area was braided with tiny rivulets, spring-fed trickles bubbling up from the earth itself. Warmer than the air, the moving water was keeping the low-growing ferns from freezing. The effect was magical, like a scene from a fairy tale.

The jangle of Traveler's bell summoned. A handful of master grouse hunters possess a sixth sense that enables them to relocate flushed birds with uncanny accuracy. I don't. But I'd gotten a reasonably good reading on the grouse's line, and as near as I could tell it had headed for a nasty clot of cedar deadfalls. At worst, it was impenetrable; at best merely semi-impassable. The bird could have hidden out in the middle of that mess until doomsday, but as I stumbled along the perimeter and Trav tried to wriggle into the inner sanctum, the grouse lost its nerve. I detected movement out of the corner of my eye, and looked left just in time to see it sprint down the trunk of a deadfall and take off, like a jet from a runway. But this bird didn't fly far.

She was a lovely, chocolate-colored hen. Traveler raced in at the shot, but I "whoaed" him; this was a retrieve I wanted to make myself. I broke the Browning, catching the spent shell and smelling the peppersweet pungence of the smoke as it curled from the chamber. Then, holding it near the muzzles, I balanced the gun on my left shoulder. I knelt to pick up the grouse, called Traveler to heel and walked back to the truck. We were done.

I hung the bird from a nail on the front porch for several days, letting its flavor develop—and admiring it at every opportunity. When I cleaned the grouse, I expected the crop to be bursting with bright-red cranberries. But it wasn't. Instead, it was packed tight with springy green ferns.

And, yes, when Trav and I returned the following April to renew our acquaintance with the woodcock, the drummers were there too.

16

THE PRINCIPALITY
OF WOODCOCK

There are regions we visit in this bird-hunting life where the magic of place is so intense, so overwhelming, that it eclipses the memory of individual events. In places like these, the specifics are fuzzy, recollected only with difficulty. You remember what happened at the edges: the way your mouth puckered when you bit into a tart wild apple; the maple tree whose indominable trunk had grown through the hub of an abandoned iron wagon wheel; the plume of dust and crunch of gravel as you sped down the road to the next wedge of cover.

And you retain a vivid impression of colors, of sky so blue you'd swear it would come off on your fingers if you touched it; of close-cropped fields clinging to their green; forests reeling with reckless swipes of gold and scarlet; a hillside thick with thornapples, their hard, red fruits pointillistic dabs of pigment against the tangled, gray branches.

The light, too, you recall, as something almost palpable, something with density and presence. It fills the landscape of your dreams like liquid poured into a mold.

At first, you travel to such a place simply in order to hunt. It is no different from any other destination, a promising spot to slip the dogs, taking delight in their craft and diligence, in the fierceness of their purpose, their joy feeding yours. But as you return, season after season, the sensations and experiences accreting into a kind of indivisible whole, you discover that your logic has swapped ends, the way a swift-moving dog does when it runs headlong into scent. It occurs to you that you no longer go in order to hunt; you hunt in order to go.

Washington Island has, for me, become such a place. The largest of the Grand Traverse chain that links Wisconsin's Door Peninsula with the Garden Peninsula of Upper Michigan, "the island" is a convenient stopover for migrating woodcock. An attractive one, too, with its patchwork of old, brush-bordered fields and long-neglected orchards, its irregular puzzle-pieces of second growth forest, its seams of alder and pockets of popple. Much of the island's relatively flat interior is stitched with solemn stone fences, which are neither here nor there as far as the woodcock are concerned, but have a profound appeal to tradition-loving sportsmen. Some of these fences date to before the turn of the century, when a wave of Icelandic immigrants washed ashore to clear the land, till the soil, and cast their nets upon the teeming waters of Lake Michigan. Judging by the letters they sent home, opinion was equally divided as to whether they'd arrived in paradise, or been relegated to purgatory.

Being stoic, stubborn Scandinavians, however, they stayed. And if they hadn't cut trees, picked stones, and planted potatoes (at least for awhile), there would be precious little woodcock cover on this 23-square-mile hump of glaciated rock. Washington Island remains the largest Icelandic settlement in the new world; barely pronounceable names like Bjarnarson and Gunnlaugsson, names that seem more properly to belong to ancient Norse sagas, are common among the several hundred year-'round residents. Tourism, which years ago replaced farming and fishing as the backbone of the island's economy, helps swell the summer population into the thousands.

This annual warm-weather migration is faintly ironic, because the secret of the island's abiding charm is its very lack of what might be called "conventional" tourist attractions. There are a couple of beautiful, largely deserted beaches, no fewer than three funky little museums, a truly quaint fishing village, a weaving school, several friendly pubs, and at least one marvelously ramshackle old resort. Clear, crackling-cold water, too, all the fresh air you can breathe, and, lest I forget, a nine-hole golf course. Sadly (but predictably), the local chamber of commerce seems hell-bent on bringing the island up to speed by attracting more faux-Scandinavian shops, more businesses, and more people. There will be fewer woodcock as a result, of course, but that's a tragedy no one is likely to notice.

No one but my pal Steve Gordon, that is. As near as I've been able to determine, he's the only island resident who hunts woodcock there. And the handful of non-residents who hunt there are, without exception, Steve's guests. For a few weeks every autumn, the island is his private shooting preserve, his personal principality of woodcock. His "native" status entitles him to immunity from the trespass laws that apply to outsiders, and extends to protect those who hunt with him in kind. My guess is that Steve's fellow islanders, glimpsing him as he ghosts in and out of sight, haunting the bogs, brakes, and thickets with his dogs, regard him as eccentric but harmless.

Frankly, Steve *is* a tad eccentric. We've been hunting together for 11 years, and I don't know much more about him now than I did an hour after we met. If I had to describe him in a nutshell, I'd say he was interesting but inscrutable, an enjoyable but enigmatic companion. He's one of those moving targets that you can never quite get a bead on.

How he manages to support himself (his awesome frugality notwithstanding) is the biggest mystery of all. Not long ago, I sold a setter puppy to a contemporary of his. "I've known Steve for fifty years," he told me, smiling wryly, "but I've never known him to work. On second thought, I guess he did run a charter boat for a while."

That's how I became acquainted with Steve: fishing for Lake Michigan trout and salmon aboard *Circe*, his 22-foot Chris-Craft. He did a bit of guiding for birds in those days as well (in addition to woodcock, the island boasts a healthy population of pheasants stocked by the local sportsmen's club), but I suspect this was chiefly a ploy to write off his expenses. When he concluded that his hunting clients didn't necessarily subscribe to the same refined ethic he does—their priority was quantity, not quality—he quit. He sold *Circe* and got out of the charter business at about the same time, circa 1987, which was a smart call because the fishery had pretty much gone belly-up.

Hard to figure though he may be, Steve, more than anyone, is responsible for shaping my sensibilities as a woodcock hunter. He showed me that the woodcock, of all the birds we pursue with dog and gun, is the one that most completely allows us to set our own terms, to establish a truly artful protocol. Hunting other game, we're essentially forced to play by their rules; hunting the woodcock, this accommodating sprite, we can play by our own and still feel the satisfying heft, the lovely rounded contours, of birds in the bag. Perfection is the goal—not gross accumulation.

Steve was the first person I hunted with who refused to shoot a woodcock in any manner other than over a point. In fact, he generally wouldn't even load his gun—variously, an exquisite sliding-breech Darne, a plain-Jane Ruger o/u, and once, when the pheasant season was also open, a Model 12 with a bizarre but gorgeous Monte Carlo stock that had been a gift from a former girlfriend—until point was called. Nor would he ever go out of his way to hunt up a missed bird. In his strict construction of fair chase, one chance was, and is, enough.

"Well, when in Rome . . .," I thought when I began hunting the island. I was, after all, a guest, and guests—especially shooting guests—have a certain obligation to follow their host's lead. But it wasn't long before I appropriated much of Steve's style as my own. It struck a resonant chord. Like a 28-gauge double or a light-footed lady setter, it seemed an elegant fit for the bird. While I confess I'm not above detouring to hunt up a marked 'cock on occasion (and I've never been comfortable carrying my shotgun in a noose-type leather sling the way Steve does), the rare birds that I kick up without canine assistance twitter away unscathed. This is not meant to sound "preachy." I'm just relating what I do, and who I learned it from. Life is what matters to the woodcock, not the circumstances of its death. That issue is left for us to grapple with.

Steve also introduced me to the pleasures of hunting a pointing dog and a flushing dog in tandem, the former to locate the bird, the latter to put it to wing. Given the claustrophobic cover woodcock frequent, this method makes great sense, especially for a solo gunner. Locating his Brittany on point, Steve positions himself for a clear shot (he hopes), and sends Suzy, his yellow Lab, in for the flush. It's exciting, but it takes some getting used to—particularly on the part of the pointing dog.

One of the Washington Island memories I can peel off at will is the time Steve directed Suzy to flush ahead of a bandy-legged, black-ticked setter of mine named Gabe. Gabe was strung as tightly as a mandolin, and she had big, expressive, deep-brown eyes. I didn't believe her eyes could get any bigger, but when Suzy started racing around in front of her, they did. Desperate to break, but knowing she should stay staunch, Gabe's entire body began to shake uncontrollably. I feared that she'd suffer a nervous breakdown, and I politely informed Steve that I'd prefer to flush her birds myself.

There have been practical lessons as well. Hunting the island, I learned that it's almost impossible for a scrap of cover to be too small to hold a woodcock. Steve once led me to a low spot in a hayfield, nothing but a clump of spindly shrubs. The dogs struck point before we got there—on different birds. The ultimate example of this, however, was the woodcock pointed and flushed from beneath a solitary old apple tree that stood in the middle of a stone-fenced meadow. I can see it, still, as solitary and enduring as a monument.

Much changes; much remains the same. Gabe and Zack, my partners when this chapter of my bird-hunting life began, are gone. So is Sam, the hard-headed, wide-ranging Brittany who was Steve's boon companion. And yet, pausing in mid-morning to water the dogs and eat an apple during our most recent hunt, it came as a genuine shock when Steve informed me that Suzy and her kennelmate, petite, sensitive, cat-footed Didi, were both pushing 11. I still thought of them as pups, and here they were, gray-muzzled veterans in the twilight of their careers. Didi had been one of the best, most industrious woodcock dogs I'd ever had the privilege of shooting over; Suzy's enthusiasm had always been boundless. Where had the time gone?

I was taken aback, too, when Steve allowed that he had no immediate plans to start a new pup. He could feel an attack of wanderlust coming on—for him, a chronic, recurring disease—and he couldn't feature boarding a young dog for months on end. It wouldn't be fair. And there was a chance he might not return to the island for, well, awhile. As usual, his plans were a bit indefinite.

But my gut feeling is that this autumn, as in autumns past, there will come a brilliant morning in early October, the dawn boiling out of Lake Michigan like lava, when I load Traveler and Emmylou into their crates and drive to Northport, where the road, and the land, ends. I'll board the car ferry there, squeezing the Blazer between the tour buses and the trucks carrying drywall for Lamperts lumberyard and produce for Mann's general store. It takes 40 minutes to cross the strait that separates the island from the mainland, the ferry's diesels throbbing heavily, the spray glittering as the steel hull shoulders its way through the waves. Seagulls hover and wheel, crying hoarsely; the border dividing water and sky seems fluid, indistinct, one element merging with the other.

I stand on the top deck, hands in my pockets, the collar of my fleece jacket turned up against the cool breeze, the island growing ever larger. As the details begin to resolve—the vertical white strokes of the birches, the rocky, foam-washed spit of Lobdell Point, the tan bulrushes bending in the Detroit Harbor backwaters—my heart beats a little faster. My skin tingles; my mind hopscotches between past, present, and future. Everything old is new again.

A member of the ferry crew recognizes me and says, "You must be going hunting with Steve. Didn't know the pheasant season was open yet."

"It's not," I answer, smiling. "We're hunting woodcock."

"Oh."

Groaning mightily, the ferry shudders into its berth. Hawsers are looped over pilings; electric winches lower the bow ramp into place. The boat opens, its cargo of vehicles spilling out. I need to clamber down the narrow stairs and start my truck. But before I do, I spot a brown Ford pickup, a real beater, parked in front of the low, nondescript building where they rent mopeds. Through the windshield, I can see Suzy peeking over the dashboard, and I know that Didi is curled up on the floor below her. Steve gets out, tilts back his sunglasses, and waves.

17

THE SPORTSMAN'S BIRD

The meeting with the bank president had gone well. He'd pledged his support for the small land trust John and I represent, and now we were sitting in John's rather spartan office a few blocks away, discussing our next move. At the same time, I was idly flipping through the appraisal done for an abandoned farm John had purchased and enrolled in our land protection program. I came to a page of photographs of the property, open meadows gradually being reclaimed by brushy successional forest—aspen on the high ground, alders in the low spots.

"Looks like good woodcock cover," I remarked off-handedly.

John stared at me as if I were sprouting antennae. "That's why I bought it!" he exclaimed. "You hunt?"

You have to understand that John knew me only through our affiliation with the land trust, most of whose members are birders, gardeners, and amateur botanists; the "brie and chablis" crowd, not the "cast and blast" bunch. It had simply never occurred to John that I might be a hunter.

Anyway, my reply was something to the effect that I owned four pretty fancy bird dogs, that if I had just one day left on earth I'd choose to spend it in a woodcock covert, and that in my opinion the woodcock is the finest table bird of all, the kind of sublime fare that will bring a brave gourmet to his knees.

"Yes!" John cried. "Yes!" It was as if he'd been wandering the desert for years, searching in vain for a kindred spirit, a fellow believer—and now, at last, he'd found one. Like many people of independent means, John is, in addition to being well-educated and widely read, a touch eccentric, and opinionated to a fault. His outrageous and inflexible attitudes had apparently cost him most of his friends, including several hunting companions, and the rest of the men with whom he shared the fragrant autumn coverts had gone to their rewards. So the part of John that loved woodcock and woodcock hunting had been alone for a long time. Now, with a sympathetic (not to mention captive) audience at hand, the floodgates opened. The memories—and the concerns—poured forth in torrents.

"I used to hunt all over the northeastern part of the state," he began. "I had a set of topo maps with all my favorite places marked, and I knew from experience when the flights would peak at each one. You could follow the migration north-to-south. Come to think of it, those maps are still around here somewhere, but now I suppose the cover's past its prime in most of my old spots. God, the birds we'd move in some of those creek bottoms! If you hit it just right, it was unbelievable.

"It was funny," he continued. "When I bought the farm"—he gestured toward the appraisal—"I thought I'd be able to predict the date the flight would come through. But it always seemed to arrive a few days late. I could never figure out why. Not that it made much difference, because I never killed more than three or four birds a season there. Woodcock are in trouble, you know. The spring singing ground counts are down, and I'm convinced they don't know what the hell's happening in Louisiana, where the birds winter. If we don't watch out, they're going to go the way of our ducks. Of course, in my opinion they should have closed the duck season five years ago and kept it closed! It just goes to show that the fish and game agencies aren't run by biologists; they're run by a bunch of damn politicians and bureaucrats."

John then went on a tirade about the grouse season, the gist of which was that it should open later and close earlier. I steered him back to woodcock with a question about his dogs.

"I always insisted that my dogs be under control," he declared. "Nothing ruins a hunt faster than a dog that runs up birds, doesn't handle . . . you know what I mean. The last dog I had, a Brittany, was a genius. I never had to tell him what to do; he just *knew*. And could he find woodcock! It broke my heart when he died, and—oh, I don't know—I guess I realized he couldn't be replaced, so I didn't even try. I've tried to persuade my wife to beat the bushes for me"—a wry smile crossed his face—"but she's not too enthusiastic about it."

John added that he trained this avatar of spaniels in French—not because it was a romantic thing to do given the Brittany's country of origin, but on the theory that if it were ever lost or stolen, the dog would appear to be a complete imbecile (at least to anyone who didn't speak French), and would thus be more likely to be returned. Like I said, John is a tad eccentric.

Finally, when the conversation moved to woodcock cuisine, John's eyes narrowed, and with precise diction he inquired, "How do you prepare them?"

It was a loaded question if I ever heard one. I had been around John long enough to know that he's a culinary snob, the kind of person who might never speak to you again if you poured an undignified wine at a dinner party.

Thinking fast, I recalled a recipe that he would surely approve of. "I like to make a salmi with Madeira sauce."

"Salmi's good," John nodded. I'm sure he half-expected me to admit to baking them in a casserole with cream of mushroom soup, or some equally heinous perversion. "But here's the way to *really* cook woodcock . . ."

John then commenced an elaborate discourse on his favorite method of woodcock cookery, complete with quotes—in French, no less—from the legendary epicures Escoffier and Brillat-Savarin. Briefly, it calls for hanging the birds—undrawn, in the European fashion—in a cool place "until you detect the most delicate whiff of the aroma you get when they're *just* beginning to brown in the oven." Plucked but otherwise fully intact, the woodcock are roasted at 500 degrees for no more than 10 minutes. They are then removed from the oven and drawn. While the birds are kept warm on a heated platter, the "trail" is minced and whisked into a sauce with the pan drippings, woodcock stock, and *foie gras*. Just before the sauce is spooned over the birds, it is flamed with cognac. Wild rice, baby Brussels sprouts, and a voluptuous red Burgundy—"Chambertin, for example"—are the proper accompaniments.

When all the meat has been devoured, the white, toothsome thighs and the spectacular, dark-red breasts, one climactic act remains: "You sever the head, hold it by the bill, and pop it whole into your mouth. The taste is . . . I can't do it justice. It is absolutely the *pièce de résistance* of the entire meal!"

Tears welled up in John's eyes as he relived this moment of ecstasy. Such passion, such devotion! Would that all of us who gun woodcock honor the bird so well! Shortly thereafter, I sent John a copy of Guy de la Valdene's poignant *Making Game*, with the inscription, *Il n'y a rien au dessus de la bécasse*—"Above the woodcock, there is nothing."

The woodcock is a bird about which opinions radically diverge, not only on the table, but in the shooting field. To some of us, it is the aristocracy of upland game, the quarry that affords gunning at its most poetic, its most introspective, gunning that most truly approaches the purity and perfection of art. An intense, stylish, tenacious pointer or setter; a nimble small-bore double; a crackling October day that smells of woodsmoke and apples and the damp, shadowed forest; aspen leaves like silhouette hearts dipped in gold; a flight of 'cock down from the north country: These are the dimensions of paradise. It is a miraculous convergence, this intersection in space and time of bird, dog, man, and gun. I can think of no loftier measure of what we call sport.

But there are others who can take the woodcock—or leave it. They view it as an incidental species; at best a "bonus bird," at worst something of a nuisance. The most obsessed grouse hunter I've ever heard of not only refuses to shoot woodcock, he tries to avoid them, period.

"The way I look at it," he told me, "is that if my dogs are pointing woodcock, they're not pointing grouse."

Such ferocious singleness of purpose is almost frightening. And gunning grouse to the exclusion of woodcock is frankly unimaginable to me. It would be like a saltwater fly-fisherman holding out for permit when bonefish are tailing all around him.

Still, while his may be an attitude I can't identify with, it's not one I can logically fault. It is perhaps the central paradox of hunting that you adore what you kill, and if you don't adore the woodcock, you shouldn't shoot it. He doesn't. This is a far more admirable position than that of another fellow of my acquaintance, a man who, as it happens, is an outdoor writer. I've always considered him a basically decent guy, even after he called a friend's 65-pound Ryman-strain English setters "Brittany spaniels"—in print. But then one day I was describing the remarkable woodcock hunting I'd enjoyed in an area about a two-hour drive from his home. It's a place unlike any other in the upper Midwest, a place out of time, a dreamland of stone-fenced fields, hillsides bristling with thornapples, ragged woodlots, gnarly old orchards, brooding swamps, and unforgettable sport.

"That's a long way to go," he sniffed, "just to shoot a woodcock."

I haven't spoken to him since, other than a curt "Hello" when avoidance was impossible. And I'm reminded, again, of an old adage (are there any new ones?) that seems particularly appropriate in this context. The gist of it is that the content of a sportsman's character is inversely proportional to the size of the quarry he pursues. By such reckoning, the woodcock is emphatically a sportsman's bird. Those who keep the woodcock first in their hearts are, with rare exceptions, a fine crew.

I heard through the grapevine that the above-mentioned individual was sneering at my habit of only shooting 'cock that my dogs successfully point. Well, if this constitutes elitism, so be it. The bottom line is that I eat what I shoot—but I don't shoot to eat. No one's going to go hungry if I come home with an empty gamebag. My premises are as follows:

A. There is no earthly reason to try to kill every woodcock that flies.

B. The bird lies incomparably well for a pointing dog, and dog work is—or should be—at the crux of woodcock hunting.

C. Woodcock are reasonably abundant in these parts, i.e., you'll get plenty of opportunities to shoot.

D. While undeniably elusive, the woodcock is, day-in and day-out, a target of average difficulty.

So why not set my own terms and add an extra element of refinement, an extra layer of challenge? No one bats an eye at the trout purist who insists on using only split-cane rods, 6X leaders, and #22 dry flies; shooting woodcock over skillful pointers with a 28-gauge is in the same league. I have one hunting partner who doesn't even *load* until his Brittany snaps onto point. (I load right away, on the off chance that I accidentally stumble across a grouse—to which sections B, C, and D of my hypothesis do not apply.) This is the same man who rarely, if ever, follows up a missed 'cock, even if he has it precisely marked down.

"We had our run at that bird," he'll shrug. "Let's find another one." Wonderful stuff, as the Brits are wont to say.

Another friend, a fine sportsman, a dedicated conservationist, and an ardent grouse hunter, passes on shooting woodcock simply because he doesn't enjoy eating them. I applaud him. On the other side of the fence, I know of gunners who kill appalling numbers of 'cock, eat a handful out of a vague sense of ethical obligation, and allow the rest to desiccate in the freezer.

This is truly abominable. They could at least make an effort to give their woodcock to someone with a sophisticated palate who would do right by them. John had a standing offer to all his hunting cronies: He'd trade them grouse for woodcock, even up. Both sides believed they were getting the better end of the deal.

More and more, I find myself taking two or three birds and quitting for the day. The law says I can kill five, but part of the maturation process as a sportsman is developing a feeling for what's "enough." Being driven to bag a limit every time out is no way to hunt, and a great deal of the charm of gunning woodcock derives from its very lack of tension—especially if you're following a dog with several seasons' experience under its collar. To be sure, woodcock hunting offers its share of drama and excitement, but it's understated, elegant. In contrast, grouse hunting involves a certain amount of bombast. If grouse are Tchaikovsky, woodcock are Debussy.

But regardless of the composer you fancy, the woodcock makes beautiful music. At dusk, we sat on the tailgate of the pickup, wishing we'd had the foresight to pack a couple of beers. Late afternoon is the best time to hunt, not because it is more productive, but because it is more mellow. The light is soft; the air has resonance.

My setter, Emmylou, had performed flawlessly. I'd grassed a brace of woodcock over her, missed a pair of grouse that were little more than blurs thundering through a morass of cedar blowdowns, and watched in bemused helplessness as several other 'cock shrewdly used my non-shooting friend as a shield. I told her that she would have to learn to handle a firearm, as she obviously has an instinctive knack for positioning herself for a clear shot.

"Too much pressure," she laughed. "I'd rather leave the shooting up to you."

She was wearing green Wellies, riding pants, a Barbour coat, and the ridiculous but necessary orange cap . . . and she looked ravishing. And now, as we sat in the twilight, in the gathering chill, an enormous umber moon rose through the tops of the birches, and a mournful, tremulous yapping drifted up from the dense swamplands to the east.

"Hear the coyotes?"

"No."

"You mean you can't hear that?"

"Those are farm dogs, aren't they?"

"There aren't any farms in that direction, love."

"Ohmygod." You can take the girl out of the city, but . . .

We were parked on the outside edge of a large, kidney-shaped clearing, and there was something coming that I wanted her to see.

The wait was not long. First, we heard the flute-like trill of wings; then, against the coral-hued canvas of the western sky, we saw them, plump, courtly, preposterous, the woodcock barnstorming their way to . . . where? A roosting cover on the far side of the beaver pond, or a creek bottom in the dairy country 50 miles south, a stop on the great migration to the balmy Gulf Coast wintering grounds?

Unanswerable, we left these questions hanging in the moonlight, like the image of the woodcock as they spiraled into the evening glow.

18

A Pheasant for Al

When Joan throws a dinner party it is not merely a gala event. It is a gastronomic extravaganza. Days of planning and preparation are invested; dozens of trips to markets, gourmet shops and specialty vendors are made—for, inevitably, the costliest of ingredients. Do you have any idea how much Stilton cheese, celery root or a decent bottle of Meursault go for? As Joan's sous-chef (i.e., galley slave), I do, and I assure you that their purchase lightens the wallet considerably. The menu never features fewer than two appetizers, two desserts, a luscious soup, a piquant salad and a spectacular entrée, all of which combine to leave guests groping vainly, even stuporously, for superlatives. The only thing missing, if you want to niggle about it, is a palate-cleansing sorbet—an oversight that will be remedied as soon as Joan saves up enough cash from her spare-time catering gigs to buy that $500 Italian ice-cream-maker she's always coveted.

So you can perhaps understand why, when I suggested pheasant as a main course for Joan's most recent soirée, she was a bit hesitant. Skeptical, even. Joan was still getting used to the idea of *eating* wild game, much less serving it. Early in our relationship, a quail dinner at the home of friends had been an epiphany for her. I had innocently asked our host, a frequent gunning partner, if the quail were game-farm birds or if they'd been part of our Thanksgiving-week bag in Iowa. When he responded they were indeed Iowa bobs— "From those coveys we got into at Sawin's farm"—Joan had nearly spilled her Chardonnay.

"You mean," she'd sputtered, "these are quail you went out and got yourselves?"

"Where did you think we got them?" I'd queried. "From a store?"

"Well, yeah," she'd replied, desperately trying to wrap her mind around the concept. "I guess I just assumed you'd ordered them from a gourmet shop in Virginia or someplace like that. It honestly never occurred to me that you could go out and get quail yourself. I mean, I know you guys hunt and everything, but I never thought about what you do with the stuff you shoot."

We'd laughed so hard we damn near peed our pants. "That's right, Joan," I'd teased. "We really ordered these birds from a catalog. Then when they arrived we stuck some shot into them for that gritty, realistic effect—part of that whole *cinema verité* thing we're into."

After that I began preparing meals of wild game for her with regularity. There was salmi of woodcock in Madeira, a classic roast grouse with bread sauce, and a complicated stuffed and braised Hungarian partridge we both agreed could use some fine-tuning. Marinated and grilled quail became such a staple that we served it at an informal Easter dinner. We enjoyed a variety of pheasant dishes—scaloppine, stir-fry, pheasant dumpling pie—but to achieve the lofty standard established by Joan's usual entrées, an enhanced quotient of elegance was required. The bottom line, as the Executive Chef herself expressed it, was this: "OK, we can serve pheasant—*if* you can find a recipe."

"May I assume that baking it *en casserole* with cream of mushroom soup is not an option?"

"That's disgusting!"

"Actually, it's not too bad if you doctor it up a little. And I promise you that it's the way 98 percent of the pheasant in America is cooked."

"Unless you want your privileges at 'Chez Joan' revoked, I wouldn't mention it in my presence again."

Needless to say, finding a suitable recipe proved no easy task. I pored over cookbooks, paged through stacks of magazines, did everything but consult the ghost of Elvis. Finally—and I am loath to admit this—Martha Stewart saved my bacon. I am loath to admit it because Martha Stewart, despite being classified a "babe" in *Esquire*'s "Women We Love" issue ("Cool but scary," they averred), makes me want to . . . well, she's just so hideously *perfect!* I have this sick fantasy about Martha Stewart being remanded to the custody of the Hell's Angels. Be that as it may, her imprimatur on a recipe is regarded in certain circles—Joan's, for example—as a kind of blessing.

And thus the decision was made to proceed with Martha Stewart's Roast Pheasant with Chestnut-Fennel Fricassee.

There were five pheasants in the freezer. Needing four, I thawed the entire quintet in case one happened to be badly mangled. As it turned out they were all in remarkably good shape. (I wish I could credit their condition to superior marksmanship—"Oh, I *always* aim for the head"—but it was much more likely that they'd been winged and retrieved by tender-mouthed dogs. In other words, not by my pointer, Traveler.) One bird did have a couple of pellets in its breast, so I returned it to the refrigerator and set about fine-cleaning the remaining four with tweezers and shears. I even went that extra mile and, with surgical skill and a stout pair of pliers, extracted the splint-like tendons from the drumsticks. The finished birds looked as if they were fresh from the neighborhood poulterer's.

"Beautiful job, Mr. Davis," commented the lady in charge.

"Come here, you little minx."

"None of that! There's work to be done. Maybe later—if you're extremely lucky."

When the doorbell rang, I was immersed in slicing a small mountain of fennel while Joan was at the stove sprinkling salt into the curried squash-and-apple soup.

"That must be Al," she said, brushing the salt off her palms. "He's putting the new sink in the basement this afternoon."

I couldn't help but smile. Everybody knows Al. Al, who's never met a stranger. Al, who keeps up a constant patter whenever there's someone within earshot. Al, with his broad face, twinkling blue eyes, close-cropped silver hair and a toothpick always sticking out of his mouth. Al, who would cheerfully give you the shirt off his back if you were in need. The first time I met Al he drew back his big right hand as if he were a gunslinger slapping leather, then extended it with a waggling, slow-motion flourish.

"Hi! I'm Al the plumber!"

"I'm Tom, the uh, boyfriend."

"Glad to meet ya! Looks like we got ourselves a 'tom-cat' and an 'alley-cat' here! That Joanie's quite a little gal, isn't she?!"

To get to Joan's basement you have to go through the kitchen.

"Boy, it sure smells good in here!" Al exclaimed as he began ferrying tools and materials into the house from his battered van. "Get the door, will ya, Tommy? Thanks."

It was about then that Zack, my ancient English setter, padded into the kitchen to lap some water. Seeing him, Al remarked, "I'll tell ya one thing, Tommy. If that dog belonged to me, I wouldn't be in here choppin' onions on a gorgeous November day like this! I'd be out huntin' birds!"

"This dog's bird-hunting days are long past," I said, reaching down to pat Zack's wise old head. "He found his share when he was younger, though. I've got two pointers and another setter in the kennel—they're the dogs I hunt over now. Yeah, normally we'd be out chasing birds on a day like this, but a higher power"—I nodded toward Joan—"ordained that I do KP for her dinner party."

Al threw back his head, laughed heartily and disappeared into the basement.

Soon assorted clanking, grinding, banging and drilling noises testified that Al was getting down to business. When he came upstairs to take a break, he said, "Mind if I ask what you're having tonight for the main course?"

"Not at all," I replied, lifting the white cloth I'd draped over the birds as they rested on the countertop awaiting seasoning. "We're having pheasant."

For the briefest moment Al was speechless. But then, as if an electrical current was surging through his veins, he fairly lit up with excitement.

"Pheasant! I'll be darned! Where'd you get 'em!"

"South Dakota," I answered. "I was out there the week before last with three of my hunting buddies. We had a dandy shoot." In fact it had been the most action-packed pheasant hunting I'd ever experienced—and I've been at it for a quarter-century. Any way you cut it that's a long time.

"South Dakota." Al let the words linger on his tongue like the taste of mellow bourbon. "South Dakota." He said it wistfully, dreamily, longingly, almost as if it were an incantation. "I always wanted to go there, but somehow it never worked out. Is the pheasant hunting as good as they say?"

"Yeah, it really is. Or at least it can be. You have to know what you're doing, and you have to be prepared to pay to get on private land. But if you don't mind hunting public land, there's plenty to go around."

"I wish I'd gone when I had the chance," Al mused. "You know, I used to hunt pheasants around here every weekend. But after my golden died—about a year ago, now—I quit. It just wasn't the same without the dog. This is the first season I haven't hunted since I can't remember when. You know what I did, though? A couple weekends ago I went out and walked a few of my old spots—a couple marsh edges, a fencerow or two. You might not believe this, Tommy, but I hunted some of those same places when I was a kid, and I just wanted to spend some time in them again."

He leaned against the counter, took the toothpick from his mouth and chuckled. "One lady stood on her porch and hollered at me to get off her land. I said, 'Ma'm, I'm just reliving my misspent youth.' She waved and said, 'Go right ahead.' I didn't flush any pheasants, but you know, it really didn't matter. It just felt good to walk the cover and think about old times. I guess I'm kind of like your setter—I found my share of birds when I was younger."

Al paused, put the toothpick back in its rightful place and continued in the same reflective vein. "I do plumbing jobs for so many old guys who don't hunt any more, but you know, it's all they talk about. They don't want to talk about their careers, or the Packers or anything else. They want to talk about hunting—the dogs they had, the shots they made, the trips they took, that kind of stuff. I used to feel sorry for 'em, but then it hit me. I don't hunt any more either, and I'm getting ready to retire. I'm turning into one of those guys myself!"

With that, Al shook his head and returned to his work in the basement.

"God, he almost had me in tears," Joan confessed.

Truth to tell, I was also thinking hard on what Al had said. It was too powerful, too heartfelt, to be written off as mere nostalgia. No, it was more than that. It was something vital, something meaningful and intensely personal that flows from the core of a hunter's being. I knew men like the ones Al described, men nearing the end of life's journey, men for whom no greater pleasure remains than to conjure memories in the company of kindred spirits. In such company the years and the insults of age melt away, the buried dogs blaze across the prairies, and the birds—the pheasants and the quail, the grouse and the woodcock, the chickens and the sharptails and the partridge—rise endlessly against a brilliant sky, their feathers limned in pure autumnal light. Late in the game, when the body is beyond redemption, the hunter returns to the places the soul has always been.

"Do you have plans for that other pheasant?" I asked, snapping out of my reverie. "The one in the refrigerator?"

"No," Joan answered. She gave me a puzzled look: but then, all at once, she caught on. "You're so sweet!" she gushed, throwing her slender arms around my neck. I seized the opportunity to give her backside an audacious squeeze.

"Have I ever mentioned that you have a world-class derrière?"

"Only about a thousand times—but I'm glad you approve."

We uncoupled at the sound of Al's footfalls ascending the stairs. "All set," he announced as he closed the basement door behind him. "Hey, you kids have a great dinner party tonight, OK? I wish *I* was eating pheasant!"

"You are," I said, proffering a package wrapped in white butcher's paper. "Here's a pheasant for you, Al. We want you to have it."

"No, no, I couldn't!" he protested, waving his hands. "You kids . . . well, maybe. Are you sure?"

"We won't take no for an answer," I admonished, pressing the pheasant into his grasp.

"Hey, Tommy, Joanie, thanks a lot. You don't know how much this means to me. I'm gonna cook this bird for supper tonight! I don't know about you, but what I like to do is bake my pheasant with a little cream of mushroom soup. When I was still hunting, that's what we had for dinner almost every Sunday evening during the season."

Joan and I exchanged knowing smiles. "*Bon appétit,*" I called as Al carried the pheasant out to his van.

Then, impulsively, I jogged after him. He'd already clambered inside and was setting his pheasant on the seat when I tapped on the glass. Startled, he rolled down the window.

"You know those bird-hunting spots you mentioned? The ones you walked the other day for old times' sake?"

"Sure, Tommy. What about 'em?" His brow was furrowed.

"Think if a guy had a dog he might be able to put up a rooster or two?"

"Yeah, I think so. The birds aren't as thick as they used to be, but my golden could always find a few. Tell ya what, get a map and I'll show ya right where to go."

"I don't want you to show me, Al. I want you to *take* me, and my dogs. What're you doing tomorrow morning?"

Once again, Al was dumbstruck. But then he broke into a grin as wide as the Grand Canyon, and his blue eyes danced a jig. He was no longer a 60-something plumber reflecting on the past, but a man to whom age was irrelevant, a man whose life still brimmed with possibilities. Pointing at me with his ever-present toothpick, Al declared, "I'll be here at a quarter-to-seven, sharp."

"I'll have the coffee and sweet rolls," I volunteered. Nothing more needed to be said; we understood each other perfectly.

The van rumbled down the driveway, Al and I exchanging waves. Then I thrust my hands into my pockets and hurried back into the house, where it was warm.

19

BACK AT ANDY'S ACRES

I'm sitting on the edge of the middle step, cleaning birds. There's a plastic bucket lined with a trash bag between my legs, a pair of game shears in my hand, and a plate on the step above me for the finished products. The birds, three woodcock and a single grouse, are on the ground at my feet, among the feathers left from the previous evening's cleaning. Emmylou is lying nearby in the open doorway of the screen porch, intently studying the blue spruces—planted long ago when this was still a working farmstead—for the squirrels that hide there; off to my left in the clearing where we park our vehicles, Traveler is curled up in his crate in the back of the Blazer. Geese are moving overhead, and the midday warmth that left the dogs panting and me wringing with sweat is giving way to the chill of late afternoon. A breeze rustles through the aspens, shaking loose a few golden, heart-shaped leaves. They drift down noiselessly. It is like a scene from a dream.

All of these particulars are familiar, yet something feels strange. It takes me a while to put my finger on it, and then it hits me: In all the years I've been coming here to hunt grouse and woodcock, this is the first time I've been alone, the first time I've been the last man in camp. Andy, who more than anyone I know truly lives the life of the globe-trotting sportsman, headed back right after breakfast to get ready for an upcoming bonefishing trip to the Bahamas (North Riding Point, to be precise); Erik, whose wife doesn't see much of him in the fall, suffered a rare pang of conscience and decided that he should pull the plug early; Terry needed to get his thirteen-year-old son Dan back home in time to finish his homework and get a good night's sleep before the bell rang Monday morning.

So I was left to close down the cabin. Actually, "cabin" is something of a misnomer; it's a house, really, with a full kitchen, indoor plumbing, TV, all the usual amenities. Andy's the owner—its official title, in fact, is "Andy's Acres"—but he pretty much gives his friends the run of the place when he's not around. It's up in the sticks of northern Wisconsin, in a wild, lightly populated corner of the state that has considerable appeal for hard-core grouse and woodcock hunters but, thank God, very little appeal for tourists. In other words, it hasn't been "discovered" (i.e. ruined) yet. Grouse crash into the cabin's windows on a regular basis; the last time it happened, the bird busted right through the screen *and* the glass, and was lying dead on Andy's bed when he found it. And we wonder why they're so easy to miss.

Because Erik would be back up the following weekend—and because his October weekends typically start at noon Thursday—closing down the cabin simply meant turning down the heat and the hot water, shutting off the pump, making sure the kitchen was reasonably spic-and-span, taking home any food that might otherwise spoil, hauling the garbage away, and locking up. As jobs go, it wasn't a big one, even without any help.

The part that felt strange, though, was cleaning birds by myself. There's usually a bunch of us clustered around the porch steps, feathers and insults flying, beers close at hand, dogs hovering in the wings like hopeful scavengers. It's a time of laughter and high spirits, a time to replay the day's events, reveling in the successes, shrugging off the failures, and marveling over those weird, inexplicable things that always seem to happen in hunting. At least one dog invariably tries to sneak off with a bird; at least one dog invariably knocks over somebody's beer. Empty threats are hurled, and the culprits slink off. The atmosphere is festive.

Cleaning birds alone, the mood is totally different: quiet, reflective, even a little somber. Holding a grouse or woodcock in my hand—each perfect, each unutterably beautiful—I am reminded again of what an awesome act it is to take a life, and of what an awesome responsibility this act confers upon us. It is one thing to defend hunting on a logical, rational basis, but it is quite another thing to accept its moral obligations on a personal level, to consciously *make the choice.*

I'd pondered these philosophical questions before, of course—but never at Andy's Acres. Even now, I don't dwell on them long. No sooner do I begin working on a woodcock than I find a jagged tooth-mark in the breast, the signature of Ilsa, Erik's golden retriever. I can't help but smile, because Ilsa, despite her occasional indiscretions, is one of those infectiously exuberant dogs that you just have to like. Erik claims he named her for Ilsa Lund, Ingrid Bergman's unforgettable character in *Casablanca;* I counter that a more appropriate cinematic allusion would be the infamous B-movie *Ilsa, She-Wolf of the SS.*

It is also the case that while Ilsa is graceful, athletic, and undeniably birdy, she's a little lacking in the looks department. Classic conformation? *Not.* One of our standard lines is "You know, Erik, that dog of yours bears a remarkable resemblance to a golden retriever." She is somewhat narrow of skull, long of muzzle, and high and short of ear, a combination of characteristics that makes you wonder if one of Ilsa's ancestors might have shacked up with Lassie. "Swamp collie" is our affectionate term for her.

But she can hunt—and that, ultimately, is all that matters to her master. Erik is about as serious and passionate a grouse hunter as I know, to the extent that he considers woodcock little more than an amusing sideshow. Function, not aesthetics, is his credo; always hungry for information in this regard, he constantly solicits your opinions on everything from boots and vests to gundog kennels. He has been in a running feud with L.L. Bean ever since they discontinued what was, in Erik's opinion, the best briar pant ever made, and replaced it in their catalogue with a "new and improved" version that—again, in his opinion—doesn't measure up. After a few polite exchanges of correspondence, they quit answering his letters. Erik's single surviving pair of these pants gives new meaning to the phrase "hanging on by a thread." But then, everything he wears is frayed, tattered and coming apart at the seams.

Erik's utilitarianism extends to his choice of firearms. His favorite grouse gun is a Remington 870 Special Field, and he regards my preference for doubles as a snobbish affectation. "Don't be a chump—shoot a pump," he likes to say. In response, I composed the following ditty:

If on your back
You sport a hump,
Chances are
You shoot a pump.

Truth to tell, it's rare for Erik and me to hunt together. As a flushing dog guy, he generally heads in one direction while I, as a pointing dog guy, generally head in the other. He's also a firm believer in the old adage "Guns don't get grouse—legs do." Combined with the fact that he is tall and fit, this translates into a pretty intense—if not downright punishing—aerobic workout for anyone not in the same kind of shape. But with Donny, his usual (and even taller and fitter) hunting partner, up in Saskatchewan chasing white-fronted geese, with me needing a break from hollering at dogs that either can't hear (Emmy) or won't listen (Traveler), and with Terry hinting that he and Dan would just as soon go off on their own, we decided to team up.

The spot we picked—we call it the Four Corners—is one of those heart-stoppingly gorgeous covers that you can spend all day in without retracing your steps. Let me put it this way: We hunted hard for three solid hours and barely scratched the surface. Our limits of woodcock came quickly—we discovered a concentration of them on a brushy sidehill—but grouse were curiously scarce. And when we did find them, they were in the damn pines and spruces, where their flushes were heard but, for the most part, unseen. I finally managed to score on a high, rocketing overhead when a bird went out above Erik, who was upslope. It's a shot I make about once a decade, and when the grouse thumped down, stoned, I figured I'd probably burned my quota of luck for the entire season.

Needless to say, I fanned a few minutes later when a grouse let me walk past before thundering out of a spruce. Then, after Erik headed for home and I turned Emmylou loose, I missed the only chance I had during one of the most exquisitely frustrating hunts I can remember. We must have had a dozen flushes in an hour's time, but other than a long left-to-right crosser that I choked on, they were blowing out so far ahead of us it was beyond laughable. If I saw anything at all, it was the leaves they left tossing in their wake. Even when Emmy got them pointed, they refused to hold; I'd take a couple of steps in her direction and *sayonara*.

Sometimes, grouse hunting is like that.

The gathering mid-afternoon heat gave me the excuse I was looking for to call it a day. Emmy was beat—she's nearing 12 and bothered by a badly arthritic elbow—and I knew that in my fragile mental state I'd come totally unglued if Traveler was in one of his frequent bull-headed moods. Besides, there's a lot to be said for quitting while you're ahead, and with three woodcock and a grouse in the bag I had no grounds for complaint.

Terry and Dan were just leaving when I returned to the cabin. Dan had recently graduated from firearms safety training, and on his first "real" hunt the day before he'd tumbled a woodcock with his 20-gauge Ithaca/SKB side-by-side. It was a proud moment in the young man's life, and we all congratulated him heartily. He hadn't been quite as lucky today, but no matter. He'd gotten a taste of grouse and woodcock hunting—its excitement, its challenge, the magical allure of the country, the deep camaraderie that binds sportsmen who share the same values—and he'd be back. His dad was ready to entertain offers for his setters—Willie wasn't handling his birds properly, and Babe just plain wasn't handling—but he'd be back, too.

I rinse the birds under the pump. The well water is shockingly cold, and it takes a minute or two to regain the feeling in my hands. Emmylou is still watching for squirrels; Traveler is still asleep in his crate. The sun is melting into the timbered hills, its last rays suffusing the clouds with a coral glow. Alone with my dogs and my thoughts, it occurs to me that this might be the one place in all the world where I would wish nothing to be different, where everything is exactly as I've always imagined it should be.

20

SHOOTING GUESTS

A fter lunch, the blanket folded and the food repacked in the picnic basket, we crossed the pine barrens and entered the range of rumpled hills that shoulders Macintire Creek. The popple grows as thickly as corn in that rough, unpeopled country, and there are patches of hazel scattered throughout it like reefs in a sea.

We stopped where a park-like grove of ancient sentinel oaks commands the height-of-land, overlooking the dark green spires of the spruces edging the creek below and the hills that rise on the other side and roll in waves to the far horizons. Andy Cook led Gary and Nancy Johnson and their brace of handsome setters in that direction; they would move woodcock in the dense alders at the bottom of the slope, and when they regained the high ground they'd be in some of the prettiest mixed-bag cover you can imagine, cover with that brushy, ragged, unkempt look that makes bird hunters weak in the knees. Randy Lawrence and I headed the other way, following Emmylou into the bristling popple, the uneven, up-and-down terrain lending the endeavor a distinctly three-dimensional feel.

I probably spend more time than I should pondering the question of just what it is that makes a hunt "good." (Blame it on my being a philosophy major.) But I think it would have been hard to improve upon the hour-and-a-half that Randy and I spent gunning over Emmylou. For one thing, we all knew our business. Emmy's at that point in her career where youthful exuberance has been replaced by a kind of tough-minded professionalism; which is to say, she doesn't screw up very damn often. The fire still burns hot, though: There are times when her intensity and resolve shock me, and I realize that the centuries of selective breeding are but a veneer that masks the ancient predator within.

And while Randy and I had never hunted grouse and woodcock together until that very morning, it was as if we'd been gunning partners all our lives. There was no wasted motion, no unnecessary noise, and when Emmylou stacked up on point, we deployed as quickly and efficiently as a couple of street-smart cops responding to a burglary in progress.

We made the most of our chances, too. Even more importantly, we had them. Not every bird we flushed afforded a shot, and not every bird we shot at fell. But walking down the rocky two-track in the mellow October light, guns balanced on our shoulders, a tired lady setter at heel, and the divided weight of three grouse and three woodcock tugging on our tattered vests, we were buoyed by the conviction that we'd done it right.

Our companions were already back, watering dogs and munching on tart apples. "Sounded like you got into them," Gary remarked in that elliptical way outdoorsmen have of asking the obvious question.

"We had," declared Randy, reaching down to stroke Emmy's finely rendered head, "one of the nicest hunts I can remember."

That being exactly the kind of experience I'd hoped Randy would have when I invited him to join us in northern Wisconsin, I couldn't have been happier. A host's pleasure, after all, is a reflection of his guests' satisfaction.

"Mankind," mused the English essayist Sir Max Beerbohm, "is divisible into two great classes: hosts and guests."

The world of wingshooting is no exception. Indeed, the guest-host relationship, along with the reciprocity and respect it implies, is woven deeply into the fabric of the sport—so deeply, in fact, that it has been taken for granted, if not overlooked entirely. Beyond *Recollections of a Shooting Guest,* George Bird Evans' memoir of Dr. Charles Norris, the starchy Philadelphian who left Evans his Purdey, the literature is largely silent on the subject. Turgenev touches on it in his *Sketches,* obviously; so do Guy de la Valdene and Jim Fergus in *Making Game* and *A Hunter's Road,* respectively. But they don't explore the territory of the relationship so much as they use it as a point of departure for their narratives.

Historically, of course, you couldn't hunt *unless* you were a host—that is, an owner of property—or one of his/her invited guests. This was particularly the case in Europe where, from the emergence of hunting as sport circa 1000 A.D. until fairly recently, it was a privilege reserved by and for the landed aristocracy. The most familiar example is probably the Edwardian "shooting party," the somewhat decadent flavor of which can be sampled by viewing the movie of the same name (coincidentally, James Mason's last significant role).

In America, not surprisingly, hunting has always been a more egalitarian, broadly accessible affair—with such notable exceptions as the old-line duck clubs and southern quail plantations. But while generally not as formal here in the colonies, the guest-host relationship remains central to our traditions, and our practice, of wingshooting. It doesn't underpin all of our bird hunting; there are times when we hunt alone or with companions of long standing, places we keep to ourselves or choose to pioneer by our own devices. I think it's safe to say, though, that most of us—and especially those of us who enjoy gunning a variety of birds—depend to some degree on the largesse of hosts.

I'm not talking about booking a week at a lodge; the concept of the paying shooting guest, which is a relatively new development on this side of the Atlantic, has a totally different politics. No, I mean the old-fashioned, no-strings-attached invitation extended by a friend/acquaintance/associate who has a *place*. It might be BLM land in Idaho, it might be a cabin in Michigan's Upper Peninsula, it might be a cousin's farm in Kansas. Regardless of the address, it's somewhere your host has established himself. He's learned the lay of the land; he knows the habits of its game. And, for any number of reasons, he'd like to share it with you.

Clearly, not all hosts have the same expectations. For some, it's enough that you enjoy yourself—whatever your terms of enjoyment happen to be—and that you make the appropriate gestures of appreciation. For others, the important thing is that you hold up your end and play by the house rules.

I have a friend in Texas who occasionally invites me down to hunt his quail lease. (All of us should have such friends.) After a morning of cooperative covey rises and crisp dog work, we were only a few birds shy of our limits by the time we broke for lunch—which was prepared by firing up one of the two gas grills mounted on his stainless-steel dog trailer. My host is a deadly shot, so with filling out a moot point I thought I'd tote a camera that afternoon instead of a scattergun.

Well, let's just say that this decision was not met with enthusiasm. He didn't tell me I couldn't carry the camera—he's too gracious for that—but he didn't hide the fact that he wasn't very damn pleased about it. I caught on pretty quickly that his guests are expected to (A) shoot well and (B) *keep* shooting until their limits are filled. Then, and only then, can you safely stop to smell the roses—or the mesquite, as the case may be.

(I learned, too, that it doesn't hurt to lavishly compliment him on his fine string of pointers. But then, praising your host's dogs *never* hurts.)

Personally, I couldn't care less about how well or how poorly my guests shoot (assuming they shoot safely, of course). Being a skilled wingshot does not necessarily make a person a principled sportsman or a pleasant companion, only a "talented butcher," to use Guy de la Valdene's eloquently sanguinary term. One of my favorite people to hunt grouse and woodcock with, Adrian Webber, scratches down a bird about every third season. But his joy at simply being there is so infectious that it spreads to everyone around him. His presence also serves to remind us not to take things more seriously than they deserve to be taken.

By the same token, the fact that Gary and Nancy Johnson happen to be exceptional shots is ultimately unrelated to the qualities that make them such lovely people to hunt with. What matters is their values, their attitudes, their abiding civility and generosity. I'd like to think that I'm cut from similar cloth. When all is said and done, this remains perhaps the best reason to welcome shooting guests: to be with members of your own tribe.

Mention of Nancy Johnson brings to mind another desirable quality in both hosts and guests: facility in the kitchen. There is an elemental connection, after all, between hunting and feasting, a connection richly celebrated in the art and literature of sport. Nancy is a caterer by trade, and she transformed Andy Cook's humble northwoods cabin into an intimate gourmet restaurant. Would you believe herb-stuffed pork *roulades* napped with a sauce of honey, mustard, and rosemary? To say nothing of her pungent chutneys, light-as-air pastries, and olive "fireballs" encased in a cayenne-laced crust. Artist Peter Corbin, who has been both my guest in Wisconsin and my host in upstate New York, wields the cook's tools as cunningly as he does a paintbrush, and I'll never forget the sauteed filets mignons with curried fried bananas that Pete Macfarlane, sportsman and bon vivant, prepared while our guest at Andy's place.

I fancy myself something of a cook, too, so when Terry Barker and I traveled to northern Iowa to hunt pheasants as the guests of his partner in crime from veterinary school, Steve Roti, a festive dinner was a must. Steve's freezer was full of fat, wild, corn-fed mallards, several of which I seared and served with a port reduction sauce. Tragically, the dish's subtleties were lost on our host, whose palate was revealed to be, shall we say, unsophisticated. Horrified by the thought of the treatment those beautiful mallards were likely to receive (some sort of mortification in a crock-pot, no doubt), we liberated as many as we could cram into our cooler. The pheasant hunting was dismal, which meant that we had a lot of room for ducks.

Dr. Roti's heart was gladdened, however, by the case of Point beer and bottle of Famous Grouse we gave him, potables of one description or another being the standard honorarium for shooting hosts. Trouble is, all evidence to the contrary, not every bird hunter drinks. I learned this hard lesson many years ago on a Mississippi quail junket when I discovered, too late, that our host was a devout Baptist who considered liquor the devil's own venom. It was not pretty.

Along these same lines, there's no surer way to disgrace yourself than to show up with about a finger of Scotch left in the bottom of your bottle and, upon finishing that off minutes after the cocktail hour is declared, spend the rest of the trip unapologetically sucking down your host's booze. Such behavior is also a reliable indicator of other character defects. While a host has a certain obligation to be accommodating, some guests, no matter how carefully screened or highly recommended, simply turn out to be boors. They don't pitch in, they don't pull their weight, they make no effort to blend in with the group—and they don't get invited back.

Another fail-safe way to see your name deleted from the invitation list is to be the owner of an uncontrollable, interfering, and/or just plain lousy dog. Sadly, some of these scoundrels belong to people who are otherwise beyond reproach. One universally well-liked fellow owns a craven Brittany that busts birds, refuses to honor a point, and is visibly despised by her four-footed brethren. His company is welcome; hers is not. Too bad they come as a pair.

And then there are the guests who don't *want* to come back. A few of the "flatlanders" I've hosted on grouse and woodcock hunts decided that clawing through alder thickets, stumbling around in cedar swamps, and taking hopeless stabbing pokes at brown blurs just isn't their idea of fun. Go figure. Another sportsman, a hardcore quail hunter whose impeccable pointers and setters double as champion field trial performers, turned me down flat when I invited him to reprise a pheasant hunt.

"I'm not about to waste my dogs' talents on those God-damned ditch parrots," he snorted. "It's like hitching a Ferrari to a honey wagon."

Just as shooting guests don't always pan out, there are some hosts you can't wait to say goodbye to. If you hunt long and widely enough, making contacts and following up leads, it's bound to happen.

How I came to be there is a long story, but some years ago I found myself, along with a couple of friends, chasing sharptails and prairie chickens as the guests of a ranch family deep in the unforgiving bosom of the Nebraska Sandhills. The patriarch was an affable sort; his wife, however, was a grim, self-righteous harpy who wore her Christianity like a badge and played the martyr at every opportunity. She was also the single most abysmal cook whose food I've ever choked down. Their older son—our nominal guide—was a rooster who held himself in extremely high regard and considered us college-educated city-dwellers a bunch of Nancy boys.

And while there were plenty of birds around, we couldn't get within a hundred yards of them—a phenomenon explained by the fact that the younger son, as we learned later, had declared open season on them approximately one month before the state of Nebraska had. (They don't have a hell of a lot of respect for governmental authority in those parts.) Needless to say, when it came time to leave we boiled out of there like a pack of scalded dogs.

Thankfully, that kind of experience is rare. Rare, too, is the experience of hunting pheasants and quail as the guests of Gary and Karen Sawin—but for totally opposite reasons. The Sawins, who run a family farm in the rolling hills of western Iowa, are simply two of the finest, kindest, most unconditionally generous people you could ever hope to meet, people I'm privileged to call my friends. Whenever Andy, Terry, and I drive down from Wisconsin, they truly treat us like royalty. Gary calls the neighbors to make sure it's OK for us to hunt their land, leads us to the best spots, and ferries us to our vehicles so we don't have to deadhead; Karen cooks up the proverbial storm.

In fact, the only problem with hunting at Sawin's is that Karen's lunches are such groaning boards—garden vegetable soup, potent chili, sandwich fixings, crunchy homemade pickles, two or three fresh-from-the-oven desserts—that it's all a body can do to push away from the table, stagger out into the biting November chill, and return to the field.

We've had a few poor days there, a lot of good ones, and a handful of spectacular ones; we've felt mild disappointment, profound satisfaction, and wild elation. I smile whenever I picture the time Andy found himself literally surrounded by roosters—they were going off like fireworks—and never drew a feather, and I can still see the covey of quail that Terry and I surprised as they fed in the picked corn. With military precision, they lined up single file and double-timed it straight down a stubble row, looking for all the world like a platoon of toy soldiers. I broke a finger at Sawin's one year when the ice at the edge of a cattail marsh buckled and my knee came down on my hand, but as I'd tumbled a cockbird over a point just moments earlier I viewed it as an acceptable trade-off.

Across the seasons, walking the heavy switchgrass (Gary calls it "red top") or working the brushy cornfield ditches, waiting for a stout-hearted dog—Zack, Emmy, Traveler—to pop out ahead and look to me for direction, I often wondered *why*. The Sawin's hospitality surpassed any I'd ever known, and while it was easy to credit this to them simply being who they are, I couldn't help suspecting that there was something else, some part of the equation that wasn't obvious, but that ultimately made all the difference.

One wintry morning, my question was answered. I was standing beside Gary on the brow of a hill, the country spilling away for miles in every direction. The brown fields were dusted with snow, the grass bowed penitently before the keening wind, the light was like a thin blue glaze.

"Some people think Iowa's boring," said this gentle bear of a man, "but I think it's beautiful."

"I do, too. I've always thought so."

That was the connection: our love of the land. It bound us together, host and guest, like an oath of blood.

21

HOW I GOT MY
NICKNAME

My name was mud. Literally. "Mud," you see, was my nickname in high school, and to make a long story short, I got it after borrowing my mom's car to go duck hunting in the Missouri River bottoms, miring it axle deep in a muddy cornfield that bordered a network of marshes, and having to have a wrecker come all the way from town—Sioux City—to extract it. The loud sucking noise it made as it pulled free of the gumbo was, I knew, the same sound I was about to make when I disappeared into the deep you-know-what waiting for me at home. I was no angel—there had been that streaking incident, among other transgressions—but this time I'd really stepped in it.

I should have known better, of course. I should have parked on the gravel and hiked the extra quarter mile. But the burlap sack I used to haul decoys got pretty heavy after awhile, and I'd spent so much time down in the river bottoms that the thought of getting stuck there seemed as remote as getting stuck in my own driveway.

Those marshes truly were my home away from home. I haunted them in every season, simply watching the ducks, as content in the spring with a pair of binoculars in my hands as I was in the fall with a shotgun. I was aware, in a dim, incomplete way, that the marshes had once been part of the Missouri proper, and that at some distant point in time the river had meandered, carving a new channel out of the sandy loam and leaving behind this crescent of stiff-stemmed cattails, waving bulrushes, and black water. It was hard for me to imagine that the marshes hadn't been there forever, but the massive wooden pilings—logs of a size that dwarfed any tree I'd ever seen (except in photographs)—and timber revetments that I'd discovered in my explorations were convincing proof. They, too, had been left behind. They were a source of wonder and mystery; they seemed like the ruins of a vanished civilization.

I should mention here that my mom's car was not the matronly sedan or station wagon you're probably envisioning as you read this. Uh-uh; it was a '65 Mustang convertible, a dazzlingly sexy turquoise job with a white leather interior (gulp) and incredibly cool knock-off hubcaps that looked like they had come off the wheels of the Roman chariots in *Ben Hur.* I wonder what the archaeologist who excavates that cornfield a thousand years from now will make of the one that stayed there.

Yeah, I was in deep, deep you-know-what. It was pretty obvious, too, that the single, scrawny bluebill I'd managed to scratch down—a candidate for the stewpot if there ever was one—was not going to help tilt the scales of justice in my favor. A variety of punishment scenarios played out on the stage of my mind, from grounding (worse than death itself in the middle of duck season) to loss of the 16-gauge Model 12 that was, at the time, my pride and joy. My future—it was the autumn of 1973—looked as bleak as Richard Nixon's.

Luckily for me, it was my 17th birthday. This served to blunt the edge of my parents' wrath, although Mom stung my guilt-ridden psyche with a lecture on responsibility (the abridged version), and Dad gave me that disgusted, what-a-sorry-excuse-I-have-for-a-son shake of the head that even now, a quarter century later, still makes me feel like something you just scraped off the bottom of your boot.

But it was my eight-year-old brother, Andy, who cut to the heart of the matter, put things into their proper perspective—and gave me my nickname. After Mom and Dad had finished working me over, he came up to me and, grinning slyly, handed me a homemade birthday card. It was nothing fancy, a piece of blue construction paper, folded in half, on which he'd hastily doodled with a black felt-tip pen. On the cover was a stick figure labeled "Tom," a balloon with the legend "2+2=5," and the caption "Pea Brain." Inside, Andy had written the following heartfelt message: "Dear Tom—I'm sorry you got stuck in the mud. Mud spelled backwards spells Dum. Happy Birthday."

As soon as my duck hunting buddies caught wind of this, it was all over but the shoutin'. "Mud Davis," they'd snicker. "*Muuuudddddd,*" they'd quack, sounding like mallards with postnasal drip. The name stuck—so to speak—and it wasn't long before everyone was calling me Mud. They even began calling my mother "Mud-Mom." She didn't mind at all; in fact, she seemed to get a kick out of it. But then, any mother who would hand her teenage son the keys to her Mustang convertible so he could go duck hunting is, by definition, a little different. I loved her for it, and I still do.

I lived for duck hunting in those years. It was possible then—and there, in that place where the broad Missouri comes slewing down from the Dakota hills to spill across the black-soil flatlands of western Iowa, filling the hidden sloughs and oxbows, pulling the wild-fowl from the prairie skies—in a way that it no longer is for me. I am not sure I have lived for anything so purely and profoundly since.

And, it's been a long, long time since anyone called me Mud.

22

SOMETHING SO RIGHT: EMMYLOU, NOW AND THEN

The other day—it's early July as I write this—Emmylou caught a baby rabbit in my wife's flower garden. The flower garden is supposed to be off-limits, of course, but you can't really blame the old girl (Emmy, I mean) for being so irresistibly attracted to it. Compared to the neatly clipped grass that comprises the rest of the yard, the garden, which is mostly tall, thickly massed perennials such as bee balm, monkshood, and prairie coneflower, must look to Emmy like a hell of a nice patch of cover. With thirteen hunting seasons under her collar, recognizing cover is something she knows a thing or two about.

And while over the course of her career she's learned not to pay much attention to rabbits, there's a certain any-port-in-a-storm law that applies to bird dogs cooped up for too long in the wilds of suburbia. The upshot is that when Emmy scented a rabbit—game!—in the flower garden, she dove in and grabbed it. She may be a canine senior citizen, with an arthritic left elbow the size of a tangerine, but when she really needs it she can still dig deep and come up with a surprising burst of speed.

I'm guessing that she pointed for a while before she broke in on the bunny—at least I like to think so—but I can't be sure because I wasn't there. We'd gone out of town for the weekend, and in our absence my saintly, 77-year-old mother-in-law was taking care of the livestock—Emmy, Traveler, my stepdaughter's good-for-nothing cat, and two goldfish that belong to no one in particular.

In any event, while my mother-in-law watched helplessly, Emmy made quick work of the cottontail. (With a little imagination, you can add your own sound effects.) Then, when she'd finished her hors d'oeuvre, she fastidiously licked up the drops of blood she'd spilled. That was enough to push my already horrified mother-in-law right over the edge. It was all she could do to herd Emmy back into the kennel before staggering light-headedly into the house, getting her best friend on the phone, unburdening herself about the grisly scene she'd just witnessed, and pretty much falling apart.

What upset her as much as anything was the idea that it was somehow her fault, and that allowing Emmylou, this blue-blooded, high-toned, pedigreed-to-the-nth-generation, dam-of-champions English setter bird dog to catch, kill, and eat a *rabbit* was about the worst thing she could possibly have done. When she told me what had happened, I felt a little like a priest hearing a confession. "Oh, Tom," she apologized, "I'm so dreadfully sorry . . ."

I just smiled and shook my head, envisioning the entire rueful scenario in my mind's eye. "Don't give it another thought," I said. "There was nothing you could have done. Emmy knows better, but she was really just doing what comes naturally to her. She'll be none the worse for it, I promise. The only thing I feel badly about is the poor rabbit."

That seemed to cheer her up. And it reminded me again of something Emmy had finally opened my eyes to, something that should have been obvious but didn't penetrate my thick skull until I was 40 years old and had been fooling with bird dogs for nearly 30 of those years. That something was this: Beneath the style and the manners and the whole sophisticated surface of the modern pointing dog beats the heart of an ancient predator. Predators do not hunt for fun; they hunt to *survive*. When a dog hunts as if her life depended on it, it's because at a deep, almost molecular level, she's convinced that it does.

Emmylou hunted that way. Still does, for that matter, when she gets the chance. (Just ask my mother-in-law.) The speed and style have faded; the focus, resolve, and intensity have not. If there is one word that perfectly captures Emmy's attitude in the field, it's *urgency*; a close second would be *purpose*. It's not as if she has to worry about where her next meal is coming from, and the conscious part of her knows that. Her unconscious being—the part where the wolf still howls—is not quite so sure. And so she hunts with all her heart, all her being, all her soul. She knows no other way to do it.

———————

Emmylou came into the world February 20, 1987. She was whelped in Ken and Sara Ridderikhoff's basement in Sturgeon Bay, Wisconsin, and spent the first few weeks of her life there. Ken owned Emmy's dam, Tara, a lovely tri-color with a fabulous pedigree—both her sire and dam were grouse champions—a ton of bird sense, and great natural ability. In short, she was the kind of dog that any shoe leather bird hunter would have pawned his soul to own. Tara's only real fault was that she ran and pointed with her tail held at back level or slightly above; in other words, not as high as is fashionable in this fashion-obsessed day and age. Truth to tell, I was more inclined to regard a low tail as a fault then than I am now, having figured out that it's what's up front—between the ears, that is—that really counts.

Anyway, I had an idea that if we linebred Tara to the right sire we could preserve all her desirable qualities while at the same time jacking up the tail carriage a few notches. I had a sire in mind, a dog standing at stud in Oklahoma named Trail's End Tomoka. He, like Tara, was royally bred: His sire, Tomoka, arguably the greatest of all the Smith/Ray Setters (which, if you know anything about setters, is saying a mouthful), was something of a legend in his own time. And while there has always been some debate in the setter camp over Tomoka's worth as a sire, I've always felt that his offspring were, if nothing else, superior bird-finders.

So I approached Ken with the following offer: In exchange for the pick of the litter, I would pay the stud fee and the shipping costs for breeding Tara to Trail's End Tomoka. The rest of the litter would be Ken's to sell. It was pretty much a no-risk, no-lose deal for him, and needless to say he agreed to it. As I recall, the stud fee was $200, or maybe $250. Add the shipping costs, and I probably spent about

$400 out-of-pocket. It was by far the best investment I ever made; no other money I've spent even comes close.

Tara whelped a litter of five—all females, all tri-colored. They were as alike as the proverbial peas in a pod, which made picking one—*the* one, I hoped—no easy task. (Curiously, these look-alike littermates would grow up to be quite different in size, conformation, and action.) Although I was leaning towards Emmylou all along, my then-wife cast the deciding vote. "She has the sweetest face," she declared. I had to agree, but I also fancied that I detected something else, a little extra sparkle that set her apart. Maybe it was there; maybe I imagined it. Either way, the events of the ensuing years have convinced me that there's no real science to picking a puppy. You do your homework and try to find the best-bred litter available; beyond that, it's largely the luck of the draw. All else being equal, a sweet face is as sound a bet as any.

We named the puppy for Emmylou Harris, the country diva whose voice, it has always seemed to me, is one of the better proofs of the existence of a divine being. Her registered name, Grievous Angel, comes from the song by the late Gram Parsons, the self-destructive genius who was Harris' muse early in her career (her heart-rending "Boulder to Birmingham" was written in his memory) and who pioneered the "country rock" sound as a member of the Byrds and the Flying Burrito Brothers. (This should give you a pretty good idea of the stuff that's in my tape player when I'm on the road.)

It's not often, in my experience, that things work out the way you plan them. In fact, it's damn rare. But it didn't take long to see that Emmylou was everything I'd hoped for—essentially a higher-tailed version of her mama. It would be overstating the case to say that I "trained" her in any meaningful way; beyond the usual whoa-heel-come yard work, I mostly just took her hunting. She did the rest on her own. It all came naturally to her: quartering, digging into the cover, going to the birdy places, keeping tabs on my whereabouts. She was staunch on point virtually from the beginning; from the beginning, too, she would back another dog from as far away as she could see it. (She would also back the occasional sun-bleached stump, dog-sized rock, or wind-blown sheet of newspaper.)

Like her namesake, Emmy was class personified. On the ground, she had terrific speed and animation; on point, she had high style and blistering intensity. And, true to her blood, she was a bird-finder deluxe. She was just eight months old when I shot the first grouse and woodcock over her points; at nine months she gave me one of the greatest performances on pheasants I've ever seen, pinning three late-season Iowa roosters absolutely dead to rights.

It was an auspicious start to her career; indeed, as a typical doubting Thomas I wondered if it might be a little *too* auspicious. The doom-and-gloom part of me couldn't help thinking that something was bound to go wrong, that Emmy couldn't possibly stay in this zone, that it was just a matter of time before the wheels came off.

But they never did. With experience and maturation, Emmy only got better. She also became more *complete.* One of the few qualities she seemed to lack, early on, was a pronounced inclination to retrieve. Then, in her second summer, I sent her to professional trainer Bob Olson for force-breaking. Bob force-broke her, but in reality he did much more than that: He tapped into a reservoir of natural ability that might otherwise have never bubbled to the surface. You'd expect a force-broken dog to be a reliable retriever; Emmy, on the other hand, became an unstoppable one.

Actually, that statement needs to be qualified. What Emmy became was an unstoppable retriever of *game*. She had about as much interest in retrieving dummies as I have in folding laundry. Knock a bird down anywhere in her vicinity, though, and she turned into Tommie Lee Jones in pursuit of Harrison Ford. A retrieve she made on a wing-tipped cock pheasant still makes me shake my head in awe. The bird fell on the far side of a strip of tall shattercane, and by the time Terry Barker and I fought through to the other side neither the pheasant nor Emmy was anywhere in sight. It was rough, hilly ground, and we stood there for several minutes, scratching our heads and wondering what the right move would be when Emmy suddenly hove into view, the cockbird—still very much alive—clamped firmly but tenderly in her jaws.

The danger, in any memoir such as this, is that it can very easily turn in to the literary equivalent of a sports highlight film: entertaining, perhaps, but not very enlightening. Reflecting on Emmy's career, the strange thing is that while plenty of brilliant moments come to mind, they're overshadowed, finally, by her sustained level of excellence. It's what my gunning companions and I came to expect of her, and what, day-in and day-out, she delivered better than any dog I've ever hunted over.

In fact, she was so dependable, and performed at such a routinely high level, that we started to take her a little bit for granted. It was only when she began showing her age that we woke up to the realization that we were spoiled rotten, and that while there were some good young dogs in our kennels, none were capable of completely filling her shoes. She had become the standard by which we judged all other pointing dogs.

Not that she was perfect, mind you. On Emmy's first trip to South Dakota for prairie grouse, the chickens and sharptails really took her to school. I mean, it was *ugly*. Emmy also had a tendency to rev a little high once in a while and forget about the guy blowing the whistle (although she was a rank amateur in this respect compared to Zack, her fondly remembered kennelmate).

The vast majority of the time, though, Emmy did it right. Ruffed grouse and woodcock were her forte—they were what she was "made" on, after all—but she had the intelligence, the physical equipment, and the sheer, unadulterated bird sense to adapt to whatever species and whatever environment happened to be on the menu. She was as comfortable mucking through a snipe bog as she was roaming the high plains; as long as there were birds to be hunted, the address didn't matter much. Nor did her approach ever change. Wherever our travels tooks us, Emmylou always hunted the same way: as if her life depended on it.

I used to believe that a big part of what made Emmy such a consummate gun dog was the quality known as "eagerness to please." But now I'm not so sure. The more I ponder it, the more I incline toward the view that it was a happy coincidence. And, to a certain extent, a planned one. She was bred to be a particular kind of dog, a dog whose style of hunting matched my own ideals and tastes. In this respect, you could say that she was born to please me. But a conscious effort? I don't think so. Emmy was—is—too strong-willed, too independent, and too laser-focused on her work to worry about anything so trivial as whether I'm happy or not. It just so happens that her way of doing things *does* make me happy.

Emmy raised three litters of puppies, by three different sires. Some turned out better than others, of course, but from everything

I've heard there wasn't a bad pup in the bunch. Three of them are NSTRA champions; the rest earn their keep as gun dogs. Willie, who belongs to my friend Terry Barker, is one of the latter—and a credit to his mama he is. He has all of Emmy's drive, an even loftier way of going, and as much stamina as any dog I've ever seen. He is also the single best prairie grouse dog it's ever been my pleasure to gun over. There isn't a shred of doubt in my mind that if Terry had been interested in field trials, Willie would be a champion many times over.

Wanting to perpetuate the line—and badly needing to start developing a replacement for my long-of-tooth veterans—I kept a female from Emmy's last litter. Daphne was breathtakingly gorgeous and fast as light, with a high-cracking tail and an effortless stride that made her look as if her feet weren't touching the ground. She, too, was a bird-finder—I shot a double on prairie chickens over Daphne in just her second season—but our relationship, which was strained from the beginning, kept getting progressively worse. It felt as if we were locked in a downward spiral, a decaying orbit in which the negative forces fed one another and grew stronger, pulling us down faster and faster. Daphne was smart as a whip, but she absolutely refused to recognize me as the leader of her pack. My patience finally wore out, and I decided I really had no choice but to sell her. It was either that or have a nervous breakdown.

The guy I sold her to loves her to death. She hasn't given him a lick of trouble. I could never get Daphne to stop barking; he cured her, permanently, with one swat on the butt with a rolled up newspaper. When I heard that, I wanted to blow my effing brains out.

Like an aging ball player who continues to see spot duty when he can no longer crack the starting line-up, Emmy has retired in stages.

It wasn't until her tenth season, when she developed arthritis in her left elbow, that she slowed down to any appreciable degree. This was brought home to me on a grouse hunt with Gary and Nancy Johnson and their superb blue belton setter, Dawn. Both dogs acquitted themselves with distinction, and the pointing and backing was a sight to behold. But it was Dawn doing most of the pointing, and Emmy doing most of the backing. I'd never seen her beaten to the birds as consistently as she was that afternoon, and while Dawn's performance certainly had a lot to do with it, I was forced to concede that Emmy had at last passed her prime.

The following autumn, when I left for my September prairie grouse trek, Emmy stayed home. Prairie grouse hunting is as physically demanding as it gets—the conditions are punishing, and there are typically a lot of miles between birds—and I didn't think she was up to it. But she still got the job done on ruffed grouse, woodcock, and pheasants, guile and wisdom having compensated for the inevitable decline in speed, range, and stamina.

Three months shy of her 11th birthday, she even upstaged Gilly on the one occasion the late Dave Meisner and I hunted together. I'd noticed Gilly lightly check his stride as he hurtled along a southern Iowa fencerow, but after feathering for an instant he put his foot back on the gas and sped on. A few moments later, Emmylou came scampering down the same fencerow—and at the spot where Gilly had merely shifted gears, she slammed on the brakes. While I stood back with the camera, Terry Barker kicked up the cockbird. (Dave was off scouting for Gilly, who by then was about two hills over.)

Bird dogs invariably suffer some loss of hearing, in part due to the normal aging process and in part due to the cumulative damage done by bells, beepers, and gunfire. A couple falls ago, I noticed that Emmy was beginning to have difficulty staying oriented to me in the woods; last season, the problem became so acute—she could no longer distinguish between the actual whistle blast and its echo—that I regretfully concluded that the curtain had fallen on her career as a grouse and woodcock dog. And a glorious career it was: Just ask Peter Corbin, who painted her; Dale Spartas, who photographed her; Randy Lawrence, who wrote about her; or any of the other sportsmen who had the pleasure of gunning over Emmy in her prime. She was splendid wherever she hunted—but in the woods she was magical.

This year, Emmy's doing her hunting in the manicured fields at Little Creek, the shooting preserve I joined a few years ago. (Among the many good reasons to become a member of a preserve is that it gives you a place to take the canine pensioners.) In the open, where there are no echoes to confuse her, she does fine. She still gets around surprisingly well—Rimadyl helps with the arthritis—and she has no prejudice toward game farm pheasants. In Emmy's world view, a gamebird is a gamebird, and its sole purpose on earth is for her to find, point, and ideally retrieve it.

As I read this over, it occurs to me that I may have conveyed a couple of false impressions. One is that Emmy, because of her extreme, all-business focus, must be some kind of joyless automaton. Nothing—*nothing*—could be further from the truth. The novelist Jim Harrison once observed that dogs are always happiest when they're doing what they were bred to do, and when Emmy hunts she does so with an air of enraptured bliss. She is purposeful, yes—but she is also passionate.

The other wrong impression is that Emmy and I have a cool, impersonal, strictly professional relationship. I'm not the best person to speak to that—it's hard to be objective about a relationship when you're one of the principals in it—but the way Emmy throws herself at me and grabs my hand loosely in her mouth whenever I open the kennel gate is pretty compelling evidence to the contrary. So is the way she presses her lovely head against my hand and makes vaguely obscene moans when I rub the inside of her ear with the second knuckle of my index finger.

But even if she did nothing else, there would be the way she looks at me. Emmy has always been one of those dogs that meets your gaze, and when we stare into each other's eyes there is nothing more that either of us needs to know.

23

A Boy and His Dog

For Mom and Dad

Growing up, I was lucky. We lived on what were then the outskirts of town, where the sideroads turned to gravel. Beyond our backyard lay a series of open fields, fields that began literally where our lawn stopped. There was no fence, just a wall of belly-high brome. Wading into it was like passing through the looking glass. In a single step, I felt as if I'd been transported, as if I'd left the ordinary world behind and entered a place that was wild, unspoiled, and even a little mysterious, a place where anything might be possible.

Best of all, I imagined that it belonged to me and me alone, the private domain of a daydreaming boy and his dog, an Irish setter named Sheila.

We roamed those fields in every season, Sheila and I, but I remember them best in winter, my red dog bounding through the snow, her progress measured in glittering white explosions. She loved to run, and she did it for the sheer, carefree joy of running, front legs grabbing for as much ground as they could purchase, hindquarters driving, flag stretched straight behind. Watching Sheila run, feathers streaming, muscles rippling beneath her mahogany coat, there were times when I thought she was the most beautiful sight I'd ever seen.

She was birdy, too. I always knew, instantly, when she'd struck scent. Her tail would start to whirl in tight circles; she'd check her stride, lower her head, and race back-and-forth, furiously searching for this thing that had brushed away the generations of ash and rekindled the small, faintly glowing ember of instinct that survived inside her. Then would come that muffled roar as a streamlined hen or brassy cockbird took wing, the pheasant silhouetted against the somber winter sky, my adored red dog in hot, heedless, happy pursuit.

These were the times when I saw Sheila through lenses of somewhat darker hue. It was my fervent dream, you see, to have an Irish setter gun dog, a dog that would hunt and point birds for me the way the dogs in Jim Kjelgaard's books did. You know the ones I'm talking about: *Big Red, Irish Red, Outlaw Red.* Not that any dog made of flesh-and-blood could have lived up to the standard set by Kjelgaard's fictional champions, but Sheila was burdened by an especially grievous handicap.

She didn't have the blood.

This manifested itself in a variety of ways. Her most significant shortcoming—about as significant as it gets, alas—was that she had virtually no inclination to point. None. Sheila was interested in birds, as I just noted, but she wouldn't display even a glimmer of a flash point before she flushed them. She'd just bore right in and put 'em up.

It wasn't as if she lacked the opportunity to get it right, either. By the time Sheila was two, she'd had hundreds of contacts with wild game, pheasants and quail both—a quantity of exposure that would have had any decently bred pup well on the road to becoming a fine bird dog. In addition to the fields behind our home, there were half-a-dozen other places within a 15-minute drive that reliably held game, and my dad—who knew the hopes I'd invested in Sheila— was unfailingly willing to provide transportation.

"Dad," I'd say, "can we take Sheila for a run?"

"Sure, buddy," he'd reply, dropping whatever he was doing and fishing his car keys out of his pocket.

With Sheila whining softly in the back of the station wagon, we'd head east into the rolling hills, or maybe south, onto the flood plain of the Missouri. "I'll pick you up in an hour," Dad would say when he dropped us off. He usually lingered for a minute or two before he left, watching us strike out across the waving grass, filled, I'm sure, with hopes of his own: hopes for his son, and for the red dog that meant so much to him.

This is something I'd never understood, or even really thought about, until I became a parent myself. Nor did I fully appreciate the lengths to which my parents went—physically, financially, and emotionally—trying to turn my dreams for Sheila into realities. I've said I was lucky—but I was also blessed.

And the birds we had then! Their abundance in the Iowa of my youth was staggering, with pheasants as common as barnyard chickens and bobwhite quail in numbers that, by the standards of this quail-destitute era, seem almost hallucinatory. To think there was a time when we'd routinely move a couple of coveys in the course of a typical day's pheasant hunt, as many as they find now in a typical day's running of the National Championship at the Ames Plantation . . . it is to weep.

The upshot is that Sheila was given chance, after chance, after chance for the point switch to be flipped to the "on" position. But it never happened, and I was forced to admit that she simply didn't *have* a point switch. The necessary genetic circuitry simply wasn't there.

This did not make Sheila unique among Irish setters. Indeed, I'd been cautioned to expect this very outcome. After falling under Kjelgaard's spell—my goose was cooked as soon as my sixth-grade teacher, Mrs. Smith, plunked a copy of *Irish Red* on my desk—I began lobbying for a puppy. My parents eventually warmed up to the idea (or maybe I just wore them down), so Dad asked the one serious "dog man" of his acquaintance if we could come over and pick his brain about the breed. Chuck had a kennelful of highly trained German shorthairs—and a pretty low opinion of Irish setters.

"They're victims of their own beauty," he told us. "Years ago, Irish setters were wonderful bird dogs—some of the best. But then the show crowd took over and bred the hunt out of them. And, as far as I'm concerned, the brains. I don't mean to sound so discouraging, but the fact of the matter is that good hunting Irish are few and far-between."

Chuck emphasized that if I was still dead-set on getting an Irish setter puppy, I should try to find one out of hunting stock—and added, sympathetically, that I should be prepared for a long wait. You'll recall that in 1969 there was no Internet, or even a *Pointing Dog Journal*, to facilitate my search, and with Dad having exhausted his resources about the only option I had, as a 13-year-old, was to scan the classifieds of the local newspaper, wishing for something like a miracle.

Then, lo and behold, something like a miracle occurred: an ad for Irish setter puppies appeared, puppies described as having "top field bloodlines." Needless to say, I couldn't dial the number fast enough, and after I'd wolfed down supper Dad drove me over to take a look at the litter. The breeder, Jon, seemed like a nice guy—he turned out to be an ex-jock whom Dad had heard of—and he explained that while Duchess, the dam, was actually out of show stock, she'd displayed "good hunting instincts" the few times he'd taken her afield.

The litter's sire, however, a dog named Shannon Redstar, was not only from "the best line of hunting Irish setters in America," but was at that very moment being groomed to compete in "major" field trials. And Jon was convinced that Shannon had put more of a "stamp" on the litter than Duchess had.

"See those white blazes on the puppies' chests?" he said. "That comes from their sire's side. The old-time Irish setter guys consider it a sign of hunting ability. A few of the pups even have white on their chins, like that little female there. I'm told that that's a trademark of Shannon's line; guess it started with a famous ancestor of his named Askew's Carolina Lady."

A couple weeks later, Dad wrote Jon a check for $100, and the little female with white on her chin came home with me. I named her

Sheila, after the lady Irish setter in *Big Red*. Dad hired someone to put up a roomy fenced run that attached to the back of our garage—I shudder to think how much it cost—and my life was as complete and unimprovable as it could possibly be. It was ridiculous to believe that a few white hairs signified *anything*, of course, but what the hell did I know? I was a starry-eyed kid with a brand new puppy—and thus, by definition, an irrepressible optimist.

Chuck had loaned me his copy of *Wing & Shot*, and I tried my best to follow the Wehle program. In retrospect, I don't think I did a terrible job of it. I certainly didn't compromise Sheila's brimming *joie de vivre*, although I was probably more sensitive to that than I needed to be. Sheila was a free spirit and a gentle soul, and because I hated to see her unhappy I tended to be a little lax on the obedience side of things.

In fact, we were obedience school dropouts: My parents had insisted we enroll, but after enduring several weeks of those relentless, choke collar-enforced drills—and observing their debilitating effect on Sheila's normally sunny disposition—I put my foot down. I don't remember what I said, exactly, but I'm sure it was cribbed from Wehle; you know, something like "This is not the proper way to develop a high-class gunning companion!"

Mom and Dad bought it, in any case. And I did continue Sheila's obedience work—after a fashion, at least—on my own.

Mostly, though, I just took her for runs, waiting for the day it all clicked, the day I'd step in front of Sheila's proud, rock-steady point and flush a gloriously long-tailed cockbird. I always imagined her with one forepaw lifted and her flag at 10 o'clock—exactly the way a particularly noble-looking Irish setter from years past, Rufus McTybe O'Cloisters, was posed in a photograph I'd seen.

One winter's afternoon when Sheila was about a year old, we started off behind the house on our usual route. But instead of turning back where the familiar fields ended, we kept going, across a golf course that was now a featureless expanse of snow, up a hill on the edge of a thick oak woods, and into a place I'd never been before, a long, shallow valley with a brushy creek meandering down the middle.

I felt like we'd made a momentous discovery—and perhaps we had. Our secret valley proved to be a kind of wildlife Eden, with pheasants beyond counting—Sheila flushed and chased so many that after a while she flopped down panting in the snow—deer (a rare sight in those days), even a red fox that I glimpsed slipping out of the cover far ahead of us.

It was blue dark by the time we got home, Sheila's feathers clumped with snow, both of us tired, cold, and hungry. But I was exhilarated, too: I felt like we'd shared a Great Adventure, that it was just the first of many more to come, and that it had brought Sheila and me closer together than we'd ever been. This feeling was so strong that I was inspired to write a story about the experience. Mom typed it up, and with the enterprising hopefulness that characterized my every move back then, I submitted it to *Field & Stream*. They turned it down, but they did it gently, and they encouraged me to continue writing—a ruinous piece of advice if I ever heard one.

Several months later, on a mild summer evening, Sheila and I got more of an adventure than we bargained for. There was a rectangle of hilly ground a few miles east of town where I liked to run her, but unlike the uniform fields of brome I was used to, it was made up of different varieties of grass: some taller, some shorter; some thicker, some sparser; some with heavy seed heads that resembled cultivated grain; some with stems that were a deep purplish-red.

Anyway, Sheila disappeared over a rise, and as I clambered up to follow her I fancied I heard barking. When I reached the top, I saw her about 80 yards down the slope on a little south-facing, sun-warmed bench. Her hackles were up, and she was sort of hopping from side-to-side, stiff-legged, barking like crazy at something in the grass.

What it might be I hadn't a clue—but when I got within 15 feet or so I nearly peed my pants. There, coiled next to its den hole, was one very irritated prairie rattler. The sizzle coming from its tail sounded like raw meat plunged into hot grease. To this day, I don't remember how I managed to coax Sheila to leave the snake and come with me; the next thing I knew, I was sitting in the road ditch waiting for Dad, heart pounding, lungs heaving, trembling arms cradling my precious red dog.

Years later, I finally put two-and-two together and figured out that the reason we stumbled upon a prairie rattler there is because it *was* prairie—a swatch of virgin tallgrass that had somehow escaped the plow. And yes, Sheila and I did return from time-to-time, although we always gave that particular south-facing slope a wide, wide berth.

That November, around the time of my 14th birthday, Sheila made her first—and last—legitimate point. The image remains as vividly clear in my mind's eye as that of Neil Armstrong walking on the moon, or Hank Aaron rounding the bases after clubbing number 715.

It was hunting season, and with Dad doing the gunning and me handling the dog, we were working a strip of marshy cover in the Missouri River bottoms. We hadn't gone very far when Sheila flushed a covey of bobs—out of range—from a plum thicket at the edge of the cattails. The majority of the singles pitched back into the cover about 100 yards dead ahead, and as we approached the area where I'd marked them Sheila suddenly threw up her head, stiffened her tail, roaded up a few paces, and froze.

"Dad!" I blurted, all but disintegrating with excitement. "Sheila's on point! She's *on point!*"

Sheila never moved a muscle as Dad circled in front of her and began kicking out the frost-browned grass. She had the bird nailed, too, and I've often wondered what might have happened if Dad hadn't missed it. I've wondered if that was, like some fleeting celestial phenomenon, the one time Sheila's settings were properly aligned, and if the reward of a dead bird at that precise moment would have locked them there, permanently.

But I don't think so. I don't think it would have made any difference at all.

In a last-ditch effort to make a gun dog out of Sheila, Dad agreed to bankroll a stint with a professional trainer who, at the time, specialized in "red setters." This was the term, I'd learned, that the hunting/field trial camp used to distinguish their smaller, lighter-coated, more athletic dogs from the big, clumsy, "show type" Irish.

To make a short story even shorter, the pro gave up on her after a month. That's when I threw in the towel, finally conceding that Sheila took after her show-bred dam—good hunting instincts, my a**—and that her field-bred daddy hadn't put any kind of stamp on her whatsoever, other than a couple meaningless splotches of white.

Well, you can imagine how disappointed I was. My dream had fizzled out; my dog was a lemon. In typical teenage fashion, I moped, sulked, and treated Sheila with unforgivable indifference. Beyond keeping her fed and watered, I barely acknowledged her existence.

I was raiding the refrigerator one afternoon—speaking of typical teenage behavior—when Mom came into the kitchen and stood at the window. "I went out to say hello to Sheila today," Mom said, looking toward the kennel. "She put her paw through the fence, and I held it and stroked it for a long time. She seems awfully lonely to me, Tom."

Leave it to your mom to lay the Mother of All Guilt Trips on you. But it was exactly what I needed to hear. It made me realize what a complete jerk I'd been, and that I was failing Sheila in a far more profound and hurtful way than she had failed me. If she had even failed me at all, for I saw now that I had asked the impossible of her, asked her to become something she could never be.

And what had Sheila asked of me? Nothing—except to be the boy I'd been, the one who thought the sun rose and set over her, the one who'd been her boon companion.

I walked out to the kennel, where Sheila greeted me with an expectantly wagging tail and an imploring gaze. My image of her no longer clouded by expectations, she seemed more beautiful than ever.

"Hey, girl," I said, opening the gate. "Let's go for a run."

24

GUERILLA QUAIL

In his acclaimed book *April 1865*, historian Jay Winik argues that the Civil War might have had a very different ending. There was tremendous support on the Southern side for reorganizing its armies into small, highly mobile units, fading into the hills, and waging a "guerilla" war, a war that would have dragged on for years and, in all likelihood, resulted in a United States profoundly different from the one we know today. Jefferson Davis himself favored this course, but to their everlasting credit Generals Lee and Johnston, commanders of the largest Confederate armies still standing, rejected it—and by so doing helped bind the nation's wounds and effect a lasting peace.

A century later, another war was fought on Southern soil: a struggle for the soul of the land itself. The victor was large-scale mechanized farming and regimented industrial forestry, and if these strike you as distinctly "Yankee" notions, you're not alone.

The loser, of course, was the bobwhite quail.

The tenant farmer with his proverbial 40 acres and a mule (not to mention the trusty .22 he used to dispatch "varmints") was the best friend the quail ever had, and as he disappeared from the landscape so, in large part, did the birds. I've often thought that it's a blessing Nash Buckingham and Havilah Babcock are dead, because if they were alive to witness the decline of their beloved bobwhite—this handful of feathers that engendered such an enormously rich tradition, and which stirs such fierce passion and devotion—their despair would surely kill them.

In the Deep South, the bobwhite quail has survived by taking measures the graycoat soldier refused to. It has abandoned the familiar fields and hedgerows—along with its "Gentleman Bob" persona—and retreated to the dim swamps, the brooding hardwood bottoms, and the briar-snarled canebrakes. From these all-but-impregnable sanctuaries, these isolated pockets of resistance against the colossus of progress, it emerges into the light of day just long enough to tantalize hunter and dog, raising their hopes, clouding their judgement, and luring them with cool, remorseless calculation onto the dark and bloody ground where it chooses to do battle.

And when the smoke has cleared and the mingled roars of wings and gunfire echo only in memory, hunter and dog are left broken, their confidence shattered, their resolve—like their skin—in tatters. Blinking dumbly and gasping for breath, they wonder what the hell hit them.

Guerilla quail, that's what.

Even in south Georgia, the closest thing to a bobwhite "stronghold" this side of Texas, the old rules no longer apply—especially when it's the end of the season, and the birds you're trying to get the jump on have been dodging radar-nosed pointers and volleys of #8 shot for the past three months. River Ridge Plantation, Tommy Mock's lease along the Flint River, is one of the few places where, for a price, you can still hunt wild bobwhite quail in the classic style: butter-smooth Tennessee walking horses, mule-drawn shooting wagons, big-going pointers, the whole heartbreakingly romantic, steeped-in-tradition tableau.

Now, with the last of his paying customers taken care of, Tommy's invited Mike Gaddis, Teddy Roberts, and me to join him on a kind of busman's holiday, running dogs and hunting birds strictly for the fun of it.

Long-time bird-doggin'/field-trialin'/turkey-huntin' buddies, Tommy and Mike go way back. They're more like brothers than most brothers are. Teddy is Mike's son-in-law—and you'd be hard-pressed to find a trio of more broadly competent outdoorsmen. They can ride, they can walk, and they can shoot; they can rise early and stay up late; they're limitlessly patient, astutely observant, and keenly attuned to the rhythms of the earth and its wild creatures.

They're physically powerful men, too. When I look at them, I see the reason the South came within a whisker of winning the war. It's easy to imagine them riding with Jeb Stuart's cavalry, swooping down on unsuspecting Federal supply trains and generally bedeviling the bluecoats.

When I regard myself, on the other hand, I see the token slack-fleshed, carpetbagging Yankee brought along for comic relief.

After two days in the saddle, though, it's clear that the quail are playing no favorites—and that the only toll being taken is on our psyches. The birds are beating the stuffing out of us, the dogs—Tommy's veteran pointers and Mike's homebred English setters—included. They're making themselves scarce to begin with, and when we do find them they're running, flushing hopelessly wild, and sometimes vanishing without explanation, the eyes of the rigid dogs going wide with disbelief when we fail to put birds to wing.

And the few gunnable covey rises we do get are in the thorniest, gnarliest, downright nastiest stuff you can imagine, arm-grabbing, barrel-clutching, canvas-ripping thickets where you shoot quickly or not at all, and where the idea of following up the singles—unless you happen to be carrying a few liters of plasma in your saddle-bags—is preposterous.

Guerilla quail, indeed.

Finally, Mike suggests we change tactics, resting the horses in favor of foot-hunting behind a single dog. "We'll slip along slow and stealthy," he explains, "and try to take 'em by surprise." He has just the dog in mind for the job: Katie, a seven-year-old snow-white setter with a wealth of bird sense, a nose that's second-to-none, and a forward, easy-handling pattern. Tommy, who has business elsewhere, directs us to a swatch of piney woods tangled underneath with catbriar and beggar's lice, and of a late afternoon we array ourselves across its width: Mike in the middle, Teddy and I on the flanks, Katie sweeping ahead.

The light is gauzy, and we glimpse the setter only briefly as she crosses to the front, as swift and silent as a wraith. Mike hardly says a word—but then, he doesn't have to. He and Katie have the kind of rapport that verges on telepathy, and their trust in one another is complete. Katie knows what's expected of her, and Mike knows that she'll give nothing less than her best—which is considerable.

It's shirtsleeve warm; there's scant breeze; the air is heavy. The thing we know—but leave unspoken—is that the scenting can't be good. The odds are stacked against her, mightily so, but in the manner of all champions, crowned or not, Katie responds to the challenge. We walk barely a hundred yards before she points her first covey, nailing it dead to rights, her entire body quivering like a javelin. Then, a few minutes later, she repeats the performance, the birds holding as if transfixed, their wingbeats like thunder in the pines.

When Katie locks up on a third covey, we're aware that something special, even magical, is happening. It's as if she's persuaded—or perhaps beguiled—the birds into shedding their guerilla ways and abiding by the old terms, meeting us face-to-face, making a stonewall Rebel stand. They put us to a stern test even then, flushing so concussively and explosively that it's like trying to draw a bead on grapeshot. I've never experienced tougher shooting; next to these Georgia quail, ruffed grouse seem as big as turkeys.

Katie's fourth and final find comes near the remains of a sharecropper's shack, little but the faint outline of a foundation and a red brick chimney barber-poled with briars. The poetry—and poignancy—of this is lost on none of us. "The old home place," Teddy muses, able to breathe again after the pandemonium of the covey rise.

It's fitting that the birds should be here, where once their ancestors fed in the pea patch and dusted in the lane, where their calls heralded the day with unfailing optimism and maybe, just maybe, their decorous presence lightened the burdens of the people who worked the land. Less than an hour has passed since Mike softly spoke Katie's name and we followed her into the woods, but it feels as if we've traveled a long, long way, as if she's guided us to a place we didn't know existed any more.

And if we haven't retrieved something lost, exactly, we've at least held it in our hands for a while.

25

PRAIRIE FIRES

Somewhere, the prairies were burning.

We smelled it first. Strange, to be walking the tallgrass, not a tree in sight within that breathless steppe, and catch a whiff of smoke. It smelled familiar, like smoldering leaves, like childhood autumns.

"Must be a grass fire," I remarked to Terry.

"West of the highway, probably," he speculated.

We knew we were in no danger, that the blaze was miles away. And it might not be a wildfire, but rather a prescribed burn, its spread controlled, its extent contained. But as haze slowly filled the immense Dakota sky, dimming the sun and cloaking the earth in a gauzy shroud, I couldn't help but think of the accounts I'd read of prairie fires, of their terror and majesty. "Fearfully grand" was how an early 19th century observer described the spectacle, the flames advancing like hell's own infantry. For their part, the Plains Indians called prairie fires "red buffalo," respectfully and poetically acknowledging their violent, irresistible power.

Of course, it's been a long, long time since a genuine red buffalo swept across South Dakota—almost as long as it's been since the brown ones grazed in herds that blanketed the horizon, herds that moved across the prairie ocean like drifting archipelagos. But they linger in imagination for those who seek them, quick and bright there in the company of the curlew's call and the marionette dancing of cranes and the other shining tokens of a vanished Eden.

I seek them, myself. And sometimes, walking the prairies with the dogs sweeping the front, the wind moving through the grass as if it were the hand of God smoothing the earth's rough coat, they become so vivid in my mind's eye that it is blinding, and if I remain certain of where I am, I am not at all sure of when.

Hunting prairie chickens is like that. The country is big, the residuum of history strong. Throw in the distance between flushes—a distance typically measured in miles and hours, not yards and minutes—and try as you might to stay keen, to stay focused, you find yourself indulging in wishful, wistful revery.

This can be ruinous, especially if the birds lift without warning and, as is the norm with chickens, they're already dangerously close to out-of-range. If you'd simply let your instincts and experience take over, you'd be fine. Instead, seized by panic at the knowledge that you weren't ready and that you've only got a split-second to react, you fall apart.

The dogs make all the difference. Nothing galvanizes your attention more comprehensively—and returns your fugitive thoughts to the here and now faster—than a dog on point. It is the prairie hunter's salvation—if not necessarily his redemption.

Wherever our thoughts might have wandered after a couple hours of birdless tramping, when Willie whirled in mid-stride and froze we set our minds on the task at hand. The setter's pretzeled posture told us that the birds were *right there,* tensed to spring beneath the waving, sun-bleached grass.

And so they were.

Upslope of Willie's stand—and too far away for a shot, sadly—I had a panoramic view of the entire tableau: the chickens rising in tight formation, dark and sensuously plump, curving away across the prairies' tawny backdrop; the high-tailed setter breaking at wing with great bounding jumps; Terry stopping in his tracks and shouldering his 20-bore.

In the universe of upland bird hunting, there is no more achingly beautiful sight than a point and flush on prairie chickens. And with every year that passes, I find myself caring less and less whether I experience it as a spectator, or as a participant. What matters are the birds, the dogs, the country—and the chance.

We watched the chickens sail across the broad valley below, a riverine swath of green flowing between buckskin hills; then, like ships that fade into the mists of legend, the birds merged with the grainy haze and disappeared.

A few minutes later, where the ridgeline flattened onto a high bench, a single blustered cackling out of the pale grama. It was a long shot, but I managed to keep my wits about me and make good on it. The bird was a big mature cock, one of those lone wolves who abjures the company of the flock and prefers to keep to himself. Or at least that's how I imagined him. He was nearly the size of a pheasant, full-plumaged, his deep breast boldly barred, his pinnae like goose quills, his eyecombs and neck sacs a rich burnt orange.

Admiring this magnificent bird, this palpable symbol of the prairies' ravaged abundance, I felt as if all my desires had been satisfied, that to ask or expect for more would be an act of the profoundest hubris. I'd witnessed a spectacular point by a grand dog—an image that would burn bright in my memory—and I'd killed as fine and handsome a chicken as I'd ever seen. A fair piece of ground lay between us and the the truck, but whatever we might or might not find there, I knew that when we returned I'd case the Superposed and leave Terry to hunt on his own.

Me, I was going to turn loose my puppy, Ernie, so he and I could take a walk on the prairies.

I rarely have much in the way of an agenda when I go afield—whether I'm sneaking out for a few hours of grouse and woodcock hunting close to home or burning the highway miles on a caffeine-fueled road trip. "Low expectations but high hopes" would be an accurate description of my approach. Over the years, I've learned that pride does indeed goeth before a fall, that humility is always a virtue, and that I should be grateful for whatever portion, meager or generous, that comes my way.

But on this South Dakota hunt, there were a couple of things I fervently wanted to accomplish. One was to shoot a few birds over Traveler, my battle-scarred old pointer. I knew that at 11 years of age, it would in all likelihood be his last big trip. And while a long stretch of the road we'd traveled together in that time had been a four-wheel-drive proposition—an "adventure" would be one way to describe it—I intended to make his farewell tour as memorable as possible for both of us.

The other item on the agenda was giving Ernie, my five-month-old setter pup, plenty of chances to run, hunt, find birds, chase them all over creation, and pretty much have the time of his young life.

Knowing Ern, I didn't think that would be a difficult order to fill. The orange-eared pup seemed born to seize the day, and in at least this one respect he was the alter ego of his namesake: Ernie Banks, the irrepressible Chicago Cubs shortstop whose battle cry was "Let's play two!" Ernie the puppy had all of Banks' boundless enthusiasm and *joie de vivre;* I could only hope that he might one day play *his* game—bird hunting—with a fraction of the skill, grace, and out-and-out class that earned "Mr. Cub" a place in the Hall of Fame.

Based on what he'd showed me thus far, though, I had to say that the pup looked like a hell of a prospect. I'd been running Ernie regularly in the woods since mid-September, and from the moment he got his first smoking muzzleful of grouse scent it was obvious that the bouncy little guy was crazy about birds—and that he had no qualms about diving into the thickest, gnarliest, nastiest cover to find them. It was almost scary, the way he ripped around in the briars, hazel brush, and assorted other heavy stuff, heedless of its effect on his hide.

It was scary, too, how quickly he caught on to hand signals. He'd pop out on the trail and look at me with that quizzically cock-eared "Where to now?" expression; I'd wave my arm in the direction I wanted him to go, say "Ernie, look in there!" and that's what he'd do. His bent toward a natural quartering pattern, criss-crossing from side-to-side but staying to the front (mostly), also put a smile on my face. Yes, it's something that can be taught—but you'd just as soon not have to.

And while Ernie still had his share of tripping-over-his-own-shadow awkwardness to outgrow, he was uncommonly well-collected for his tender age, with a flowing gait and the hard-whipping "cane cutter" tail that I've always thought of as the hallmark of classic English setter action.

"If he goes on point," my friend John McMahon marveled, "I'm afraid his tail'll break off."

In fact, Ernie's style and intensity on point were superb—even if 15 seconds was about as long as he'd hold one of his quivering, bug-eyed poses before busting the bird and giving it a ride. The staunchness would come in time; the important thing now was that he liked to point, and that he looked good doing it.

Obviously, I was delighted that Ernie seemed to have the right stuff. But I can't honestly say that I was surprised. You see, I knew his blood, and having terrific natural ability is what he'd been bred for. It was his birthright.

And it was his burden.

I hadn't been looking for a pup. Yes, I badly needed to begin grooming a replacement for Traveler, but after taking a hard look at my situation and its demands—home in the suburbs, 13-year-old stepdaughter, wife who works full-time, blah-blah-blah—I'd decided that a started dog was the more intelligent choice. A devastating experience with Daphne, the last puppy I'd had, played no small role in this decision, either.

But when Sam Vainisi called to say he was planning on breeding Bella, his lovely daughter of my adored and irreplaceable Emmylou, my goose was cooked. And when he bred her to a fine young dog whose sire and dam I greatly admired—and who was himself a grandson of Emmy's—I was done to a turn. I was still hesitant, still worried about my ability to do right by a pup and live up to the responsibilities and obligations that comprise the tacit contract of puppy ownership. But I knew that if I *didn't* get a pup from this litter—this litter shaped by Emmy's genetic influence to a degree that I'd likely never find again—I'd twist myself into knots with obsessive second-guessing.

I knew, too, that to be fair to the pup I'd have to minimize the temptation to compare it to its grandma. So, before I'd laid eyes on the litter, I'd decided to pick a male and, if possible, a white-and-orange one. As it happened, there was only one pup that fit that description, so the choice was essentially made for me.

But what was ultimately even more important, I think, was my resolve from the outset to let the puppy be a puppy and, for as long as it took, focus on nothing but making him my buddy. That had been my great failure with Daphne, whose talent was breathtaking—but who, for reasons I won't dwell on, I'd been unable to firmly bond with. I hoped that if I could earn Ernie's loyalty and affection, he'd become the enjoyable companion and good canine citizen that Daphne never was. Once that battle had been won, the rest—trusting as I did in the mandate of blood to guide his development afield—would largely take care of itself.

I'll spare you the details of the sleepless nights and bleary-eyed days, the piles on the living room rug and the puddles on the kitchen floor, the toppled lamps, the upended bowls of cereal, the shoes sacrificed to needle-sharp teeth. To anyone who's lived with a pup in the house, it's a familiar litany. While Ernie perhaps leaned a bit toward the hyperkinetic end of the spectrum, by and large he was no more or less destructive than the usual run of puppy. And he had such a goofily endearing personality, embodied by a sort of lopsided grin and squinty-eyed way of looking at you, that no matter how flagrant the infraction, you couldn't stay mad at him for long.

So we just palled around, Ernie and I, roughhousing in the backyard, going for rides in the truck, taking walks in the alfalfa field on the edge of town. No agenda, few expectations. Sometimes, when we walked in the cool of the evening, I'd bring along a wing strung on an old fishing rod, and after snatching it from Ernie's eager jaws a time or two he'd invariably tighten up on point. There he'd stand, barely taller than the green alfalfa, looking proud but tentative, perhaps even a little perplexed at the source of the power that had suddenly overwhelmed him, that had turned his limbs to stone.

It's almost unbearably thrilling to watch a pudgy puppy—a baby, really—making his first points; you smile at the serious expression he wears—like a kid charged with some critically important "grown up" task—and you marvel at the sheer force of the instinct, this defining act hard-wired into the genetic code. It's like a seed planted long ago that, upon at last receiving the water and sunlight it craves, blossoms instantaneously into full flower.

And it's as close to pure magic as anything I know.

In the bird hunting/dog training business, you hate to say that things are going according to plan. To do so is to tempt fate—and it's not as if the gods need another excuse to smite you, after all.

But everything really *had* gone pretty much the way I'd hoped it would. We'd shot several roosters over Traveler, giving him all the work his arthritic old pins could stand and making his valedictory trip to South Dakota a rousing success.

As for Ernie, well, he'd had more fun than the rest of us put together. But at the same time, he'd learned some important lessons. He'd made the acquaintance of cactus and cocklebur, slithered through his first barbed-wire fence, regarded a jackrabbit with befuddlement as it loped away from him. The jack was nearly as big as Ern was, which is the only reason I can think of that he didn't chase it to Saskatchewan.

Ernie had also discovered the ringnecked pheasant—a meeting I was counting on to take the next step in his introduction to the gun. I'd been routinely firing a .22 blank pistol when he flushed a grouse or woodcock, and as the report had no perceivable effect on him I decided that I'd let fly with the shotgun the first time he rousted a ringneck. I figured I'd simply shoot in the air while he was under a bird—but, offering further proof that the stars were aligned in my favor, I was able to have my cake and eat it, too.

Ernie was about 25 yards to my left in some patchy, weedy grass when a rooster flushed from a sorghum food plot about ten yards to my right. I hit the bird hard, Ernie whirled at the shot to see it thump down, and as he buried his muzzle in the cockbird's steaming feathers I knew that the gun-equals-birds connection had been forged, that from now 'til doomsday the *whump* of a shotgun would be, to Ernie, the most heavenly sound on earth.

Now, though, on the last afternoon of the trip, with that lesson completed, with Trav resting his weary bones, and with my account filled to overflowing by the gift of a prairie chicken, I had no desire to carry a gun. I just wanted to turn Ernie loose and follow him over that sea of grass, reveling in his undiluted joy as he raced across the swells, eyes glazed with purpose, nose sifting the wind, tail cracking hard. Leaving the truck, I noticed that the smoky haze had cleared; unveiled, the low, late sun cast an alchemizing light.

But as I walked the ageless prairie with my puppy, pulled by the slipstream of the thing that burns white-hot inside him—an ember of which glows in my own soul—I was buoyed by the conviction that the fire still raged.